WHY SHAKESPEARE?

D0048476

WHY SHAKESPEARE?

CATHERINE BELSEY

palgrave
macmillan

First published 2007 by
PALGRAVE MACMILLAN
Houndmills, Basingstoke, Hampshire RG21 6XS and
175 Fifth Avenue, New York, N.Y. 10010
Companies and representatives throughout the world

PALGRAVE MACMILLAN is the global academic imprint of the Palgrave
Macmillan division of St. Martin's Press, LLC and of Palgrave Macmillan Ltd.
Macmillan® is a registered trademark in the United States, United Kingdom
and other countries. Palgrave is a registered trademark in the European
Union and other countries.

ISBN-13: 978–1–4039–9320–5 paperback
ISBN-10: 1–4039–9320–3 paperback
ISBN-13: 978–1–4039–9319–9 hardback
ISBN-10: 1–4039–9319–X hardback

This book is printed on paper suitable for recycling and made from fully
managed and sustained forest sources.

A catalogue record for this book is available from the British Library.

A catalog record for this book is available from the Library of Congress.

10   9   8   7   6   5   4   3   2   1
16   15   14   13   12   11   10   09   08   07

Printed and bound in China

To the memory of my Irish grandmother

Contents

Preface *viii*

1 Shakespeare's Singularity *1*

2 *As You Like It* and 'The Golden Goose' *21*

3 *King Lear* and the Missing Salt *42*

4 The Exiled Princess in *The Winter's Tale* *65*

5 Fairy Tales for Grown-ups in *A Midsummer Night's Dream* *85*

6 *Hamlet* and the Reluctant Hero *108*

7 *Twelfth Night* and the Riddle of Gender *129*

8 Cultural Difference as Conundrum in *The Merchant of Venice* *149*

Postscript   Happy Ever After? *169*

Further Reading *171*

Abbreviations and References *174*

Notes *176*

Index *187*

Preface

It all began when my mother died. Her books included the Brothers Grimms' *Household Tales* in a reprint from 1918, when she would have been five years old, and it seemed well thumbed.

I realized that, although I felt I knew the classic fairy tales, I had never consciously *read* one. Out of a combination of curiosity about the stories and piety towards my mother, I started on 'The Golden Goose'. To my surprise, the outline of Dummling's story, narrated in early nineteenth-century Germany, seemed to bear a close resemblance to Orlando's in *As You Like It*. The third and youngest son, ill-treated at home, was kind to a little old man, who gave him a gift in return, and this eventually enabled him to marry a princess.

Did Shakespeare know 'The Golden Goose'? Probably not, or not, at least, in the form the Grimms recorded. But perhaps he didn't need to. Instead, his play reproduces a classic pattern that still feels familiar to audiences who probably don't know 'The Golden Goose' either. And isn't that, I reflected, one of the reasons why Shakespeare's plays remain iconic now?

Someone who knows more about music than I ever shall, but not all that much about Shakespeare, described to me her experience of seeing the plays. 'For five minutes', she said, 'the language seems impenetrable. Then you get into it, and the words are no longer an obstacle.' Yes, indeed. To some of us, accustomed to the language, the words are the pleasure. But not for everyone, and not always in the first instance. What enables us to get into it is often the recognition of a storyline we already know.

On 27 March 2006 *Time* magazine illuminated its cover with images of an equally familiar domed head, turned into a screen print and repeated, like Andy Warhol's Marilyn Monroe. Inside, six brightly coloured pages stressed the money still to be made out of this exceptional dramatist four centuries old. It was not just that three British theatres were making a living out of Shakespeare, as were the replica Globes springing up all over the world, but some 600 films had also cashed in on the plays, not to mention an organization that used them to inculcate management skills, and a descendent of Monopoly called The Bard Game.

The question is why. It would be hard to think of another author, however famous and influential, who has this sort of international standing. What differentiates Shakespeare from other writers? There is certainly more than one reason for his extraordinary continuing pre-eminence, and no single answer to that question will or should be definitive. But it is worth noting that a whole genre of fireside stories has shown even greater durability, and a parallel adaptability in many languages. The third Arden edition of *Hamlet* quotes with approval a description of the play as 'the world's most filmed story after Cinderella'. Perhaps that conjunction is not as coincidental as it sounds.

When it comes to sources, scholars have generally preferred to see Shakespeare in their own image, sitting in a library diligently studying books in quest of material he could reassemble to make his case. Shakespeare evidently was a voracious reader: he worked through everything that came his way, from Ovid's Latin poetry through Montaigne's French scepticism to his English predecessor, Chaucer, as well as the latest writers, Spenser and Marlowe, alongside popular romances and racy Italian narratives in translation, only to put it all to work in sometimes unexpected ways. But have we tended to overlook another debt – to the unwritten stories that must have been in circulation among the country people in Warwickshire and the old wives of London? *but how to explain how this becomes familiar to us (if indeed it is)*

Half a century ago, the editor of Arden 2 commented scathingly that Snow White had been 'unconvincingly' cited as a source of *Cymbeline*. At that time it seemed unthinkable that our greatest writer should have drawn on such a humble genre as the folk tale. But the parallels seem to me inescapable. A beautiful queen, wicked stepmother of the heroine, tries to poison her stepdaughter; the heroine leaves the court and keeps house in the woods for huntsmen *[handwritten annotations:] Shk's plays echo, perhaps uncosly, fairy tales; hence tired familiarity, phaps also uncosly, for audiences — the stories are ours too. Impo of this for SA? poco culture — the industry*

who love her, just as the dwarves love Snow White; both step-
mothers eventually succeed in poisoning their victims, although
not fatally, it turns out; and in the end both protagonists live
happily ever after.

Source-hunting tends to privilege what was going on in the
author's mind at the expense of the play's appeal to an audience.
Who knows whether Shakespeare consciously thought of 'Snow
White' when he composed *Cymbeline*? Probably, playgoers don't
consciously think of this traditional story, either. And yet it might
just be a less specific sense of recognition that makes them feel
strangely at home with the plot as it unfolds on the stage.

Until recently fairy tales, especially popular with children in
Shakespeare's time, as now, have subsisted beneath the gaze of
academics eager to find Shakespeare's aspirations as lofty as their
own. One major obstacle to the perception of the fairytale element
in the plays has been the requirement that fiction should be true,
convincing, realistic. The more I think about this demand, the odder
it seems. There are other modes available to those who want truth:
history, biography, science. Fiction is – well – fiction, and it tells
stories. Are such stories obliged to replicate the world we know? Or
can we also allow certain genres to map a landscape of dreams and
desires just as powerful as the everyday reality we also inhabit?

Shakespeare's plays show no sympathy whatever with the pedants
of his own day. Perhaps, instead, he shared with Walter Benjamin
the conviction that the old fireside narratives do in practice resurface in later fiction. 'The fairy tale', Benjamin urged, 'secretly lives
on in the story. The first true storyteller is, and will continue to
be, the teller of fairy tales.' Whether or not he consciously recognized this secret life, Shakespeare was surely too canny a dramatist
to let a good narrative go to waste, whatever its origins. Meanwhile,
the independent survival of the traditional tales themselves may
go some way, in turn, to account for the continuing vitality of
Shakespeare's plays.

At the same time, the plays also distinguish themselves from the
tales they reinscribe, and this accounts for their appeal to audiences
who believe they have left fairy stories behind. Complex where folk
tales are often simple, elaborate where they are commonly austere,
Shakespeare's plays remake this material in another image, at once

from perhaps to definite statement

evoking and transforming the genre they rework. In the last century, structuralists reduced folk tales to a handful of components, and then reduced all stories to folk tales. In the process, they lost their sense of the distinctions not only among the tales themselves, but among and within the works that rewrite them. My emphasis will be on the differences the parallels make visible.

This book, then, is designed to test a double proposition: Shakespeare rewrites familiar narratives – but always with a difference. I shall discuss the plays in a sequence that aims to develop a case. To begin with, *As You Like It* demonstrates that the reinscription of fairy tales may be anything but artless. Indeed, *King Lear* goes on to show how a simply recounted folk tale can constitute the starting point for a tragedy at the limits of language. *The Winter's Tale*, it is widely agreed, opens with something like realism, and abruptly turns into fairy tale in Act 4. But which logic prevails in Act 5, when Hermione returns from the dead? *A Midsummer Night's Dream* displays a degree of scepticism towards the fairies who superintend its romances. Is the play an escapist fantasy, or a serious engagement with the power of fiction to represent the workings of desire? Hamlet's ethical dilemma, meanwhile, is prompted by an apparition with strong roots in folklore. And if *Twelfth Night* is structured as a riddle, it differs radically from the fireside tradition by allowing its enigmas to include the gender of the protagonist. Finally, *The Merchant of Venice* treats one of the many riddles that compose it as a matter of life and death. *Why Shakespeare?* thus unfolds a continuing argument but, so that people can dip in and out, I have also tried to make each chapter relatively self-contained. I hope readers will forgive the small element of repetition this entails.

While I have been thinking about the issues, many people have helped me to bring them into focus. I am grateful in a range of ways to Neil Badmington, Andrew Belsey, Ian Blyth, Claire Connolly, Catherine Dahlström, Herbert Foltinek, Janette Graham, Tara Hanley and Year 13 of Theale Green Community School, Christa Jansohn, Alessandra Marzola, Helen Phillips, Susanne Reichl, Virginia Richter, Jonathan Roper, Marie Rutkoski, Susan Sellers and Ben, Alan Sinfield, Frances Spalding, Julia Thomas and Michael Wood. Kate Wallis entered fully into the spirit of the project from the beginning. The detailed comments of John Drakakis and Kiernan Ryan were most helpful. Alan Dessen has been more than generous with his immense knowledge. I have enjoyed discussing a number of the issues with Hugh Mellor: he may recognize parts of the outcome – up to a point. And I also thank my longtime friend and colleague, Terry Hawkes, who has posed the question the book addresses so compellingly that I have felt obliged to look for an answer.

1

Shakespeare's Singularity

Survival

Let me begin with a question. What do the following expressions have in common: 'high and mighty'; 'every inch a king'; 'the be-all and the end-all'; 'make short work'; 'the primrose path'; 'the green-eyed monster'; 'suit the action to the word'; 'more in sorrow than in anger'; 'poisoned chalice'; 'sea-change'; 'mind's eye'; 'tower of strength'; 'the milk of human kindness'; and 'the crack of doom'? They all sound proverbial. More precisely, however, they are all drawn from Shakespeare.[1] In some ways these two observations amount to the same thing: Shakespeare is part and parcel of English-speaking culture, and not only high culture. In Britain now, phrases from the plays are still current, woven into the fabric of everyday life four hundred years after they were spoken on the early modern stage.

Like the Bible, Shakespeare is full of quotations. He also offers an endless supply of titles: *Pomp and Circumstance*, *Brave New World*, *Salad Days*, *Perchance to Dream*, *Look to the Lady*, *Cakes and Ale*, *Present Laughter*, *Sad Cypress*, *Band of Brothers*, *This Happy Breed*, *The Weaker Vessel*, *The Dogs of War*. On in London for decades in Agatha Christie's version, *The Mousetrap* originally ran for one night in *Hamlet*.[2]

Meanwhile, Shakespeare has proved nearly as influential in other countries. Many Germans feel, not entirely without justification, that Shakespeare belongs to them. Slogans from Shakespeare were used to inspire soldiers in the trenches on both sides in the First World War.[3] The old Soviet Union made films of Shakespeare that cast the plays in a new light: in 1971 Grigori Kozintsev's version of *King Lear* brought out its concern with the link between property and power. In Japan Akira Kurosawa's *Ran* (1984) drew on the Noh tradition to foreground the element in *Lear* that links power to performance.[4] Shakespeare is also well known in India, although his reputation there suffers from his appropriation for colonial education in the mission schools.

Cinema's love of Shakespeare has reinforced his international currency. Early films included a trailer for Sir Herbert Beerbohm Tree's *King John* in 1899, and an extract from Sarah Bernhardt's *Hamlet* made in 1900. Any number of silent renderings followed. In 1929 D. W. Griffith made *The Taming of the Shrew*, 'with additional dialogue by Sam Taylor'. There have been at least nine mainstream English-language *Hamlets* since the Second World War, while Baz Luhrmann's *Romeo + Juliet* broke records in 1996. Surely, no other dramatist quite possesses this continuing status, for better or worse? Would *Aeschylus in Love* have had the same box-office appeal, I wonder?

If not, why not? What is it that differentiates Shakespeare from other writers? One consensual answer has been the endless adaptability of his work. Modern directors reset the plays in a contemporary world and discover new meanings. But then, every generation notoriously perceives its own preoccupations in Shakespeare. He has also regularly invaded other genres: retold for children as *Tales from Shakespeare* by Charles and Mary Lamb in 1807, the plays also threaded their way through a number of classic novels and a great many Victorian paintings;[5] nineteenth-century composers made music out of them. In these instances, as always, appropriation necessarily reworks what it borrows, testifying in the process to a vitality that is open to repeated reinscription.

Besides filming the plays, Hollywood has also adapted Shakespeare with enthusiasm, often on the basis of successful Broadway musicals. In *The Boys from Syracuse* the music of Richard Rodgers and the lyrics of Lorenz Hart re-energized the plot of *The Comedy of Errors* (Jules Levey, 1940), while Cole Porter's *Kiss Me, Kate* reframed *The Taming of the Shrew* (Jack Cummings, 1953). *The Tempest* surfaced anew as *Forbidden Planet* (Fred M. Wilcox, 1956) and *West Side Story* updated *Romeo and Juliet* with music by Leonard Bernstein (Robert Wise, 1961). No doubt taking its cue from the success of *10 Things I Hate About You*, based on *The Taming of the Shrew* (Gil Junger, 1999), and *O*, which rewrote *Othello* to centre on a basketball player (Tim Blake Nelson, 2001), *She's the Man* set the plot of *Twelfth Night* in a school called Illyria (Andy Fickman, 2006). This teen flick shows Viola disguised as Sebastian in order to join a soccer team captained by Duke Orsino. Malvolio, meanwhile, turns out to be a tarantula.

Somehow, the stories stick, even when all about them changes. In 2005 the BBC rewrote Shakespeare. Preserving the names but very few of the words, four new plays took Shakespeare's titles and relocated them to our own era. *Much Ado About Nothing* made a plausible romantic comedy, set in a regional newsroom and played out between two presenters. Hero did the weather. The Shrew was a Conservative Party candidate; Macbeth was a successful chef. These plays were highly watchable, and more immediately accessible, of course, than the originals. What they demonstrated beyond doubt was that Shakespeare tells a good story. It seems that his plots include a degree of irony and a measure of suspense that has lasted into the twenty-first century. They have also generated modern spin-off novels by well-known authors, including Angela Carter's *Wise Children* (1991), Jane Smiley's *A Thousand Acres* (1992), and John Updike's *Gertrude and Claudius* (2000).

A black hole

How can we account for this pervasive power? What singles out Shakespeare for such continuing attention? The Victorians had an answer. Shakespeare was a genius; his plays depicted human nature in universal situations; and he inscribed timeless moral truths in immortal poetry.

Possibly. A century later, however, a sceptical academy developed radical doubts about this view. We were deluding ourselves, so the story went, misled by the Shakespeare industry, which had editions to sell and souvenirs to market. Theatres needed audiences: it was in their interest to promote Shakespeare as a reliable source of revenue. Hollywood itself was also party to this deception, it appeared, and with the same motive. The construction of Shakespeare as icon went back a long way: Britain needed a national poet – and Shakespeare represented the obvious candidate. Generations of critics, it was urged, had not only made careers out of interpreting Shakespeare; they had also *created* the extraordinary dramatist they presented as no more than an object of knowledge. To Gary Taylor, for example, no less a figure than one of the editors of the Oxford Shakespeare, there is nothing exceptional about the plays. Shakespeare was never special, or not in the way his admirers imagine. Taylor puts it so vividly that the passage is well worth quoting:

> If Shakespeare has a singularity, it is because he has become a black hole. Light, insight, intelligence, matter – all pour cease-lessly into him, as critics are drawn into the densening vortex of his reputation; they add their own weight to his increasing mass . . .
>
> But Shakespeare himself no longer transmits visible light; his stellar energies have been trapped within the gravity well of his own reputation. We find in Shakespeare only what we bring to him or what others have left behind; he gives us back our own values . . .
>
> Before he became a black hole, Shakespeare was a star – but never the only one in our galaxy. He was unusually but not uniquely talented . . . He was no less and no more singular than anyone else.[6]

Cultural materialism

In this challenge to the Victorian veneration of the dramatist, Gary Taylor makes two related points. First, he denies Shakespeare's singularity; and second, he maintains that the plays have disappeared behind centuries of interpretation. All we can see in Shakespeare is our own image of him, he argues, and this in turn is the cumulative effect of successive rereadings. If Taylor is right, the answer to the question, 'why Shakespeare?', is to be found not in the works but in the history of their reception.

How has it come to this? The answer requires a brief excursion into recent critical debates, and readers who have no interest in the story of competing approaches to Shakespeare are invited to proceed directly to the section on 'The plays'. For the rest of us, it is worth emphasizing that Taylor's is by no means an isolated voice. Shakespeare has been relativized. In English departments on both sides of the Atlantic a concern with historical difference has called into question traditional beliefs in human nature, universal situations, and timeless truths.

While new historicism (mostly American) has been busy pushing Shakespeare firmly back into his own period, cultural materialism (often British) has concentrated on the way the plays have been put to work since then, and enlisted or appropriated in support of specific causes. Shakespeare has been invoked to defend political passivity (*Julius Caesar* can be played to show resistance as hopeless), as well as imperialism (Prospero, the colonial oppressor, has been held up for admiration), in addition to Nazism (*Coriolanus* was a favourite in Germany between the wars). Cultural materialists have also scrutinized the education system to discover that Shakespeare has been interpreted on behalf of right-wing individualism and a divisive class structure, not to mention racism and sexism. The case is now incontrovertible: in the course of time Shakespeare has been made to speak from a range of positions, some more appalling than others, and each masquerading in its day as the truth about Eternal Man.

Roland Barthes in *Mythologies* had already removed the mask from the face of Eternal Man to reveal the history beneath it. Timeless human nature, Barthes affirmed, is an illusion societies foster to prove their own specific values and practices inevitable, or *natural*. The social arrangements that currently prevail in the West, he indicated, are one way of organizing the world; they have come into being historically, not naturally; and the attitudes they encourage are as much their consequence as their cause. The myths we live by transform history into nature in order to legitimize and perpetuate existing social practices.[7] Wherever 'human nature' makes its appearance, it is likely that change is being held at bay. *really??*

A historicized Shakespeare is no longer widely credited with enshrining human nature. But the evidence that the works can be so radically reread has generated not only a healthy scepticism towards any interpretation that proclaims itself definitive, but also, in extreme instances, a relativism so severe that it effectively erases

Shakespeare's own writing. If the plays can be invested with such different meanings, we have no access, purists urge, to Shakespeare, but only to what has been made of Shakespeare; there are no texts, they insist, only readings. The playwright whose meanings are reducible to existing interpretations is the Shakespeare who no longer transmits visible light, but is lost in the black hole of his own reputation.

We find in Shakespeare no more than we bring to him, Taylor asserts. I have never been able to see the force of this argument. Texts exist in their difference as the material inscription of meanings. Our interpretations are the effect of an interplay between what we bring and what we find. The sense we make of Shakespeare will not be exhaustive or final; it will be made in the present and in the light of current knowledges; but the process of making sense does not come to an end because a succession of editors, directors, critics, or examiners have previously made other senses of the same works. Whenever it pronounces the plays inaccessible behind their own celebrity, cultural materialism closes off the question why it should be *Shakespeare* who is so repeatedly adapted and enlisted, and excludes the possibility that some aspect of the plays facilitates such appropriation. OK; but how, for our purposes, to extricate this from their history :)

Performance criticism   Use?

Meanwhile, other voices were announcing the disappearance of the texts from a quite different angle. Shakespeare works wonderfully in the theatre. From the gallery at the Old Vic I craned forward as a schoolgirl to catch every detail of the unfolding action. (In retrospect, I am not entirely sure in my own mind whether the primary lure was Shakespeare or Richard Burton, who played most of the star roles at that time.) Although I knew almost none of the plays in advance, I had no sense that I needed to read a synopsis, and no difficulty in following the course of events. It is on the stage that the plays come alive.

But their meanings have been ruled inaccessible, ironically, by the redefinition of the texts as *no more than* scripts for performance. While the cultural materialists were developing their case, a generation of theatre historians were arguing that the real Shakespeare existed *only* on the stage. The surviving texts were merely spectral pointers to possible productions. A play that lives only in the theatre lives in one particular incarnation at a time, and is subject to perpetual revision. According to the strong form of this view, then, there are no texts, but only successive productions, and if we want to understand Shakespeare's continuing pre-eminence, we should look to the theatrical record. No it doesn't. This is unnecessarily polemical

Once again, this deflects any appeal to the plays for an answer to the question, 'why Shakespeare?' Although I have no quarrel with performance criticism, it does not, in my view, tell the whole story. The materiality of the texts is reaffirmed, however, perhaps surprisingly, by the proposition that versions of the plays printed in the dramatist's own lifetime were designed for reading. In *Shakespeare as Literary Dramatist* Lukas Erne makes the detailed case that the texts originally led a double life – as scripts for performance on the one hand, and as reading matter for an increasingly literate public on the other.

Although it may not have been Erne's primary project, the effect of his argument is to undermine the view that the plays have no meaning outside individual productions, and can do no more than reflect the values of any moment at which they happen to be performed. If we concede that the plays also once made at least a degree of sense on the page, we reassert their intelligibility as texts, and confirm in the process that meaning depends on what we find there, although always in conjunction with what we bring to the task of interpretation.

The plays

Shakespeare does more, in my view, than give us back our own values. The works exist in their material inscription, and therefore in their difference from subsequent cultural norms, as well as in their resemblance to them. We can recognize the undoubted adaptability of Shakespeare, and the range of possible interpretations, without giving up on the plays, or declaring them dead and buried under the weight of their own fame. Moreover, I believe the time has come to assess whether there is something in these works that makes them especially susceptible to appropriation. In the end, we do not have to choose. Of course Shakespeare's visibility promotes his reputation; it is also possible that the plays contribute to his continuing visibility. Whether Gary Taylor likes it or not, the plays have proved 'singular' in the specific sense that they have been singled out to an exceptionally high degree for re-creation. This might be because we are all sheep, foolish enough to follow any institutional lead without question. And it might also be thanks to some feature of the plays themselves.

That term, 'the plays themselves', cannot, of course, be invoked without very considerable caution. What we read may be some way from anything Shakespeare actually wrote. None of his works have survived in manuscript (although a passage from *Sir Thomas More* may be in his hand). Sometimes individual plays appeared in one or more quarto editions, printed in Shakespeare's own life-time; in other cases we owe them entirely to the Folio collection of *Mr. William Shakespeares Comedies, Histories, & Tragedies*, assembled after his death by his colleagues in 1623. When there are consecutive early printed texts, there is no way to tell for sure how far the differences between them are the effect of revision in the theatre, with or without the dramatist's approval, as the plays reappeared in the repertory over the years. Since then, editors have modernized, modified, 'improved', and explained, to the point where Shakespeare's own designs are beyond reconstruction.

On the other hand, precisely because there are no authoritative or *authorized* versions of Shakespeare's plays, they represent paradigm instances of the unstable nature of all textuality. In practice, we have no access to the intentions of an author 'behind' any text. Interpretation of the texts works with what there is, and concedes all the undecidability that implies. Shakespeare's texts are just a little more undecidable than most.

The language

Can we, despite the difficulties, and without reverting to simple value judgements, which are no more, in the end, than the inscription of changing tastes, find a feature of the plays that would go some way to account for Shakespeare's iconic status? Many people, when asked, 'why Shakespeare?', are likely to mention the language, and they are surely right. Shakespeare's vocabulary is immense, his linguistic innovations way in excess of other writers', while the sheer density of the imagery can be breathtaking. 'The words drop so fast', Virginia Woolf noted in her diary, 'one can't pick them up.'[8] There are, first and foremost, the grand set pieces, such as Mark Antony's oration over Caesar's body (*Julius Caesar*, 3.2.74–243). It is hard not to be moved by Antony's appeal, even though the play makes clear that his rhetoric is designed to manipulate. Then there are the cosmic comparisons: 'O sun,/ Burn the great sphere thou mov'st in! Darkling stand/ The varying shore o'th' world!' (*Antony and Cleopatra*, 4.15.10–12). It is not necessary to understand medieval cosmology, with its concentric crystalline spheres each inhabited by a star, to grasp the scale of Cleopatra's pain at the sight of the dying Antony. Shakespeare could have seen the random indentations of the earth's shorelines on a globe, still a relative rarity in the period.

This image of a darkening world, perceived as if from beyond the earth, invests Cleopatra with a superhuman stature that has nothing to do with mere morality. I was brought up to worry about the relation between heroism and piety, and to question whether Shakespeare's tragic protagonists 'learned from their experience', as if tragedy were a variety of Sunday school. Some do, some don't; but most of them are rendered magnificent by the way they speak. 'There is nothing left remarkable', Cleopatra laments, 'beneath the visiting moon' (4.15.69–70). Hearing these words, could an audience doubt the grandeur of the dead Antony, however poor his moral judgement might have been?

Moreover, the breaches with convention, in many instances almost blunted for us by familiarity, can still on occasions surprise an audience, or at least a reader, who has time for reflection. When Macbeth imagines the end of the world, he sees the pity he is about to abandon not as a conventional ministering angel, but 'like a naked new-born babe,/ Striding the blast' (*Macbeth*, 1.7.21–2). This simile, apparently so pictorial, in practice almost defies visualization, but it specifies Macbeth's horror at the brutality of his own projected crime, as the vulnerable infant paradoxically rides triumphant on the gales to bear witness at the Last Judgement. The 'blast' that heralds the apocalypse may also be suggested, in the manner of the free association that characteristically links one element of Shakespeare's vocabulary with another, by the trumpet(-tongue)s of the angels calling the dead to account (*Macbeth*, 1.7.19); it leads on to the cherubim bestriding the storm to disseminate the image of Duncan's murder, like dust invading all eyes, so that 'tears shall drown the wind' (25).

None of this, it is worth pointing out, is particularly lifelike. Not even heroes talk – or think – like this at times of stress. Indeed, many of us do not at such times talk or think at all: anxiety is more commonly registered physiologically, as is pain, in accelerated heartbeat, or tears. It is not a good idea to look to Shakespeare for realism. Critics who condemned the improbability of *Titus Andronicus*, because Marcus laments over the raped Lavinia when he should be administering first aid, were missing several points at once. On the other hand, Shakespeare's descriptions suggest a sharp eye for detail, ridiculous, as well as sublime. The 'ages of man', although they varied in number, were a commonplace of the period, but the precise comments of Jaques were not. His schoolboy, for instance, is closely observed, 'with his satchel/And shining morning face, creeping like snail/ Unwillingly to school' (*As You Like It*, 2.7.145–7). Classes began at six o'clock, and the boy's face gleams in the horizontal light of dawn. This is not from pleasure, evidently, but because it has been scoured with cold water, probably at the pump. As the day wears on, the shine will give way to grime from the schoolroom, not to mention smears of ink, as the lad struggles to construe or imitate passages of Latin.

It is extraordinarily difficult to talk *in* language about why an inventive image or a witty observation gives pleasure. But if the language we learn is the source of our world picture, a surprising collocation or an unexpected verbal association can make us see that world differently, at least for a moment. At the same time, the ultimate undecidability of meaning, the trace of an alternative that haunts all interpretation, tantalizes in itself, giving rise to new readings. I shall revert to Shakespeare's language at intervals here, and shall have more to say in the course of the book about its share in the responsibility for Shakespeare's continuing pre-eminence. But the language alone would not account for the success of the many adaptations and offshoots that discard the words of the plays. While it contributes critically to Shakespeare's singularity, the language cannot, in my view, constitute the whole explanation.

Familiar stories

So what does make Shakespeare's plays so extraordinarily adaptable or explain the renewability that Marjorie Garber aptly calls 'an uncanny timeliness'?[9] I suggest that the plays seduce audiences in the first instance by their capacity to tell good stories.

'You mean the *plots*? But surely Shakespeare didn't invent his plots?' No, on the whole he didn't. He assembled them from any number of sources: Latin poetry, Roman comedy, Chaucer, popular romance, and racy Italian narrative, among others. At the same time, he also drew on a genre he and his audiences must have known from their childhood onwards, tall tales of magic and witchcraft, apparitions, oppressed maidens and wronged wives, poor boys who win princesses, as well as heroes who kill giants or solve riddles to save lives. These are the familiar stories that we gather under the general heading of fairy tales.[10]

In a number of instances, Shakespeare's plays retell these traditional fables with a difference and, in doing so, they strike a chord with successive audiences, much as they must have done in their own period. Some of these same stories have been kept alive by anthologies of fairy tales, the British pantomime tradition, picture books for children, and Disney movies, but also by repeated reinscription for grown-ups in contemporary guise. Their generic characters and clear distinctions between vice and virtue offer every opportunity for rewriting in the light of changing concerns. Each time a poor heroine marries someone whose status might be expected to put him beyond reach, every time an ordinary man stands up to a huge corporation, the fairytale pattern is reinvested with modern preoccupations. Cinderella lives in Elizabeth Bennet and Jane Eyre as surely as she does in *Pretty Woman* and Bridget Jones. While their stories are not reducible to folk tale, when *Mr Deeds Goes to Town* or *Mr Smith Goes to Washington*, or Truman stands up to the creator/director of his *Show*, they evoke 'Jack the Giant Killer' (and *Tom Jones* and *Nicholas Nickleby*) as well as 'Dick Whittington' and tiny Tom Thumb who, in his early modern incarnation, outwitted the giant Garagantua. Perhaps, then, the adaptability of Shakespeare echoes the renewability of the fairy tales he also reinscribes.

Fireside tales

Although Shakespeare's London was growing fast, the rest of England was still predominantly agricultural, and farming in a northern climate left dark winter nights idle. The calendar was still agricultural, too, and the long Christmas holidays were determined by the short hours of daylight and the impossibility of working frozen soil. Candles were expensive, but the fire provided light, as well as warmth. In 1590, when Shakespeare's theatrical career was at an early stage, the anonymous author of *The Cobbler of Canterbury* marketed his collection of stories by drawing an idealizing picture of their popular use: 'When the farmer is set in his chair turning (in a winter's evening) the crab in the fire, here he may hear, how his son can read, and when he hath done, laugh while his belly aches.'[11] Similarly, the author of the first surviving printed assembly of fairy tales in English urges his readers, 'you must imagine me to sit by a good fire, amongst a company of good fellows over a well-spiced wassail bowl of Christmas ale, telling of these merry tales which hereafter follow'.[12] This cheap edition of *Tom Thumb*, marketed, no doubt, by pedlars like Autolycus, is confidently ascribed to Richard Johnson, and although the earliest copy we have is dated 1621, the majority of Johnson's work was roughly contemporary with Shakespeare's.

Puritans were just as ready as the storytellers to occupy the space the calendar made available. In *The Country Man's Comfort*, which first appeared in 1588, John Rhodes offers improving songs to answer the question, 'what shall we do in the long winter nights; how shall we pass away the time on Sundays, what would you have us do in the Christmas holidays?'[13] But more frivolous options probably tended to prevail. In the early seventeenth century Robert Burton named the recreations available in winter. These included games (cards, dice, chess), singing and dancing, jests and riddles, and, of course, 'merry tales', mainly romances and fairy stories, 'of errant knights, kings, queens, lovers, lords, ladies, giants, dwarves, thieves, cheaters, witches, fairies, goblins, friars, etc'.[14]

Fireside tales were not all cosy. Horror stories ought also to have featured on Burton's list. In 1584 the sceptical Reginald Scot, who had no time for such things, insists that people have been so frightened in their childhood by stories of 'spirits, witches, urchins, elves, hags, fairies', as well as giants, enchanters and changelings, and 'Tom Thumb' itself, that 'we are afraid of our own shadows'.[15] Christopher Marlowe's Jew of Malta remembers 'those old women's words,/ Who in my wealth would tell me winter's tales,/ And speak of spirits and ghosts that glide by night'.[16] The tradition lasted well. A painting of *A Winter Night's Tale* made by Daniel Maclise in the 1860s shows one of the listeners looking apprehensively towards the corner furthest from the fire.

Maclise depicts a whole family enthralled by the narrative. The poet, Philip Sidney maintained, tells 'a tale which holdeth children from play, and old men from the chimney corner'. Sidney's 'poet' is a maker of fictions, and although Sidney might not have approved, at least officially, of fairy tales, he *did* like Aesop's fables.[17] Others probably had broader tastes. The traditional stories evidently had a special appeal for children, but Richard Johnson claims a wider audience for his popular chapbook:

> The ancient tales of Tom Thumb in the old time have been the only revivers of drowsy age at midnight; old and young have with his tales chimed matins till the cocks crow in the morning; bachelors and maids with his tales have compassed the Christmas fire-block [yule log].[18]

Of course, not everyone lived in a cottage, especially not the ideal cottage of these nostalgic images. But there is reason to suppose that urban and elite groups were also familiar with the fireside narratives, even when they had not learnt them at their mother's knee. Reginald Scot blamed 'our mothers' maids' for transmitting them to the next generation. Looking back on his childhood in the 1630s, John Aubrey recorded how the servants sat up by the fire recounting such fictions. And, he adds, 'My nurse, Kath Bushell of Ford, was excellent at these old stories'.[19] No doubt *Tom Thumb* was expected to sell just as many copies in London as it did in the country and, one way or another, might reach the homes of both the well-to-do and the poor.

Old wives

As Marlowe's protagonist and Maclise's painting indicate, these fables were the special province of women. This tradition has a long ancestry. It was while they were weaving and spinning that Ovid's daughters of Minyas told some of the best tales in the *Metamorphoses*, including 'Pyramus and Thisbe'. Nearly two thousand years later, Maclise's spellbinding old woman sits behind her spinning wheel, casting a shadow that hints at the witchcraft involved in relating a story. Women's household tasks, tedious and repetitive as many of them must have been, were lightened by spinning good yarns, and passing them on as 'gossip'. The Cobbler of Canterbury, whose printed tales are not English fairy stories but translations from Boccaccio, goes on to affirm that 'the old wives' who have hitherto confined their attention to Robin Hood and other native folk heroes 'may here learn a tale to tell amongst their gossips'.[20] The example of an 'Old Wives' Tale' he himself includes is preceded by a description of the teller, a toothless, bristly old woman, who likes to gossip over a drink. Edmund Spenser's old wife, Mother Hubberd, by contrast, is 'a good old woman', although she speaks bluntly. Mother Hubberd tells a moralizing fable of a fox and an ape.[21]

Evidently, the ascription of these stories to old wives is not always derogatory. Burton exemplifies the merry tales he lists as winter recreation with an instance he could expect his readers to remember: 'such as the old woman told of Psyche in Apuleius'. This crone's captivating story of Cupid and Psyche, told to cheer up a maiden abducted by thieves, was a favourite of Shakespeare's period. The youngest of three sisters, the old woman recounts, Psyche is cursed for her beauty and doomed to marry a hideous serpent. She is told she must never look at her husband, who shares her bed only in darkness and vanishes before day. Even so, she falls in love with this unseen partner. Urged to breach the rule by her envious elder sisters, however, one night she lights the lamp, only to reveal the god of love himself lying beside her. Cupid flies away at once, but Psyche, more deeply in love now than before, pursues him through the world. To regain the god, she must complete a series of impossible tasks. Creatures and objects miraculously take pity on her, and in the end she fulfils all the obligations. Cupid appeals to the king of the gods, who makes Psyche immortal, and they live happily ever after.[22]

The story demonstrates the close relationship between romance and fairy tale. Although 'Cupid and Psyche' is no longer part of our repertoire, the pattern of events is familiar to us from the stories of 'Beauty and the Beast', 'Cinderella', and others who win through, against the odds, with magical help. Many of these fairy tales were equally familiar in Shakespeare's period. A variant of 'Beauty and the Beast' features in Giovanni Francesco Straparola's mid-sixteenth-century Italian collection of stories, *Le piacevoli notti*; 'Cinderella' itself can be traced back at least a thousand years.

There is always a difficulty, of course, in dating fireside tales precisely: their origins are literally lost, since they generally belong initially to an oral tradition. We know about their history only when they make their way into the written record. But there are enough traces of specific stories to guess that many fairy tales would have been familiar to the range of social classes that made up Shakespeare's audience, whether they learnt them from their mothers and grandmothers, from nurses and servants, or from printed texts.

Shakespearean allusions

How familiar were these fables to Shakespeare himself? Very, I shall propose, and the main evidence lies in the plots of the plays themselves. But a number of incidental allusions confirm that he knew – and assumed his audience would know – some of the tales in oral circulation at that time. For instance, it seems that childhood stories resurface in madness. 'They say the owl was a baker's daughter', intones the crazed Ophelia (*Hamlet*, 4.5.42–3), alluding to a folk tale about a young woman turned into a bird for withholding bread from Jesus.[23] Meanwhile, Poor Tom shows that he knows what folk-tale ogres conventionally say:

> Child Rowland to the dark tower came,
> His word was still, 'Fie, foh and fum,
> I smell the blood of a British man'. (*King Lear*, 3.4.178–80)

I remember a similar incantation from 'Jack the Giant Killer' at the moment when the giant registers the approach of his young antagonist.[24] Richard Johnson ascribes much the same formula to Garagantua as he senses the presence of Tom Thumb.[25]

Fairytale motifs are to a high degree interchangeable.[26] The Jack of my childhood was a peasant variant of Poor Tom's noble Child Rowland, youngest of three sons, who set out to rescue his sister from the Dark Tower of the King of Elfland. Instructed by Merlin, Rowland traced his sister to a room in the Tower, but the King of Elfland burst in, saying, 'Fee, fi, foh, fum,/ I smell the blood of a Christian man . . . '. Rowland defeated the king in combat and compelled him to release his sister and his two elder brothers.[27]

Ogres recur elsewhere in Shakespeare. Celia mentions Gargantua's huge mouth (*As You Like It*, 3.2.222). It is possible that Shakespeare knew Rabelais' giant in the original French, but as Richard Johnson's *Tom Thumb* indicates, 'Garagantua' had a place in English popular culture. Meanwhile, Bottom teases little Mustardseed by reworking a dish of roast beef with mustard as a tale of a flesh-eating giant and his diminutive prey (*A Midsummer Night's Dream*, 3.1.183–5).

Many of these references are ironic or comic, but they assume a familiarity with the tales they deprecate. When Benedick mocks Claudio's reluctance to confess he is in love, 'Like the old tale, my lord: "It is not so, nor 'twas not so: but indeed, God forbid it should be so"' (*Much Ado About Nothing*, 1.1.205–6), his words include a blood-curdling allusion to marriage. Benedick is quoting Mr Fox, an early version of Bluebeard, the serial-killer husband of folk tale, who repeatedly denies his crimes with this refrain.[28] And when the man in the moon features in *A Midsummer Night's Dream* (5.1.134) and *The Tempest* (2.2.136–7), the plays allude to the story of the thief who was sent there as a punishment for gathering sticks of thorn on a Sunday.[29]

Neglect

There has not been a great deal of critical interest in Shakespeare's links with such fireside tales. The Victorians of the folklore revival took the issue seriously,[30] and incidental later references show that their work made some impact on twentieth-century Shakespeare critics, as well as folklorists. But the divergence between these two disciplines has often combined with a distrust of fairy tales to distance Shakespeare from such childish associations.

The issue is realism. 'Fairy tale' is more or less synonymous with untrue, implausible, unreal; old wives' tales are by definition unlikely, based on terrors of the night, wish-fulfilments, dreams. How could a great dramatist have any connection with such improbabilities? From Coleridge to A. C. Bradley and beyond, Shakespeare's plays were understood as if they were nineteenth-century novels, aspiring to depict complex characters in convincing settings and situations. Inheriting this tradition, twentieth-century critics conceded an element of fantasy only where the evidence was inescapable – in *Macbeth*, for example, or *A Midsummer Night's Dream*. When novelistic criticism gave way to historicism, the plays were read alongside early modern social practices, at the expense of their intertextual affiliations. Even if the 'truth' they told was now historically relative, the plays were still expected to reflect reality.

But a century of modernism has itself relegated realism to soap opera, which does it perfectly well. Only anachronism confines Shakespeare to a mode that would have had very little meaning in his own time. Now, nearly a hundred years after James Joyce, fifty years after Samuel Beckett, or in the light of Tom Stoppard, we are surely ready to see that fiction may be exactly the place for fears, anxieties, dreams, and desires. Those of the past may not be identical with ours in the present, but the adaptability Shakespeare shares with fairy tale has allowed successive generations to uncover their own concerns in the fictions of a vanished epoch.

Peele

Shakespeare's culture was more ambivalent towards fairy stories than most of his earnest twentieth-century academic interpreters allowed. In *The Old Wives Tale* George Peele makes entertaining comedy precisely out of the naivety of fireside narratives. Three town lads, lost in the woods after dark, take shelter in the cottage of an old smith and his wife, Madge. What shall they do to pass the time, the smith wonders: 'Lay a crab in the fire to roast for lamb's-wool' (mulled ale), or play cards, perhaps? After singing a song, the boys opt for a story, 'Look you, gammer, of the giant and the king's daughter and I know not what'. Madge embarks on her tale about a beautiful princess, 'as white as snow and as red as blood',[31] but the old wife makes such a hash of it, forgetting the details and muddling the order of events, that the characters themselves come on to enact the rest of the story. What follows weaves together several old and highly improbable folk tales in an affectionate parody of the genre's inconsequentiality, and the play manages to bring the whole farrago to a happy resolution in the end.

The Old Wives Tale was printed in 1595, but probably performed earlier, in the late 1580s or early 1590s, when Shakespeare's career was getting under way. The play retells fairy tales with an ironic difference, distancing itself from the very material it also indulges. And it positively celebrates its own unlikelihood.

Royal entertainments

What was good enough for Peele was also good enough, it seems, for more than one queen. In 1591 Elizabeth I visited Elvetham, one of the houses belonging to Sir Edward Seymour, ninth Earl of Hertford. As was the custom on such royal occasions, her host put on the most lavish pageantry to welcome his sovereign. This mainly drew on classical mythology, but on the morning of the fourth day, as soon as Elizabeth was ready to look out of the window, she was greeted by the Fairy Queen, who paused in a dance with her maidens to salute her fellow ruler. There was enough allusion to the fairies' subterranean life and their nightly rings to ground this courtly episode in popular lore. The Fairy Queen presented the mortal monarch with a chaplet of flowers given her by Oberon, king of the fairies, and joined in a part song in praise of Eliza. Her majesty was so delighted that she asked to hear it again.[32]

By now a salutation from the fairies had become a feature of royal progresses. At Woodstock in 1575 the Queen of the Fairies appeared to Elizabeth in a wagon of state drawn by six little boys. As a token of her admiration, she presented the Queen with a richly embroidered gown. Three years later, as Elizabeth left Norwich, she was hailed by seven fairies, played by boys, who came out of a hedge to dance before her on the grass. The gods had already honoured her; should the spirits of the air do less? The design of the author, Thomas Churchyard, was to amuse the Queen, he records.[33]

It seems, then, that while the classical deities took precedence over the native fairies, the humbler local spirits were also worthy of inclusion. Even Ben Jonson, who deplored improbability on the stage, felt impelled to invoke the fairy queen in the entertainment he devised to meet the new Queen Anne at Althorp as she made her way south to join James I in 1603. Jonson's Queen Mab helps or hinders the churning in the dairy, pinches young women who neglect the housework, and misleads midwives into ponds at night. What the young Danish consort from Scotland made of this quintessentially English fairy queen, with the anarchic propensities of Shakespeare's Puck, is not recorded.[34]

Whether coincidentally or not, the folktale encounter at Elvetham in 1591 followed the publication the year before of the first three books of Edmund Spenser's epic tribute to Elizabeth herself, *The Faerie Queene*. Spenser's poem draws on a range of sources, including medieval literary romance, but the world it depicts includes fairytale giants and dragons, as well as wicked witches and evil enchanters, among its knights and ladies drawn from the Arthurian narratives. Properly habited, old wives' tales could, it seems, be presented at court without incongruity.

Enchantment

In all these instances, the popular fireside stories are reinscribed with significant differences. Disparaged at the time as trivial, and despised for their simple manner, fairy tales are put, nevertheless, to serious work in early modern texts that are neither inconsequential nor artless. The differences contribute as much as the parallels to the meanings of the texts. In Shakespeare's case, I shall propose, the resemblances of the plays to fairy tales constitute the secret of both their familiarity and their adaptability. The distinctions, meanwhile, between the plays and these models invest them with another kind of magic. A conjunction between tradition and novelty in Shakespeare's plays exercises an enchantment at once renewable and altogether singular.

2

As You Like It and 'The Golden Goose'

Old tales

With a view to encouraging Rosalind and Celia to stay and watch the next stage of the wrestling, Monsieur le Beau embarks on an account of the story so far. 'There comes', he relates, 'an old man, and his three sons—' (*As You Like It*, 1.2.111). But Celia interrupts his narrative: 'I could match this beginning with an old tale' (112).

And so, of course, she could – with any number, in fact. One of them is recorded by the Brothers Grimm as 'The Golden Goose': 'There was a man who had three sons, the youngest of whom was called Dummling', or simpleton. The first two sons in turn went into the forest to cut wood, each taking with him a packed lunch of sweet cake and good wine. In the forest the eldest brother met a little old man who asked if he would share his lunch with him. The lad refused out of hand, and shortly afterwards he wounded himself with his own axe. The second brother's story repeated the first's, and then Dummling wanted to try his hand. It seemed unlikely that a simpleton would succeed where his brothers had failed, and he was given only an ashcake and sour beer. But Dummling gladly shared this poor meal with the little old man, who in return gave him a goose that had feathers of pure gold.

In the course of his travels Dummling met people eager to steal a feather, but each one stuck fast to the bird the moment they touched it. In this way, the young man with the goose under his arm acquired a procession of seven followers, who were obliged to walk where he walked and run when he ran. It happened that he came to a city where the king's daughter never laughed. Her father promised the hand of the princess to anyone who could amuse her.

When she saw Dummling with his goose and his train, she laughed out loud, as if she would never stop. But the king was reluctant to let his daughter marry a peasant, and imposed three seemingly impossible tasks, so Dummling went back to the little old man, who helped him to accomplish all three. At last Dummling and the princess were married; in due course he became king; and they lived long and happily.[1]

There are many local variants of this story.[2] One Scottish version concerns Silly Jack, who is once again the youngest of three sons, and despised for his compassion to his poor widowed mother. This time, each brother in turn faces three tests of fitness to marry an heir. After sharing Jack's food, the little old man gives him a magic sword that helps him to win through. Jack duly marries the lord's daughter, and sends for his mother to live with them in the castle.[3]

Le Beau's tale continues differently, however. The three sons are all injured, in danger of death. In most respects the wrestling match in *As You Like It* follows the source text, Thomas Lodge's *Rosalind*. This romance was first published in 1590, and so popular that it was reissued two years later, as well as in 1596, and again in 1598, the year before Shakespeare's play was probably first performed. But in *Rosalind*, as in *its* source, *The Tale of Gamelyn*, the old man has *two* sons who challenge the champion. In the folk tradition, however, siblings commonly come in threes: Cinderella has two ugly sisters; the heroic Child Rowland, mentioned in *King Lear*, is the youngest of three brothers (3.4.178–80).[4] Shakespeare's tiny alteration of his source in *As You Like It*, together with Celia's teasing interruption, has the momentary effect of reminding the audience of the fireside tales they would have known since their childhood. Shakespeare's new genre of romantic comedy, in other words, positively foregrounds its allegiance to the popular narrative tradition.

Orlando's tale

Celia's 'old tale' might equally be *Gamelyn* itself, a mid-fourteenth-century poem mistakenly attributed to Chaucer and regarded as one of the *Canterbury Tales*. Gamelyn, too, is the youngest of three sons, divested of his inheritance by his elder brother. *The Tale of Gamelyn*, derived from a French text, also has roots in the oral tradition, this time from Scandinavia. The hero's generic name comes from 'gameling', meaning son of an old man.[5] In the folk tradition, of course, most fathers are old and most sons are young, and the characters tend to have generic names, or none at all. ('Jack' is generally a poor lad and an unlikely hero.) *Gamelyn* begins, as does *Rosalind*, with a father on his deathbed, distributing his possessions among his sons.

But if Celia's 'old tale' resembles *Gamelyn*, it also bears a marked similarity to Shakespeare's own play. In the interests of economy, *As You Like It* dispenses with the deathbed scene, and opens as Orlando complains that his eldest brother has withheld both his inheritance and his education, while the second is doing well at school. It is not until lines 55–6 that Orlando affirms his identity in so many words: 'I am the youngest son of Sir Rowland de Boys.' But by then the audience has been encouraged to recognize a pattern so familiar that it must have gone virtually without saying. Indeed, in the Romany story of 'The King of England and his Three Sons', the narrator can take for granted the wickedness of older brothers, observing laconically, 'To make my long story short I shall follow poor Jack, and let the other two take their chance, for I don't think there was much good in them.'[6]

'From the outset, *As You Like It* was to be a fairy tale.' This, according to John Bowe, who played Orlando, was how Terry Hands directed the Royal Shakespeare Company's production of the play in 1980. 'A boy, Orlando, meets a girl, Rosalind, and each falls instantaneously in love with the other. The boy undergoes a trial of his manhood against the champion of the wicked Duke, and wins.'[7] Bowe might have added Orlando's second and third trials, to find food for Adam and to kill the lioness. These test his humanity, as well as his endurance and skill. Orlando succeeds on his own merits, without the help of magic, and wins the Duke's daughter.

Even so, the little old man also has a role to play in his story. Adam features as Orlando's ally in both *Rosalind* and *Gamelyn*, but here again *As You Like It* deepens its own resemblance to folk tale by adding specific details. In 'The Golden Goose' and 'Silly Jack', only the youngest son treats the little old man with respect and compassion; the elder brothers rudely brush him aside. And in *As You Like It* Orlando confides in Adam, while Oliver dismisses him as 'you old dog' (1.1.79). What is more, Shakespeare's Adam warns Orlando of the plot against his life and goes on to give him the gift of his life savings which, if not magical, certainly helps the hero to find his way to the side of the princess without reduction to beggary. As a result of these modifications of the source, when Orlando insists on food for Adam, just as he does in *Rosalind*, the parallel with the shared meal of the fairytale tradition seems the more marked.

Moreover, if Orlando is not exactly a simpleton like Dummling and Silly Jack, the play follows through the implications of his missed education. This, Orlando complains, undermines his 'gentility' (1.1.20). Young gentleman were conventionally instructed in Latin and Greek, in riding, hunting and hawking, and above all in good manners, the courtesy that enabled them to find their proper place in Elizabethan society, both at court and in the community. There is no doubt about Orlando's good heart, just as there is none about Dummling's or Jack's; there is, however, some uncertainty about Orlando's command of the conventional courtesies. When the two brothers grapple in the opening scene, older editions are careful to make Oliver strike first, but there is no warrant for this in the Folio, the only early printed text of the play. Instead, the dialogue suggests that it is Orlando who first has recourse to physical violence. Here is the exchange without the subsequent editorial stage directions:

> ORLANDO   I have as much of my father in me as you, albeit
>   I confess your coming before me is nearer to his
>   reverence.
>   OLIVER   What, boy!
> ORLANDO   Come, come, elder brother, you are too young in
>   this.
>   OLIVER   Wilt thou lay hands on me villain? (1.1.48–54)

Oliver's 'boy' is a verbal insult, which Orlando returns by accusing him of inexperience in fisticuffs ('this'). And it is while refusing to let go of Oliver (64) that Orlando protests, 'you have trained me like a peasant, obscuring and hiding from me all gentleman-like qualities' (66–8).

The same lack of instruction makes the desperate Orlando demand food in the forest with drawn sword, incurring the Duke's reproach:

> Art thou thus bolden'd man by thy distress?
> Or else a rude despiser of good manners,
> That in civility thou seem'st so empty? (2.7.92–4)

We readily excuse him, as the Duke does, but we might also remember his embarrassment when Rosalind's gift leaves him speechless (1.2.239–48), not to mention his bad poems, so easily parodied by Touchstone. These are not sonnets, as would befit a gentleman, but rustic doggerel, however sincerely meant. In the source the differences of rank and wealth between the youngest son and the princess are a cause of anxiety, however momentary, to both Rosalind and Rosader (Shakespeare's Orlando).[8] But in the folk tradition marriage between Jack and the princess fulfils in fantasy a wish for wealth and power that a peasant audience might be expected to share. Ironically, Shakespeare's play is less inhibited by 'realism' than Lodge's romance. Oliver is glad to marry Aliena, believing her to be a keeper of sheep, and willing to 'live and die a shepherd' himself (5.2.12). In Orlando's case, nurture, *As You Like It* assumes, can easily be acquired by a gentle nature. Once Rosalind has satisfied herself that Orlando is 'a gentleman of good conceit' (intelligence, 5.2.53–4), there is no further impediment to their marriage.

Reinscriptions

Oddly enough, Orlando's story seems to remain recognizable to audiences who have long forgotten 'The Golden Goose' and never knew the tale of Silly Jack. Fairy tales are kept alive not only by their own retelling in the nursery, or in film and pantomime. The unlikely hero, despised yet compassionate, recurs in subsequent fiction as Henry Fielding's foundling, Tom Jones, for instance. Tom's name is as unpretentious and almost as generic as Dummling or Jack. Since in the folk tradition the second brother's story commonly duplicates the first, novels generally do without him. In

Tom Jones, first published in 1749, the hero's generous nature gets him into any number of scrapes, some of them brought to light by his self-centred, avaricious and hypocritical half-brother, who in this instance is younger than the protagonist, but legitimate, and therefore heir to the family wealth, like Oliver. High spirits and sexual adventures finally lead Tom into trouble and he is sent away to seek his fortune with very little money in his pocket. Even so, at the first inn on his travels he generously resolves a dispute about the bill by paying it himself. Tom is tested again and again in the wicked city, but good-heartedness is finally rewarded and he wins an estate and a rich squire's beautiful daughter.

But in case *Tom Jones* is not as familiar as it once was, here is a modern rewriting of that story, as well as Jack's and Orlando's. A boy with an unassuming name, brought up by his aunt and uncle, is treated with contempt at home, where his spoilt cousin, only a little older than he is, grows up selfish and greedy. When the time comes for them to go to secondary school, the cousin parades himself in the expensive uniform of a private institution, while the bespectacled orphan, undersized and unassuming, is to go to the local comprehensive in second-hand clothes. But a strange-looking old man with magic powers intervenes, and enrols him in a school for wizards. On the train he shares his picnic of pumpkin pasty and chocolate frogs with his new friend, Ron, whose family is too poor to pay for treats. With the special protection of the old man, Albus Dumbledore, Harry Potter's resources and skills are tested until he overcomes the evil Voldemort. Subsequent stories trace his further adventures, and at this moment it is too early to tell whether he will in due course marry a nobleman's daughter.[9]

In between, Charles Dickens, second only to Shakespeare when it came to the reinscription of fairy tales, rewrote the story for a succession of heroes, most notably David Copperfield, who read *Tom Jones* as a boy,[10] and who had no siblings but discovered a surrogate older brother in his dangerous schoolfriend, Steerforth. (Did J. K. Rowling redraw Steerforth as Malfoy, perhaps?) Dickens's darkest version of the story, *Great Expectations*, begins with an orphaned Pip who supplies food for a hungry man, but under duress. Any compassion in Pip's nature is well and truly suppressed by his acquaintance with Miss Havisham, who is as close as the nineteenth-century novel permits to a wicked fairy, and he has to relearn to be kind at great cost. As Dickens originally wrote the story, Pip is redeemed but not rewarded. For Dickens' friend and fellow writer, Bulwer Lytton, however, the imperatives of the fairytale pattern were so strong that he induced the novelist to rewrite the ending. The published version implies that Pip will go on to marry Estella, once so far above him in rank and wealth that she might as well have been a princess.

Difference

If reinscription depends on similarity, it also presupposes difference. When cultures tell and retell familiar fictional narratives, they necessarily change them in the reworking. This is partly a question of genre; it is also one of appropriateness – to a specific audience or a particular historical moment. Fielding rewrites the folk tale for a sophisticated eighteenth-century readership, for instance, and alters it almost – but not quite – beyond recognition. Here both difference and familiarity contribute to the meaning of the novel. Fairy tales are commonly short, austere, sparely told; *Tom Jones*, by contrast, is a populist epic and fills 900 pages with intertextual allusions: quotations from Shakespeare, Miltonic references, and parodies of Homer and Virgil. *Tom Jones* also specializes in the convoluted sentence structure of the epic simile. The book satirizes contemporary social values, and stands as the written analogue of Hogarth's images, to which it also alludes. Where 'Silly Jack' offers itself as fully intelligible to the most naive audience, Fielding expects his readers to be at home with philosophy and theology, as well as the literary tradition in English, Latin and Greek.

And yet the folktale component is also crucial to the meaning of *Tom Jones*. Although he makes any number of mistakes, its cheerful and unreflecting hero demonstrates in his way of life the value of 'natural' virtue. Experience, not theory, we are to believe, is the best teacher. As an innocent man of the people, Tom is precisely a latter-day folk hero. The wit of this prose epic depends on the gap between the high style of the narrative and the low activities of its central figure. At the heart of one of the most textually elaborate works in all English literature, we are invited to find, in order to understand its project, a simple, homely story of a simple, familiar protagonist.

Fielding's rewriting makes something new, just as J. K. Rowling's does. All repetition, after all, is by definition both the same and different: the same, or it would not be repetition; different, or it would be the original itself and not a repetition of it. Repetition, or iteration, reproduces the earlier version, but at another time, in another place, and above all *as* repetition, as citation. 'Iteration alters, something new takes place', as Jacques Derrida says, with uncharacteristic brevity.[11] What happens when one text cites another? Tom Jones, Harry Potter, Pip and Orlando all evoke the tradition of the unlikely folk hero who wins through against the odds, and the citationality of their stories, the evocation of the fireside tradition in a quite different frame, plays a part in the meaning of the texts. In other words, these stories are not simply reducible to folk tales. Citation of this tradition in another setting, manner, context is itself a component of their import for us. In the same way, the differences between Shakespeare's courtly romantic comedy and 'The Golden Goose' signify as sharply as do the resemblances.

Rosalind's tale

One of the most prominent of these differences must be the transformation of the nameless princess who constitutes the hero's reward into Rosalind, who effectively dominates the play. She sets the pace of Orlando's courtship, makes most of the jokes in the process, and engineers the happy ending. As it happens, Rosalind's story recapitulates yet another familiar narrative, the put-upon young woman who undergoes her sufferings with patience and good humour. We know her story from 'The Goose Girl', as well as 'Cinderella' and its endless variants, not to mention the subsequent remoulding of these protagonists as Elizabeth Bennet, Jane Eyre and Bridget Jones. *As You Like It*, in other words, cites two familiar tales for the price of one.

Shakespeare, or his audience, evidently liked this second story as much as we do, and told it again and again, in the histories of Viola, Cordelia, Imogen, Marina and Perdita. I shall discuss the pattern in more detail in Chapters 3 and 4. Here, instead, I shall dwell on one major difference between *As You Like It* and the fireside tale of the oppressed heroine: while disguise often conceals the fairytale protagonists' wealth and beauty, they do not generally go so far as to impersonate the opposite sex. Cinderella, like her English counterpart, Rushen Coatie, is reduced to poor clothing, her face besmirched by cinders from the hearth;[12] the Goose Girl does not unbind her golden hair before the court;[13] Cap o' Rushes hides her fine clothes under a rush cloak; and Catskin puts hers away in favour of a coat made of animal pelts.[14] But though her own motive is also self-protection (1.3.105–19), only Rosalind, by becoming Ganymede, turns oppression into carnival. In this sense, the folk-tale pattern constitutes no more than a recognizable framework for quite unexpected developments. Ganymede's elusive sexual identity raises questions about the objects of desire; his scepticism intermittently recasts as irony the romantic love that also drives the plot.

Gender

'If I were a woman', the epilogue runs, 'I would kiss as many of you as had beards that pleased me (5.4.212–14). The speaker is ostensibly Rosalind, 'the lady', as she identifies herself (197), but the tease that permits her to evade any commitment to work her way round half the audience is that opening 'If'. Rosalind, it declares, is not a woman, or not exactly. The epilogue, in the margins of the play, neither inside the fiction nor outside the performance, permits the boy-actor to speak partly in his own person, but *only* partly. Is it a boy, then, or a girl, who is offering to kiss the men in the audience? Or does the speaker magically, miraculously, participate in more than one sexual identity? Evidently, the appeal of the boy-player is to a degree homoerotic, but not exclusively so. If the speaker is seen simply as a boy, the joke is lost: 'And I charge you, O men, for the love you bear to women—as I perceive by your simpering none of you hates them . . . ' (209–11).

The mood of the epilogue is conditional: 'If I were a woman, I would kiss . . . '. 'Much virtue in If', Touchstone wisely observes, explaining how to avoid a quarrel (5.4.101). If Rosalind were indeed a woman, let alone a lady, she could hardly risk so suggestive an offer without loss of decorum. As a boy, on the other hand, 'she' is licensed to talk like a 'saucy lackey' (3.2.291–2), while evading the consequences with a conditional 'If'.

Ganymede is a 'pretty youth'. Orlando thinks so, of course; Phebe thinks so, too, although she tries hard not to; and Jaques confirms it (3.2.328; 3.5.113; 4.1.1). At this time, adolescent boys seem to have entranced and enticed both men and women. A more advanced age of puberty, perhaps as late as seventeen,[15] meant boys combined the playfulness of children with the precocious knowingness of adults. Six years earlier, in 1593, Shakespeare had written the story of 'Rose-cheek'd Adonis', object of desire for the goddess of love herself (*Venus and Adonis*, line 3). The beautiful youth rejected her suit and, when he died, Venus turned him into an anemone, most delicate of wild flowers. The poem was an instant success, especially with male readers. Meanwhile, in the same year Christopher Marlowe composed *Hero and Leander*, dwelling on the physical beauty of its male protagonist, object of desire not only for the heroine but also for the god Neptune, who dives into the water as Leander swims, to 'pry/ Upon his breast, his thighs, and every limb'. When Leander does his best to repel these advances, pointing out that he is not a woman, Neptune merely smiles and renews his attentions. *Hero and Leander* was published in 1598, five years after its author was killed over a tavern reckoning, and one year before *As You Like It* was probably performed. Marlowe's Neptune initially mistakes Leander for Ganymede, the beautiful boy desired by Jove himself. In the temple of Venus, where Hero worships, a mosaic floor depicts the amorous exploits of the gods, among them 'Jove slyly stealing from his sister's bed,/ To dally with Idalian Ganymede'.[16]

Shakespeare takes Ganymede's name from Lodge, whose heroine also masquerades as a boy, and the titillation associated with the classical story of Ganymede may well have contributed to the success of *Rosalind*. As king of the gods, Jove generally had his own way, but the desires of Neptune and Venus seem to be reinforced by the indifference of the boys they pursue. Indeed, thwarted by the death of Adonis, Shakespeare's Venus proclaims that from now on love will always be 'perverse', wayward, obtuse, running counter to reason and expectation (*Venus and Adonis*, 1157). As the goddess of love, she has the power, of course, to make her curse come true, and the perversity of desire is borne out in *As You Like It*, where Silvius loves Phebe in spite of her scorn, while Phebe falls in love with Ganymede because of his. Unattainability, in other words, seems to deepen desire: the combination of beauty and indifference proves tantalizing. In a parallel way, it is surely the promise at once given and withheld by the 'If' of the epilogue that offers to seduce the audience.

Meanwhile, a similar conditional deepens Orlando's passion. Rosalind-as-Ganymede teases Orlando both with what she (pretends she) is and with what she (pretends she) is not: 'Come, woo me, woo me; for now I am in a holiday humour and like enough to consent. What would you say to me now, and I were your very very Rosalind?' (4.1.64–7); 'I would cure you, if you would but call me Rosalind and come every day to my cote and woo me' (3.2.414–15). *Much* virtue in If. Their genuine courtship is made possible on the basis of false pretences. Both speak more openly than they otherwise might: Rosalind excites Orlando's protestations in order to 'cure' him, while Ganymede intensifies them by indifference; Orlando relishes both the opportunity to rehearse his love and the incitement to reiterate it in order to overcome Ganymede's scepticism (4.1.85–6).

The promised 'cure' is, of course, an equivocation. Rosalind has no intention of dispelling Orlando's love: instead, she will alleviate the pain it causes – eventually. In the meantime, she will enhance his desire by deferring the moment of reciprocity, tormenting him with inconsistency, now disdaining, now encouraging his overtures, 'full of tears, full of smiles' (3.2.401). This changeableness is, it seems, the common ground between boys and women (403–4): both are 'effeminate' (399). Alan Sinfield points out that male effeminacy in early modern culture was not associated specifically with homosexuality. On the contrary, men could become 'effeminate', which is to say emotional, unstable, above all as a result of spending too much time with the women they loved. The term was a way of policing masculinity: manly men were reliable, cool, rational, and perpetually ready for war. Too much feeling (heterosexual love, for instance) could undermine the state of manliness, making men capricious, inconstant, shallow, 'for every passion something and for no passion truly anything' – like boys and women (401–3).[17] (When Oliver calls Orlando 'boy' (1.1.51), he accuses him of excitability – and Orlando responds by threatening violence.)

At the same time, the perceived parallel between boys and women, their teasing inconsistency, makes both more provocative, more seductive. And the capacity to effeminate their suitors, to tease and torment, to put men – or gods and goddesses – at their mercy, invests boys and women, who have little enough of it in a general way, with a fleeting power. *As You Like It* makes clear, however, that they hold this brief ascendancy only over their suitors. Not for nothing does romantic comedy focus on courtship. As Rosalind knows only too well, and is licensed to say in the person of the cynical Ganymede, 'men are April when they woo, December when they wed' (4.1.140–1). Hymen, as the god of marriage, puts a stop to all equivocation with 'Peace ho! I bar confusion' (5.4.123). At the level of plot, very little happens in *As You Like It*. The suspense, where it exists, resides in the tantalizing deferral of the union with Orlando that Rosalind-as-Ganymede both promotes and prohibits.

Impersonation

Rosalind's success in impersonating Ganymede must have been much more apparent when the fictional heroine was played by a boy. The modern stage, where women play women's parts, has largely lost the ambiguity of the early productions, and the printed text irons out differences by doggedly attributing Ganymede's speeches to Rosalind. But from the point of view of an audience watching a boy-player, and without sight of speech prefixes, two virtually distinct voices can be heard. One belongs to a romantic heroine fathoms deep in love (4.1.198), and the other to a sceptical boy who claims, 'Love is merely a madness' (3.2.389). The first figure 'cannot be out of the sight of Orlando' (4.1.207–8), while the second 'had as lief be wooed of a snail' (49). Discontinuity divides Rosalind from Ganymede: Rosalind faints at the sight of Orlando's blood, but Ganymede calls the swoon 'counterfeit' (4.3.157–72). Ganymede names legendary lovers, Chaucer's

Troilus and Marlowe's Leander, only to call their stories lies: 'men have died from time to time and worms have eaten them, but not for love' (4.1.101–2). And Ganymede's misogyny prompts Celia to remind Rosalind who she is (193–6). Depending on the skill of the actor, either voice, romantic or mocking, might be audible when Rosalind-Ganymede urges Orlando, 'Alas, dear love, I cannot lack thee two hours' (171). Is it a playful boy or a heroine in love who impels Celia to perform a marriage ceremony at a time when many people believed the declaration of the couple to be binding?

Modern productions and printed speech prefixes both urge us to take it that Rosalind is only pretending to be Ganymede. And so, in a sense, she is. But in another sense, Shakespeare's own stage effaces that 'obvious' distinction between them. In his account of the seven ages, Jaques proposes that 'one man in his time plays many parts', and the 'playing' he goes on to describe is not a pretence: 'At first the infant . . . '. We do not *impersonate* infants, or lovers or, indeed, geriatrics, 'sans everything': instead, we *are* all these in succession; in other words, we experience a series of different states (2.7.139–66). Paradoxically, the speech indicates, selves are at once continuous and discontinuous. Jaques makes clear that his world-stage is metaphorical, but the metaphor has repeatedly been celebrated and the speech anthologized for its 'truth'. One age morphs into another; the infant turns into the schoolboy; the soldier becomes the justice. And figuratively, fictionally, in this fairy tale, just as mice become Cinderella's horses and a pumpkin her coach, Rosalind turns into Ganymede – and back, as occasion offers. In this Shakespeare reinscribes Lodge's *Rosalind* with an inevitable difference. The romance calls its disguised protagonist a 'girl-boy', and refers to her-him as Ganymede or Rosalind, according to choice. Moreover, the pronouns vary just as unaccountably: 'Ganymede, who still had the remembrance of Rosader in his thoughts . . . '; 'Aliena was awakened by Ganymede, who, restless all night, had tossed in her passions'.[18] Shakespeare's comedy, which does not need a narrative voice or the corresponding reiteration of names and pronouns, can allow its boy-actor to play Rosalind or Ganymede, inhabiting the place of a woman or a boy, depending on the mood of the speech.

Love

If Rosalind and Ganymede represent distinct states, one in love, the other mocking lovers, which of them gives a true account of love itself? While Hymen delivers a resolution of the plot, it is not so clear that the play's assessment of love is equally resolved. There are plenty of grounds for scepticism. Jaques satirizes the lover, 'Sighing like furnace, with a woeful ballad/ Made to his mistress' eyebrow' (2.7.148–9). The portrait is absurd, of course – but not so very remote from the play's own image of Orlando hanging bad verses on trees. What Orlando's poems lack in poetic skill, they make up for in idealization: '*From the east to western Inde,/ No jewel is like Rosalind*'. And yet Touchstone's parody brings love down again from this high plane to the level of an animal imperative: '*If a hart do lack a hind,/ Let him seek out Rosalind./ If the cat will after kind,/ So be sure will Rosalind*' (3.2.85–6, 99–101).

What, then, the play asks, is the nature of love itself? The lovers provide one answer to the question:

SILVIUS	It is to be all made of sighs and tears,
	And so am I for Phebe.
PHEBE	And I for Ganymede.
ORLANDO	And I for Rosalind.
ROSALIND	And I for no woman.
SILVIUS	It is to be all made of faith and service,
	And so am I for Phebe.
PHEBE	And I for Ganymede.
ORLANDO	And I for Rosalind.
ROSALIND	And I for no woman.
SILVIUS	It is to be all made of fantasy,
	All made of passion and all made of wishes,
	All adoration, duty and observance,
	All humbleness, all patience and impatience,
	All purity, all trial, all observance;
	And so am I for Phebe.
PHEBE	And so am I for Ganymede.
ORLANDO	And so am I for Rosalind.
ROSALIND	And so am I for no woman. (5.2.82–100)

Love comes across in this account as intense and pure. It is enduring, attentive, exalted. These parallel exchanges unite the lovers in fervent romantic aspiration. And yet the formal repetitions also prompt the reflection that identical protestations can be uttered and reaffirmed unreservedly by all the lovers. Whatever its charm, this set piece also demonstrates the iterability of love: a seemingly unique emotion, different in each case, nonetheless follows a predictable, interchangeable script.

Love, the most personal of experiences, is also, in a sense, the most conventional, and thus the most banal. And what is the outcome of all these sighs and tears? 'Hymen peoples every town' (5.4.141). Marriage is, after all, mating. Alongside its high sentiment, the play also offers Touchstone's view of marriage, which is a good deal less elevated: 'As the ox hath his bow sir, the horse his curb, and the falcon her bells, so man hath his desires, and as pigeons bill, so wedlock would be nibbling' (3.3.73–5). The sceptical Ganymede duly puts a stop to the iterated declarations, including Rosalind's own: 'Pray you no more of this, 'tis like the howling of Irish wolves against the moon' (5.3.109–10).

The play does not, in my view, resolve the question it raises about the nature of love. It impels us to want the happy ending it provides for all the lovers, and especially the marriage of Orlando and Rosalind. *As You Like it* dramatizes its central romance from the heroine's point of view, and if we remain indifferent to the denouement, the play as a whole falls flat. At the same time, it offers an ironic purchase on the love it also invites us to care about. Shakespeare effectively invented romantic comedy, and while he might not have recognized the term, his new genre entitles audiences to expect the pleasures of romance, in conjunction with the distance conferred by comedy. *As You Like It* is ultimately a fairy tale, and no one ever supposed that fairy tales were true. They deliver what their audiences would like to believe, an ideal world, not a factual one. To the degree that romantic comedy is rooted in fairy tale, the genre can accommodate both wish-fulfilment and scepticism. Perhaps the clue to the evaluation of love in Shakespeare's play lies in the title.

Intertextuality

At the same time, if *As You Like It* reproduces the pattern of an old wives' tale, its elegant, courtly manner is a long way from the austerity of oral narrative. *As You Like It* is a fairy tale; *As You Like It* is one of Shakespeare's most sophisticated comedies. These two propositions are not necessarily antithetical or contradictory. Within the folktale frame of the plot, the play creates a space in which a range of intertextual allusions 'blend and clash', as Roland Barthes puts it. Like all writing, 'The text is a tissue of quotations drawn from the innumerable centres of culture'.[19]

Charles the wrestler's incidental invocation of a familiar folk hero exemplifies the way intertextual references blend and clash to produce meaning in this new context: 'They say he is already in the Forest of Arden, and a many merry men with him; and there they live like the old Robin Hood of England' (1.1.111–13). The comparison illuminates the Duke's exile and brings with it a range of associations. Robin and his merry men were known at the time as riotous lowlife outlaws, heroes of popular ballads and the Whitsun play-games enacted in a wide range of English and Scottish parishes in the sixteenth century. But at the same time, a smoother Robin Hood had recently appeared on the London stage in the 1590s, most notably in Anthony Munday's plays of 1598, *The Downfall* and *Death of Robert, Earl of Huntington*. These were performed by the Admiral's Men, rival company to Shakespeare's. Munday's hero is moralized and gentrified; in his plays people converge on an Arcadian greenwood, attracted by Robin's utopian politics; and the plots are characterized by sudden repentances and ready forgiveness. Charles the wrestler's brief allusion permits *As You Like It* to subsume all this, including the contradictions between the anti-authoritarian folk hero and the righteous Earl, in the invocation of an ideal authority that represents an alternative to the corrupt law of the usurping Duke Frederick.[20]

In either of the incarnations invoked here, Robin Hood is quintessentially English. 'They say,' Charles goes on, 'many young gentlemen flock to him every day, and fleet the time carelessly as they did in the golden world' (116–19). And yet this carefree life in the golden world is not in the first instance English at all, but classical. Ovid describes as golden the first age of the world, when there was no need for law or war, and when the earth brought forth her produce naturally, without necessity for human labour.[21] Charles's evocative account of the Forest allows these folk and literary references to blend and clash without disharmony, and probably announces the design of Shakespeare's play to surpass Munday's into the bargain.

Pastoral

Silvius and Phebe, meanwhile, belong to a different literary genre. They are classical shepherds, drawn from a pastoral tradition that can be traced back to the Sicilian poet, Theocritus. Pastoral was generally regarded as a humble, unassuming mode, as if its practitioners were rehearsing for something grander, even though this modesty was often deceptive. Pastoral could be political; at the very least, the innocence of the shepherds' life threw into relief the corruption of court and city, as does the golden forest world of the rightful Duke Senior. Virgil wrote poetic dialogues between shepherds as a prelude to becoming Rome's epic poet, and Shakespeare's contemporary, Edmund Spenser, began with *The Shepheardes Calender* in preparation for his English epic, *The Faerie Queene*. Is Shakespeare's most pastoral play similarly self-deprecating? Does it, perhaps, represent a promise of more serious genres to come?

Or, alternatively, does *As You Like It* put forward a new assessment of pastoral itself? In my view, the play goes some way to revalue its own pastoral genre and, in the process, perhaps romantic comedy's reinscription of popular narrative too. For example, it perceptibly expands the pastoral to absorb other literary modes. In the first instance, *As You Like It*'s appropriation of the classical tradition draws on recent English love poetry. If Silvius is a thoroughly pastoral shepherd, he has learnt to practise courtship from the English Petrarchan lyric tradition. Phebe, meanwhile, who is not in love, draws attention to the conventionality of Petrarchan poetry by resolutely and comically refusing to enter into the spirit of hyperbole it entails (3.5.8–27). Meanwhile, when her turn comes to fall in love, Phebe will respond not with English Petrarch, but with a direct quotation from Marlowe's sexy, Ovidian narrative, *Hero and Leander*: 'Dead shepherd, now I find thy saw of might,/ "Who ever lov'd that lov'd not at first sight?" ' (81–2).

Shakespeare's incorporation of other genres into the pastoral is not inappropriate, since in classic pastoral shepherds' 'songs' are conventionally understood as poems, and shepherds themselves represent poets. Had not the 'Dead shepherd' Marlowe already identified himself with this tradition in his own more conventionally pastoral lyric poem, 'The Passionate Shepherd to his Love'? There is reason to suppose that these intertextual allusions are more than incidental, however. Marlowe, as well as Ovid himself, has already surfaced in 3.3, where the action pauses for Touchstone's pronouncements on poetry. The occasion is his intention to marry Audrey, who, as a goatherd, is not 'poetical'. The exchanges of 3.3 do not notably advance the action of the play: in the event, Sir Oliver Martext is dismissed without conducting the marriage. But Touchstone's observations reflect on the nature of poetry in general, with possible implications for the unassuming genre of *As You Like It* in particular. 'Capricious' (goatish, lecherous) Ovid is explicitly named (7), while Marlowe also appears obliquely in the allusion to the 'great reckoning' which caused the quarrel that killed him, and the 'little room' where his miserly Jew of Malta gleefully stored infinite riches (14).[22] When Touchstone goes on to affirm that 'the truest poetry is the most feigning' (18–19), therefore, we might construe that this is more than a passing paradox uttered by a cynical clown.

If we see Touchstone here as one of Shakespeare's wise fools, then, what does he mean? For one thing, of course, that if poetry is all lies, and if he were able to woo Audrey in poetry, he would not be bound by his own promises. And for another, that if Audrey were a lying poet, she might be less chaste than she claims, and he might not have to marry her. But at the same time, in a context where Touchstone has just compared himself to Ovid, supreme poet of desire, his aphorism might make additional meanings available to his theatre audience. First, if the truest poetry is genuinely the most feigning, true poetry is not an outpouring of emotion, but the exercise of skill in simulating (feigning) that emotion. It was to be two hundred years before the Romantics would suppose that good poetry could come from the spontaneous overflow of powerful feelings. Second, however, in emending the Folio's 'faining' to the more familiar 'feigning', the modern editor has erased a pun. To fain is to wish or to long and, since 'lovers are given to poetry' (19), the truest poetry is also about desire (faining), like Ovid's perhaps, or Marlowe's – and Shakespeare's own in this play.

Here, at least for a moment, the comedy offers to vindicate its own romantic subject matter: love is not necessarily less elevated, or less truly poetic, it proposes, than the themes of epic or, indeed, history and tragedy. If the truest poetry is the poetry of desire (faining), and in its most artful guise (feigning), it follows that the play's own pastoral genre, not to mention romantic comedy and the fairytale tradition it reinscribes, are not quite so trivial after all. On the contrary, when it invokes Ovid and Marlowe, the play aspires to a high intertexual lineage.

But how seriously should we take Touchstone's proposition, put forward, apparently in passing, by a Fool, and mocked by the satirical Jaques, who finds it incongruous, as well as self-seeking (9–10, 30)? Jaques dismisses Touchstone's knowledge of Ovid as 'ill-inhabited, worse than Jove in a thatched house' (9–10). Should we assume on these grounds that the play discounts in advance its own revaluation of pastoral, and with it romantic comedy's reinscription of fairy tale, as the place of the truest poetry?

In practice, the satirist's contribution only complicates the issues. The reference of the knowing Jaques to the unexpected presence of the king of the immortals in a cottage cites Ovid again but, in the event, his allusion does not bear out his contention. As Ovid tells the story, when Jove and Mercury entered the humble thatched cottage of Philemon and Baucis, however inappropriate the setting, they were, it turns out, surprisingly well inhabited. Indeed, they experienced the ideal hospitality of the simple life and encountered an instance, rare in Ovid, of an old married couple so happy together that they asked the gods for the privilege of dying in the same hour.[23] If, in spite of learned dismissal, a Fool can be wise about poetry, and a cottage may prove a suitable place for immortals, perhaps the humble pastoral genre, as well as romantic comedy, with its debt to the modest folk tradition, are fit for the gods, after all? (And what is more, perhaps Ovid, as the greatest poet of love, would not always endorse the play's most cynical comments on marriage.)

These issues are a long way from the simple fireside tales that, I have suggested, encourage the audience of *As You Like It* to feel at home in the play. But perhaps the form that Shakespeare invented is capacious enough – intergeneric enough – to accommodate all tastes. The many literary allusions in *As You Like It*, sometimes too fleeting for an audience to follow through in any detail, would have been more readily accessible to readers. Indeed, the play seems to have been prepared for quarto publication in 1600, but 'stayed' at the critical moment. Their density is no impediment, however, to success in the theatre. *As You Like It*'s intertextual references combine to constitute a work that is anything but simple or naive. Instead, the text reflects self-consciously and, indeed, wittily on its own artfulness, as well as on love, without ever lecturing its audience on what they ought to believe. Then, as now, spectators could take or leave the allusions, as well as their implications for the practice of comedy.

William

The unassuming qualities of the fireside tradition and the most artful intertexuality surely converge in William. If I had to name a favourite character in all of Shakespeare, it might well be William. This country bumpkin with 'A fair name' (5.1.22), as Touchstone approvingly points out, who comes from the Forest of Arden and complacently lays claim to 'a pretty wit' (28), has no origins in Lodge's romance. Moreover, his one short scene, like Touchstone's discussion of poetry, is virtually unmotivated by the story. As Audrey's rejected suitor, he makes no detectable contribution to the plot. Nor is the episode apparently designed to make time for changes of costume. In the event, the imperturbable William has very little to say for himself, displays no wit whatever, and, in the face of Touchstone's threats and his scathing irony, retreats with an amiable 'God rest you merry, sir' (59).

Authors in the pastoral genre conventionally appear, appro-priately masked, among their own fictional shepherds. Virgil plays his rustic pipe as Tityrus; Spenser speaks as Colin Clout in *The Shepheardes Calender* and elsewhere. Meanwhile, in the English poetic heritage, Geoffrey Chaucer not only represented a model for early modern poets, including both Spenser and Shakespeare; he was also thought to be the author of *The Tale of Gamelyn*. Chaucer's persona, the Geoffrey depicted in the texts, is consistently slightly bemused, inarticulate, not quite in control of events, a fictional target for his author's own wit. Is Shakespeare's William a tribute to Chaucer's Geoffrey, a stand-in for the playwright himself?

The dramatist is known to have acted in his own plays. It would surely have delighted the audience if he had originally played the fairly named William, who values his own wit, while apparently remaining quite unable to demonstrate any such attribute. It would also have placed Shakespeare in a direct line of descent from the greatest English poet to date.

There is no contradiction between the fairytale structure of the plot and the play's artistic and literary elegance. On the contrary, the familiar iteration of events and the generic situations of fairy tales leave every opportunity for amplification and elaboration. Popular narratives arguably survive because they so readily adapt to different historical moments and cultural contexts. Moreover, reinscription necessarily entails difference as well as similarity. *As You Like It* at once knowingly reproduces and radically modifies the fireside stories it rewrites, leaving us to place the emphasis wherever we choose. On the one hand, we may enjoy it as a disarming old wives' tale; on the other, we might relish it as an artful display of the paradoxes of desire, or as an accomplished demonstration of the scope of the playwright's new genre. Shakespeare leaves us free, in other words, to interpret this play as we like it.

3

King Lear and the Missing Salt

'Love like Salt'

Once upon a time there was a rich man who wanted to know how much his daughters loved him. The first said she loved him as her own life; the second answered, 'Better than all the world'; but the third replied in a riddle: 'I love you as fresh meat loves salt'. The father was enraged by this answer, which seemed to belittle him, and drove his youngest daughter out of the house.

The young woman gathered rushes in a fen, and made them into a cloak and hood to hide her fine clothes. Then she became a scullery maid in another house. One night there was to be a dance a little way off. Cap o' Rushes secretly shed her cloak and hood and went to the dance, where the master's son fell in love with her. But she left without saying who she was. The next night the same thing happened. On the third night, the master's son gave her a ring, but she slipped away as usual and returned to her scullery. When the young man pined and grew ill, Cap o' Rushes was allowed to make him some gruel, and she put the ring in it so that he found it at the bottom of the bowl.

At their wedding feast Cap o' Rushes gave instructions to the cook: there was to be no salt in the food. Her father came to the feast without recognizing the bride, and when no one could eat any of the dishes, which tasted disgusting, he burst into tears. At last he had got the point of his daughter's riddle, but too late, he thought: for all he knew, she might be dead. It was not too late, however. Cap o' Rushes embraced him and they were happy ever after.

This story was told in Suffolk in the nineteenth century,[1] but variants of it are recorded all over Europe, and literary treatments appeared in France and Italy early in the sixteenth century.[2] In one French version the rich man is a king, and he resolves to divide his property among his three daughters. A servant advises against this course, but the king is adamant, giving instructions for his youngest daughter to be killed when she disappoints him. Next day, his elder daughters marry, take possession of the castle, and turn their father out. The compassionate servant frees the youngest daughter and she finds employment minding turkeys. A prince falls in love with her at a ball, but she runs away on the stroke of midnight. The third night, she escapes as usual, but drops a shoe. The rest you know from the story of Cinderella – except that the turkey-minder will not marry the prince until he drives out the wicked sisters and restores her father to his throne.

A Corsican variant makes no reference to salt but the story otherwise follows a similar pattern, and the youngest child becomes a goatherd. Her elder siblings have dethroned the king and imprisoned him in a dungeon. It takes the third daughter a year of devoted care to restore him to his senses.[3]

Origins of *King Lear*

In the earliest form of it we know, the story of Lear is nearly as old as the folk tale. Like the tale itself, Geoffrey of Monmouth's twelfth-century history of King Leir has a happy ending. Cast out by the perfidious elder daughters who have claimed to love him so well, the king makes his way to Gaul to throw himself on the mercy of his youngest child. He is hungry and in rags, reduced to a single companion. With supreme tact, Cordeilla sends him enough wealth to equip himself like a king before he makes his formal appeal for aid at her court. The French army defeat her sisters and Leir regains his throne, to be succeeded in due course by his favourite daughter. Later on, Queen Cordeilla kills herself, but that's a different story.

Geoffrey's *History of the Kings of Britain* depicts a world of signs and wonders, populated by heroes and giants. His first king is Brutus, great grandson of Aeneas, who sets out for Britain in response to a dream: the goddess Diana has promised him a second Troy, beyond the setting sun, and further west than Gaul. No one knows for sure where Geoffrey found his material. He himself claims to be translating into Latin an ancient book written in the British tongue,[4] but such appeals to written authority guaranteed credibility in the

Middle Ages, and it seems more likely that he drew mainly on legends and folk tales. The consensus is that the story of King Leir and his three daughters represents an adaptation of 'Love like Salt'.

Geoffrey's account replaces the riddle of the salt with another, however. While Gonorilla and Regan protest that they love him more than anything in the world, Cordeilla assures Leir that she loves him as a father. But if he demands more, she has this to say: 'Look how much you have, so much is your value, and so much I love you.' Like all riddles, this one is ambiguous: is Cordeilla talking about property, or something less quantifiable? Leir interprets it according to the letter and grows angry. In due course, however, he comes to understand her meaning in reference to her sisters:

> While I had anything to give they valued me, being friends not to me, but to my gifts: they loved me then indeed, but my gifts much more: when my gifts ceased, my friends vanished.[5]

Cordeilla does not vanish, but weeps to learn of her father's suffering, and returns to take his part.

Familiarity

Both Shakespeare and his audience may have known this account from a manuscript source. Geoffrey's *History* was widely diffused by the Tudor monarchs in their quest for the ancient British roots of their own dynasty. On the other hand, there were plenty of intermediary versions of the Lear story, not least the additions of 1574 to the influential *Mirror for Magistrates*, as well as Holinshed's chronicles, sources of Shakespeare's history plays, and Spenser's *Faerie Queene*, not to mention the old play of *King Leir*, published in 1605, in which Shakespeare himself may have appeared early in his stage career.[6]

But whether or not the first audience already knew the story of Shakespeare's play, they might well recognize the folktale pattern of the opening scene. Knowing that the youngest child is conventionally the one to trust, they would be fully aware of the dramatic ironies involved in Lear's choice. If so, they were also in a position to see the difference Shakespeare made by his reinscription of the traditional narrative. On the basis of a tale that promises a happy ending, he produced what many see as his most desolate tragedy. And in the light of the daughters' contrasting speech acts, he pushed language to its limits, and perhaps beyond.

'Cinderella'

Two centuries later Coleridge grudgingly acknowledged the resemblance between a 'nursery-tale' and Lear's staged competition.[7] This is as arbitrary and unmotivated as any folk love test. Shakespeare's rendering emphasizes its own ritualistic character in its set demands for set responses, and the predetermined allocation of set rewards. The play stresses the proper sequence of replies: 'Goneril,/ Our eldest born, speak first' (1.1.53–4); 'What says our second daughter?' (67). And it confirms the traditional expectation that the third child will be the best: 'But now our joy,/ Although our last and least ...' (82–3).[8] These formal introductions of Lear's daughters are there to inform the audience, and what they present are not singular individuals but the generic characters of fireside tales. It follows that the first audience had every reason to suppose Cordelia would not reproduce the extravagant rhetoric of her elder sisters, but would tell something closer to the truth. They were encouraged, in other words, to *know where they were* with the opening scene of this play.

And so, in another way, are we, as long as we allow ourselves to acknowledge the resemblance between one of the grandest of all tragedies and popular narrative. 'Love like Salt' is no longer part of the repertoire of stories told to children, but 'Cinderella' certainly is. Here, too, a prince chooses between three sisters, and opts for the youngest and humblest, making the right choice in spite of outward appearances. Sigmund Freud noticed the parallel with 'Cinderella', and also connected Lear's choice among his three daughters with Bassanio's choice among the three caskets in *The Merchant of Venice*. Each time, a man is choosing a woman.[9] Then, as now, the correct choice is always the unassuming one: arrogance, grandiloquence, and greed are inappropriate; humility and reticence are endorsed. Shakespeare's audience is invited to choose Cordelia, since the audience may be expected to have more sense (which is to say more sense of the conventions) than the exorbitant old man who offers land for love.

Cinderella's story was well known in Shakespeare's period. Marina Warner, who also noticed the resemblance to *Lear*, finds a version of it in ninth-century China: the heroine is beaten by her stepmother and stepsister, and protected by a magic fish. In the end, the king traces her tiny golden slipper and marries her. Warner reproduces a woodcut of our own Cinderella weeping by the hearth, printed in early sixteenth-century Nuremberg.[10]

Cinderella owes her continued familiarity now not only to fairy tales, Christmas pantomimes, and Walt Disney, but to later analogues. The same humiliation, the same uncomplaining patience prepares Jane Eyre to marry Mr Rochester. The orphan Jane has no elder sisters but, as a child, she dusts and tidies after her Reed cousins, including the headstrong Eliza and the spoilt Georgiana. Later, Jane's rival is not a relation, but the Honourable Blanche Ingram, grand, glittering and haughty, while Jane is no more than a governess, and stays in the shadows when company comes to Thornfield Hall. Jane Eyre, in turn, is clearly in a direct line of descent from Fanny Price, who is upstaged by *her* cousins, Maria and Julia Bertram, and who also has a glittering and deceptive rival in Mary Crawford. Thereafter, the elder 'sisters' often disappear, but Esther Summerson and Lucy Snowe are clearly heirs of Cinderella, even before Jane Eyre had given rise to the long line of governesses and nannies who would eventually marry their employers in *The Sound of Music* and a whole genre of supermarket romance.

More recent versions of the Cinderella story probably include *Pretty Woman* (Garry Marshall, 1990), where the daily life of the prostitute-heroine is about as far from Cordelia's as possible. Successive social arrangements are stratified in different ways, but stratified they remain. The roles of prince and skivvy morph easily into executive and sex worker. Bridget Jones, meanwhile, is yet another modern Cinderella, and if the big knickers of *Bridget Jones's Diary* (Sharon Maguire, 2001) are not traceable to folklore in themselves, they surely update the humble dress that masks Cinderella's true beauty, or the cap of rushes that disguises the heroine of 'Love like Salt' as a scullion.

Happy endings

Like Shakespeare's own Perdita, the exiled princess I shall discuss in Chapter 4, Fanny Price, Jane Eyre, and the protagonist of *Pretty Woman* live happily ever after, or at least they live on in contentment. All the versions of the Lear story before Shakespeare's also end well. And when Nahum Tate rewrote Shakespeare's version for a late seventeenth-century audience in obedience to the rules of genre, his Cordelia restored her father and married Edgar, himself a wronged brother who had endured exile with patience and compassion. Tate's version prevailed with audiences throughout the eighteenth century: somehow, it seemed right. It was not until 1823 that *King Lear* recovered its tragic conclusion, and it was 1838 before Shakespeare's own words returned to the stage.

Tate might have been surprised to know that he was restoring the fairytale ending. However much he was influenced unconsciously by the pattern of popular narrative, his conscious project was to replace what seemed most arbitrary in the play with what he called 'probability'. ''Twas my good fortune', he tells us, 'to light on one expedient to rectify what was wanting in the regularity and probability of the tale, which was to run through the whole a love betwixt Edgar and Cordelia.'[11] Tate's 'probability' amounts largely to providing explanations at the level of plot for the patterns derived from the old wives' tale that survived Geoffrey's and Shakespeare's reinscription and continued to exercise its own imperatives.

Since the love test itself is highly improbable according to the canons of realism, Tate's *History of King Lear* 'explains' it by reference to Lear's old age and impetuous temperament (1.1.53–5). Without a sense of the folk tale that motivates the play, Cordelia's reticence can seem perverse. In love with Edgar, however, Tate's Cordelia doesn't want to marry Burgundy in the first place, so she has no motive for emulating her sisters to win a rich husband. But it is surely altogether less probable, in our sense of the term, that Poor Tom should happen to find himself in the very 'field' where Cordelia was to be threatened with rape, or that he would have no trouble in rescuing her from the two 'Ruffians' who have seized her for the purpose (3.4). In practice, most of Tate's changes have the effect of increasing the *coherence* of the story, rather than its likelihood. He found, he says, 'a heap of jewels, unstrung and unpolished', but 'dazzling in their disorder';[12] his reworking of Shakespeare's play strings them together and orders them, reducing its remote, ritualized plot to domesticity in the process.

Tate's happy ending implies a providential cosmos. His regularization of the action in favour of justice introduces a strong element of wish-fulfilment, since 'poetic justice' is nothing more than the gratification of a desire to ascribe the order of events to benevolent design. In Tate's version, the good end happily and the bad unhappily. Evidently, he believed with Oscar Wilde's Miss Prism that 'that is what Fiction means'.[13] Folk tales, too, commonly fulfil the wish that virtue or patience will be rewarded, and in 'Love like Salt', 'Cinderella', and Tate's *Lear* they are. Here Tate was defended by no less a luminary than Dr Johnson, who admitted to being 'shocked' that in Shakespeare's version of the play Cordelia dies. In Johnson's view, 'all reasonable beings' love justice, and no play can be the worse for depicting it.[14]

Nor was it only the eighteenth-century rage for regularity that impelled this longing for a happy ending. In 1904, while he dismissed Tate's revisions as 'sentimental', the influential critic A. C. Bradley acknowledged that he understood the 'wish' that prompted them. Indeed, he himself not only shared this wish, but believed Shakespeare would have provided a happy ending if he had written the play a few years later. Although the stage had now banished revision of the text to satisfy the demand for poetic justice, criticism would restore the happy ending by other means. According to Bradley's reading, suffering so ennobled the protagonist that Shakespeare's 'poem' might justly be called *The Redemption of King Lear*. In his view, Cordelia might have tried harder to deal tactfully with her father's question. Lear himself, however, eventually pays the price of his folly and then goes on to die happy, believing his daughter alive; good, and not evil, remains 'the principle of life and health in the world'.[15]

The eminent Shakespearean critic probably did not suspect that his interpretation was motivated by old wives' tales. And he was not alone. A generation later, G. Wilson Knight was to draw on the theory of evolution to invest the play with yet another kind of happy ending. Beyond the events of the final scene, and beyond the remorseless, amoral naturalism of the *Lear* universe, Wilson Knight finds in the 'miracle' of Cordelia's love the evolutionary goal of humanity. Since the evil-doers are finally crushed, he maintains, the play shows that good is the ultimate aim and object of human nature.[16]

Shakespeare's ending

It would be hard to find a modern critic who shares this optimism. Perhaps something in the events of the twentieth and twenty-first centuries has led us to distrust the beneficence of evolution or the likelihood that love will prevail in the end. But there is also the evidence of the text, or, strictly, texts, since the 1608 quarto (Q), published in Shakespeare's lifetime, differs in certain particulars from the Folio edition of the plays (F), compiled in 1623 by Shakespeare's colleagues. The final words of the play, spoken in Q by Albany and in F by Edgar, involve no affirmation of the triumph of good. Rather, the negatives there might be taken to imply at best resignation, at worst despair: 'We that are young/ Shall never see so much, nor live so long' (5.3.324–5). And F adds, as if to confirm the pessimism of the utterance, '*Exeunt with a dead march*'.

The lasting image of the final scene must be the entry of Lear with the body of Cordelia in his arms. When the dead Goneril and Regan are brought on stage, Albany draws attention to the 'justice of the heavens'. The Folio text changes this to the 'judgement of the heavens' (230), as if by this tiny change to move closer to the Last Judgement, and so anticipate here the apocalyptic reaction to the death of Cordelia:

> KENT   Is this the promised end?
> EDGAR   Or image of that horror?
> ALBANY Fall and cease. (261–2)

This 'image' of 'the promised end' compares the scene we see on the stage to the Doomsday paintings over the chancel arches of innumerable medieval churches. These must have remained unforgettable in Shakespeare's own time, even though many had been whitewashed over in the Reformation zeal for obliterating depictions of God. In these representations of the Last Judgement, desolation obtains on earth, as the dead push up their gravestones and the damned troop into hell. But Albany's 'Fall and cease' takes us beyond the moment identified in the Doomsday paintings, where the chancel arch itself is echoed in the arc of the heavens, and God enthroned is shown at their apex, in providential control of the terrifying events below. If, as Albany urges, the sky itself should fall, and 'Strike flat the thick rotundity o'the world' (3.2.7), both heaven and earth themselves would pass away (Luke 21: 26, 33).

At the same time, there is another possible reading of Kent's rhetorical question. The dead Cordelia in her father's arms is precisely *not* the end promised by the folktale beginning of the play, or by the rescue and reconciliation effected in Act 4. The image of Lear holding the body of his dead daughter is the more unbearable for that, as if Shakespeare's play has delivered the promised end in a previous scene, and then replaced it at the last minute with this dark parody of an embrace. Cheating the audience of the happiness every other version of the story affords them, *King Lear* comes across as bleak to the point of nihilism.

Indeed, Shakespeare's play maintains the suspense till the bitter end, tantalizing the audience with the wish it repeatedly fails to fulfil. Surely, Edmund's last-minute repentance will save the day? It does not: 'She's dead as earth', Lear insists. But then at once, 'Lend me a looking-glass;/ If that her breath will mist or stain the stone,/ Why then she lives' (5.3.259–61). And again, 'This feather stirs, she lives' (263). The commentary of the other characters shows Lear to be deluded, and yet, in a play where words have so often proved misleading, we badly want imagination to prove true. 'Cordelia, Cordelia, stay a little. Ha?/ What is't thou sayst?' (269–70). Lear's ironic reiteration of his original question here takes us back, as does the salt-free wedding feast in the folk tale, to the beginning of the story. This *ought* to be the moment when everything comes right.

The appeal of tragedy

Again it does not, and the end of the play diverges irreversibly from the fireside narrative to which it owes so much. The performance history of *King Lear* shows that for nearly two hundred years people have been increasingly willing to pay good money in order to watch this tragic story unfold, not only on stage but at the cinema. Grigori Kozintsev's intense Russian film of 1970 was quickly followed in the same year by Peter Brook's grainy, abridged version, based on his own unrelenting production of the play. Akira Kurosawa's film, *Ran* (1984), adapts the plot for medieval Japan; Edward Bond's play, *Lear* (1971), and Jane Smiley's novel, *A Thousand Acres* (1992), rewrite the story for the modern world.

Evidently, then, the pleasure of the text does not depend on happy endings. The reason why people enjoy tragedy has always been a puzzle. Aristotle's catharsis represents a possible description of the experience, but not, in my view, a motive for seeking it. In Aristotle's view, tragedy arouses pity and fear, in order to purge them, as the community might purify itself by an annual ritual or, indeed, the body might expel unclean material.

All the indications are that we enjoy pity and fear, and any number of other intense emotions, especially when these are experienced safely, in response to stories told in novels, films, or newspapers. But this does not seem adequate on its own to explain the appeal of tragedy. Freud perhaps comes closer in *Beyond the Pleasure Principle*, and then backs away again in a retraction that, as so often in Freud, reveals more than the original affirmation. Discussing the case of his little grandson, who learned to deal with his mother's absence in a game by alternately rejecting and retrieving a wooden reel, Freud comments that the child threw away the spool far more frequently than he pulled it back. The gratification, it seems, lies as much in its disappearance as in its recovery. In the same way, Freud goes on,

> the artistic play and artistic imitation carried out by adults ... do not spare the spectators (for instance, in tragedy) the most painful experiences and can yet be felt by them as highly enjoyable. This is convincing proof that, even under the dominance of the pleasure principle, there are ways and means enough of making what is in itself unpleasurable into a subject to be recollected and worked over in the mind.

The implication is that tragedy brings pain to light, retrieves it from repression, and renders it bearable to the degree that it is also made intelligible and thus mastered. But that argument does not satisfy him in the context of his own discussion of what lies *beyond* pleasure. These ideas ought to be studied by 'some system of aesthetics', he says dismissively. They are of no use to *him* because they presuppose the dominance of the pleasure principle. 'They give no evidence', he goes on, 'of the operation of tendencies *beyond* the pleasure principle, that is, of tendencies more primitive than it and independent of it.'[17]

Freud here casually discards his own wooden reel, and does not stay to retrieve it. But in the process he indicates – at least to a Freudian reading of his own text – where a psychoanalytic account of *King Lear* might lead. What if we were to discover that the play does exactly what Freud says tragedy doesn't, but he wishes it would? Or what, in other words, if we found that *Lear does* point – pleasurably – to tendencies beyond pleasure? This would imply that beyond the suffering it makes intelligible, and thus masters, it gestures towards something 'more primitive' that it cannot name.

Lacanian psychoanalysis

Fascinated by Freud's inconclusive efforts to identify what lies beyond pleasure, Jacques Lacan reread Freud to find a tragic mismatch between words and things. Language fails to map the world and leaves a realm of the unnameable, which Lacan calls the real. The little human animal gains by acquiring the capacity to signify: from now on, the child can indicate its real bodily imperatives in a network of differences more nuanced than a gurgle or a cry. Distinct forms and locations of joy and pain can be distinguished from one another in language, but only on condition of a certain alienation, as each state is named within an order of symbols learnt, in the first instance, from other people, not from the world. The moment they belong to this symbolic order, the wishes of the speaking being never quite fit the organic needs they promised to name.

Culture, which includes stories, is among the compensations for the alienation we undergo. At the same time, while the advent of the signifier cuts us off from any direct access to the organism we also are, the materiality of the real is only relegated, not excised. In Lacanian psychoanalysis the capacity to symbolize, combined with the impossibility of finding precise signifiers for what we want, creates a paradox, a speaking being, a signifying animal that is at once inextricably wedded to both culture and the real organic world, and tragically subject to the mismatch between the two.[18]

'Love like Salt' unfolds with perfect logic. The father makes a serious mistake; he learns the error of his ways; he is forgiven by the daughter who truly loves him; and they live happily ever after. *King Lear* follows the first three phases of the folk tale, but withholds the last. What logic, or what alternative to logic, drives Shakespeare's tragedy? In my view, Lacan can help us begin to answer that question.

Lacan had a number things to say about Lear himself, none of them very favourable. Lear doesn't measure up to Oedipus, he insists. Instead, he 'makes the ocean and the earth echo' with his rage, but he 'doesn't understand a thing'. 'The old fool', Lacan calls him – not, of course, without reason.[19] But suppose we tried to bring the Lacanian account of language to bear on Shakespeare's play in more detail? Is there more to it than an old fool who misses the point? Or, to put the question differently, what exactly is the point he misses?

Words and things

In the first place, a Lacanian might argue, Lear does not understand how language works. In this most eloquent, most poetic of plays, the dramatist whose own mastery of language is unexcelled explores the limitations, as well as the capabilities, of the signifier.

Prompted ultimately, perhaps, by the story of the folktale daughters who profit by their hypocritical declarations, the play becomes preoccupied by the implications of the potential gap between words and things. It is not simply that what people say cannot be trusted; nor is it merely that letters can be forged, like the one Edmund ascribes to Edgar, or misappropriated to incriminate in another context, like Gloucester's or Goneril's. The problem is not reducible to the fact that people tell lies. Rather, it is that, while we cannot be sure whether they are lies or not, words matter: they are dangerous because they have material consequences. Honest or dissembling, speech can incur banishment or earn property, and it hardly matters for the purpose whether the words match anything outside themselves. As Cornwall laconically tells Edmund of the stolen letter to his father, 'True or false, it hath made thee Earl of Gloucester' (3.5.17–18).

Speaking beings cannot help relying on language to name the world, but this reliance has no secure grounds. Lear counts on the hypocritical words of his elder daughters; Gloucester believes in the forged letter. Both are proved wrong in the event, but the problem, the play indicates, is that, while we cannot be sure when the signifier matches the world it seems to represent, language makes things happen just the same. Sincere or deceitful, speech *acts* on the world. Lear's choice, enacted in words, changes everything, enriches his daughters, disempowers him.

In short, speech invades reality; the signifier changes the material world. At the same time, reality inhabits the signifier. In the medieval society the play depicts, names are more than labels. As so many of the names in the play make clear, titles, acquired by heredity, literally *entitle*: France, Burgundy, Gloucester, Kent, Albany, Cornwall. To name a person is to specify land, wealth, and the power that corresponds to them. Lear fondly believes that he can give away his kingdom and keep his kingship:

> only we shall retain
> The name, and all th'addition to a king: the sway,
> Revenue, execution of the rest,
> Beloved sons, be yours. (1.1.136–9)

But the right to declare that he will spend a month with each daughter, and the entitlement to the 'addition' of the honours and respect due to a monarch, including a retinue of a hundred knights, were backed by the 'sway' and 'revenue' ensured by the territory he has now transferred to the next generation.

Lear's identification as king, in other words, is at once intrinsic, a matter of birth, genealogy, succession, and extrinsic, the consequence of the territory and the corresponding power named by the title. In so far as kingship depends on succession, Lear is and remains every inch a king (4.6.106). And yet, from the moment he gives away his land, his commands have no authority, no longer act on the world. The dual meaning of 'title' as both form of address and ownership are not as easily divisible as he imagines. 'Let me not stay a jot for dinner; go, get it ready' (1.4.8). But in Goneril's house, where he is now no more to the servants than 'My lady's father' (77), his orders carry no weight. Imperatives, it turns out, ensure obedience only when they are supported by the wealth that comes from possessions, and are uttered by one who has the material capacity either to reward or withhold patronage and payment. The guarantee of effectivity lies elsewhere, not in language, but in power.

The commands of the disempowered king become increasingly parodic as they grow both more extravagant and more ineffectual. His curse, however appalling when delivered by a father, does not cause Goneril to relent; nor, presumably, does it influence her fertility (1.4.267–81). Although his repeated imperatives offer to create the sounds of the storm in the imagination of the audience, they have no effect on the uproar they merely echo (3.2.1–9). At once heroic and absurd, Lear's defiance edges towards the grotesque. In this light, even his prayer, justly celebrated as a moment of recognition, also carries its own element of irony, coming at a time when he is furthest from any personal capacity to implement what he has learnt:

> Take physic, pomp,
> Expose thyself to feel what wretches feel,
> That thou mayst shake the superflux to them
> And show the heavens more just. (3.4.33–6)

Minutes later he will enter the hovel, which is the only 'superflux' his own situation affords.

A riot of signifiers

The storm scenes juxtapose the riotous capabilities of the signifier with the needs of the vulnerable human organism. An arrangement of words, images, and sound effects alternates the discord of the elements with the three distinct voices of a Fool, a king fast becoming foolish, and a Bedlam beggar. It is as if, since speech can no longer be seen as either trustworthy or effective, all three are liberated by varying degrees of madness to luxuriate in the possibilities that language confers when it is no longer answerable to the expectation that it will match the world point for point. Snatches of intertextual allusion and citation mingle scraps of the existing culture, demonology and the Bible, popular song, astrology, and the folk tradition. It is Poor Tom who invokes the old fairy tale of the King of Elfland, seeking human prey in his dark tower (3.4.178–80).[20] During the storm the 'rustling of silks' that betrays illicit love (94) succeeds the 'looped and windowed raggedness' which defines extreme poverty (31); emblematic 'pelican daughters' lead on to 'Pillicock' (penis) by free association (74–5). Meanwhile, despair personified proffers knives, halters, and ratsbane as sources of suicide (53–4); but even the fire of hell (51) is not adequate to allay the insistent, repetitive cold (57, 77, 82, 112), as the wind blows 'Through the sharp hawthorn' (45–6). Some of what they say seems relevant to these three people in the storm; some of it sounds like language on the loose. This anarchic concatenation of signifiers leads a life of its own, now acknowledging, now deferring the actuality of their plight.

'The thing itself'

Then Lear glimpses a way out in Poor Tom's nakedness, in what he suddenly sees as Tom's reduction to organic being, the real:

> Is man no more than this? Consider him well. Thou ow'st the worm no silk, the beast no hide, the sheep no wool, the cat no perfume. Ha? Here's three on's are sophisticated; thou art the thing itself. Unaccommodated man is no more but such a poor, bare, forked animal as thou art. Off, off you lendings: come, unbutton here. (3.4.101–8)

'Unaccommodated', unfurnished, he might escape the signifying inequalities of silk and wool, leather and perfume, reduce his own wants to those of an unclad human animal, dispossessed, unassuming, apparent for what it is, to become, as he imagines, Poor

Tom, 'the thing itself'. In place of F's final 'Come, unbutton here', Q has 'Come on, be true', as if to acknowledge the real condition of our material being. 'Allow not nature more than nature needs,/ Man's life is cheap as beast's' (2.2.458–9). That option – to be like the other animals – formerly a threat, now seems like a promise of release from the 'sophistication' of ceremony, hierarchy, obligation, perhaps even speech itself. Clothing defines people, just as names do. The signifier, as the inscription of human knowledge and human relationships, has come to represent a burden, and Lear seeks a place outside the culture that invests them with symbolism.

But there is for speaking beings no place beyond the symbolic order. Even to unbutton his clothes here is to make a signifying gesture: only death releases the organism from signification. Moreover, there is no survival for a poor, bare, forked animal in such an unaccommodated condition. Without the coats that protect other mammals against the elements, and born unable to fend for ourselves, we depend more evidently than most animals on the support of others. As if to underline the point, this is the moment when Gloucester arrives to lead Lear and his companions to human shelter. In the Folio he carries a flaming torch, the fire itself a signifier of the light and warmth of human habitation, and in addition, perhaps, as the gift of Prometheus, the civilized arts that constitute culture.

Non-sense

Madness seems to offer an escape from the symbolic order, divorcing words from any semblance of reference to the world. But, paradoxically, this only intermittently evades the world it tries to efface. What makes the mad Lear's encounter with Gloucester so painful is the succession of oblique allusions to actuality, including his own age and vulnerability, and the Duke's blindness, incongruously linked with his adultery. When Gloucester wants to kiss his hand, Lear answers, 'Let me wipe it first, it smells of mortality'. 'Dost thou know me?', Gloucester asks. 'I remember thine eyes well enough. Dost thou squiny at me?/ No, do thy worst, blind Cupid, I'll not love' (4.6.128–34). And there follows Lear's grand denunciation of 'authority', where power masks vice and shields it from justice (153–68).

In the same way, the Fool mingles wisdom with childish riddles, so that, as Q points out, he is 'not altogether fool' (1.4.144). His satiric 'prophecy' (3.2.80–95), given in F but not in Q, draws on a folk genre to depict a world where the proprieties are turned upside down, bringing the realm to confusion: 'When priests are more in word than matter,/ When brewers mar their malt with water ...'. The beginning of the speech lists current social abuses but then slides, without any change of form, into ideal improbabilities: 'When usurers tell their gold i'the field,/ And bawds and whores do churches build ...'. As utopian prophecy, this form of utterance resembles a traditional version of indefinite postponement (compare 'when hell freezes over'). Folklorists call it 'the locution for never'. But in so far as it satirizes contemporary evils, even if ironically, the list of inversions depicts a perpetual present, and thus constitutes 'a locution for always'.[21] Undecidably suspended between the two modes, the Fool's prophecy represents a kind of non-sense that renders absurd the world he inhabits and comments for the audience on the events the play depicts. And yet his conclusion reverts to a jingle that seems to trivialize what has gone before, while chronology reinserts the present of the play in an ancient world, long superseded:

> Then comes the time, who lives to see't,
> That going shall be used with feet.
> This prophecy Merlin shall make, for I live before his time.

Neither entirely sense nor wholly nonsense, the speeches of the Fool and of Lear's madness parody a great deal of human exchange. Generated out of prior utterances, now familiar, now wayward, unaccountable to the world of things, they are sporadically intelligible as truth to the degree that we find in them astute observations on the world we (think we) know.

Cordelia's bond

If there is no place outside the signifier, there is only an uneasy place inside it for a human animal that learns to make meanings from elsewhere, from a signifying network that pre-exists the learning process, and belongs in the first instance to others. Where does kinship reside? Both inside the culture that specifies the meaning and obligations of the family, and beyond it in the genetic link that makes the family possible. Love, itself learnt in the first instance by the little human animal dependent on a carer for the satisfaction of its organic needs, is the location where the uncertain conjunction of speech and organism becomes most apparent.

In one psychoanalytic case history, where should we locate the pain of the father who wakes up rather than continue to dream he hears the appeal of his dead son to save him? As Freud records, a father watches by his son's sick bed until the boy dies, when he goes into the next room to rest. While the exhausted father snatches a moment of sleep, the body of the child is incinerated by the flames of the candles round his deathbed. But the father is *woken* when he hears the voice of the child in his dream: '*Father, don't you see, I'm burning?*'[22] Why does a dream wake him up? Because the dream is even more unbearable than the reality. What wakes the father, in Lacan's rereading of Freud, is the terrible vision of the dead son appealing for help to a father who cannot save him. And why is this dream more unbearable than the waking reality? Because, Lacan says, 'no one can say what the death of a child is, except the father *qua* father, that is to say, no conscious being'.[23]

In waking life no one can name this pain, although a dream might touch it. Parenthood, in other words, is not a purely symbolic, emotional, or even psychological relationship. A father is not a father only at the level of the signifier, or in terms of a consciousness constructed in culture. The anguish of the child's death is compounded for the father *as* a father, in the inextricable real of that intimate, organic, generative, genetic bond, and the death that breaks this bond, like the real that is its location, is all the more intolerable in that the character of the suffering it causes cannot be named at the level of consciousness, cannot, in other words, be specified and mastered by the signifier.

If Lear misunderstands the meaning of kingship, he also tragically misconstrues the nature of kinship. Like kingship itself, heredity is both intrinsic and extrinsic. Lear can determine how much land he bequeaths to each daughter; he cannot, by definition, 'disclaim ... Propinquity and property of blood' (1.1.114–15), as he imagines. The love test he imposes on his daughters places the emphasis on the utterance: 'Which of you shall we *say* doth love us most?' (emphasis added, 1.1.51). Even the unloving Goneril concedes the problem that also confronts Cordelia, the inadequacy of language when it comes to defining a condition that is not purely linguistic. Placing love at the limits of what it is possible to say, Goneril claims to love her father 'more than word can wield the matter' (1.1.55), but then goes on regardless to tell him what he longs to hear. Regan has apparently no such scruples, and yet she too lays the emphasis on the signifier: 'I *profess*/ Myself an enemy to all other joys' (72). (There are no italics in the original texts, but the position of 'profess' at the end of the pentameter invites the actor to linger moment- arily on the word.) Only Cordelia, unwilling either to lie or to equivocate, directly confronts the impossible challenge of the task Lear imposes: 'What shall Cordelia *speak*? Love and be silent' (62); 'I am sure my love's/ More ponderous than my tongue' (77–8).

When Lear turns to his youngest daughter, the form of the ques- tion compounds the problem: 'what can you say to draw/ A third more opulent than your sisters?' (85–6). Whether by accident or design, the king explicitly sets up the test as a rhetorical compet- ition for a material prize. Cordelia's initial 'Nothing' answers the question according to the letter. There is nothing she can say to outdo the protestations of her sisters.

Asked to declare her love, the heroine of 'Love like Salt' propounds a riddle. Geoffrey's Cordeilla substitutes another. Does Shakespeare's Cordelia also reply with a riddle? 'I love your majesty/ According to my bond, no more nor less' (1.1.92–3). What is this 'bond' that specifies the measure of Cordelia's love? Allegiance? Obligation? The duty of the child to honour its parents, in accord- ance with the fifth commandment? All this, and perhaps more. Under pressure from her father, Cordelia goes on to gloss the word herself: 'You have begot me, bred me, loved me. I/ Return those duties back as are right fit,/ Obey you, love, you, and most honour you' (96–8).

Critics have found the term cold as a way of defining a daughter's love. A. C. Bradley thought Cordelia could have been more tactful at this moment. But could she? Whatever the nature of this bond, parallel usages in the play itself identify it as precisely binding. The hypocritical Edmund claims the same bond as the reason why he has allowed himself to be wounded rather than conspire against Gloucester. He has confronted his 'unnatural' parricide of a brother, he asserts, to remind him 'with how manifold and strong a bond/ The child was bound to the father' (2.1.50, 47–8). When Gloucester himself complains of 'the bond cracked 'twixt son and father', the image compares it to a rigid material, perhaps flint or iron (1.2.108–9). Lear himself sees it as organic: 'The offices of nature, bond of childhood' (2.2.370).

Kinship in the play remains binding, for better or worse. It depends on and inhabits physiology itself. Repudiating Goneril, Lear concedes, 'But yet thou art my flesh, my blood, my daughter,/ Or rather a disease that's in my flesh,/ Which I must needs call mine' (2.2.413–15). Kinship is inextricable, an effect of generation, beyond mere affection, or any duties inculcated by society. When his elder daughters ignore the bond that binds them to their father, the play calls them 'degenerate' (1.4.245; 4.2.44), and the term carries its full etymological weight. This degeneration of their children is what links Lear and Gloucester: 'Our flesh and blood, my lord, is grown so vile/ That it doth hate what gets it' (3.4.141–2).

The bond of kinship cannot be cancelled without cataclysm. Both Edgar and Cordelia experience this bond as absolute, unconditional. Lear expects justice at Cordelia's hands:

> If you have poison for me, I will drink it.
> I know you do not love me, for your sisters
> Have, as I do remember, done me wrong.
> You have some cause, they have not.

But Cordelia is bound to her father by an absolute law, beyond the equivalences of crime and punishment: 'No cause, no cause' (4.7.72–5).

In a society where lineage confers both title and property, the bond of blood takes on a metaphysical character than cannot be conjured away by behaviour, good or bad. Lear rejects his daughter; Goneril and Regan reject their father; Edmund rejects both father and brother; and the social order gives way. Gloucester's list of abuses (1.2.106–14) is paralleled in the action of the play: guests torture their hosts; servants kill their masters; sisters poison one another; and language is released from its apparent moorings in the world of reference.

Cordelia's bond of love represents both a social contract and an indissoluble tie between kin, between parent and child. Her term names this conjunction of duty, the obligations inculcated by culture, and the otherwise unnameable imperative that exceeds the limits of social exchange. Could she have been more tactful? I don't think so. The alternative to what she actually says is not another way of putting it, or the series of rhetorical affirmations that come so readily from her unloving sisters. Because the term alludes to something that cannot be named, the only other option is silence.

Language at its limits

Cordelia's death, unpredicted, virtually unmotivated, accidental, brings Lear up against the limits of language in another sense. Until this moment, Shakespeare invests his tragic protagonist with extraordinary eloquence. The play is full of linguistic innovations, while the storm episode is intelligible as a proto-modernist poem. Edgar's account of Dover cliff constitutes an overt instance of the power of verse to create illusions (4.6.11–24). But in the final scene, it is as if Lear's anguish is beyond formulation, except in the flattest signifiers of a practically physical pain. 'Howl, howl, howl, howl', he exclaims, as he carries on the body of his dead daughter (5.3.255). Is this an imperative addressed to the bystanders, or a representation of the sound the actor is to make at this moment? Either way, the repeated monosyllable stands in radical contrast to the whirling words of the earlier scenes. Previously elaborate or tortured syntax now gives way to blank parataxis: 'She's dead as earth'; 'He's dead and rotten' (5.3.259, 283).

The play daringly attributes to its tragic protagonist a remarkably unheroic last speech:

> And my poor fool is hanged. No, no, no life!
> Why should a dog, a horse, a rat have life
> And thou no breath at all? O thou'lt come no more,
> Never, never, never, never, never.
> Pray you undo this button. Thank you sir. O,o,o,o. (304–8)

Q prints this in prose with incidental variants. After a button, a last courtesy and the four 'o's that probably represent a cry of pain, Lear urges, 'Break, heart, I prithee break'. F, which ascribes this last appeal to Kent, adds two lines that justified for Bradley his discovery of a happy ending, but which we are more likely to attribute to dementia: 'Do you see this? Look on her: look, her lips,/ Look there, look there!' (309–10). And then the hero dies.

This is an extraordinary conclusion. In the other tragedies, Othello lays claim to his former stature when he says, 'I have done the state some service' (5.2.339). Macbeth dies with armour on his back (5.5.52) and Cleopatra turns to marble before our very eyes (5.2.238–9). But there is no such grandeur for Lear. If the bond names – and fails to name – the unnameable relationship, beyond obligation, between parent and child, the final scene of *King Lear* dramatizes – and fails to dramatize – the unspeakable pain of its loss. This grand admission of inevitable inadequacy casts in an ironic light the concluding speech of the play: 'The weight of this sad time we must obey,/ Speak what we feel, not what we ought to say' (5.3.322–3). Yes, indeed, but how? The difficulty of doing just that is exactly where the tragic events of the play began. True, the symbolic order may prescribe 'what we ought to say'; learnt from others, belonging, as it does, to a culture that always pre-exists the individual, however, it doesn't always allow us to 'speak what we feel'.

For speaking beings there is no place outside language. But there is no simple way of speaking the truth inside it, either. Drawing ultimately on a spare, austerely told folk tale about the power of words to deceive, *King Lear* builds a monumental demonstration of the capabilities of language. By its difference from the same folk tale, the play brings into focus the tragic mismatch between words and things that both defines and drives the signifying human animal.

This tragedy exists in culture; it tells a story that gives pleasure; and its performance history demonstrates that it has consistently drawn audiences to its depiction of distress. The play offers to seduce with a dazzling surface, a festival of signifiers, now lurid, now lyrical, while, paradoxically, it also throws into relief the limits of language, the inability to specify a pain no conscious being can name. In the process, it points to a component of human experience that exceeds culture, a suffering beyond the reach of the pleasurable signifiers that compose it. Out of a fireside narrative about lies and a riddle, *King Lear* constructs a veil of signifiers that curtains off a direct encounter with this pain, and yet alludes, even so, to a realm beyond pleasure that culture cannot choose but screen.

4

The Exiled Princess in *The Winter's Tale*

What's in a name?

According to A. W. Schlegel in a lecture of 1811, delivered two hundred years after Shakespeare's play was probably first performed, *The Winter's Tale* has a particularly good title. This work, he argued,

> is as appropriately named as *A Midsummer Night's Dream*. It is one of those tales which are peculiarly calculated to beguile the dreary leisure of a long winter evening, which are attractive and intelligible even to childhood, and which ... transport even manhood back to the golden age of imagination. The calculation of probabilities has nothing to do with such wonderful and fleeting adventures, ending at last in general joy.[1]

Schlegel may gild the play in his own imagination, but he is surely right about the significance of its name. The 'dreary leisure' of long winter evenings in earlier centuries can hardly be imagined by a generation that takes electric light and television for granted, not to mention central heating. In a society with no such advantages, by contrast, any story must have been exceptionally welcome, no matter how improbable the tale, at a time when darkness and bad weather kept people at home.

This was evidently the context in which fairy tales flourished. A decade after the play's first performance, Robert Burton listed the 'ordinary recreations' of winter, including 'merry tales of lovers, lords, ladies, giants, dwarfs'. Burton augmented *The Anatomy of Melancholy* with each successive edition, and by 1632 this list had come to include a number of other figures, who also feature, no doubt coincidentally, in *The Winter's Tale* itself, including kings and queens, as well as thieves and confidence tricksters.[2]

When Shakespeare named *The Winter's Tale*, the title identified a genre. Thomas Campion's *Two Books of Airs*, published in 1613, includes a song in praise of an idealized country couple. Their skills include the ability to 'tell at large a winter tale'.[3] But the phrase was already current by the time George Peele wrote *The Old Wives Tale*, in the late 1580s or early 1590s. Peele's comedy begins when three pages, lost in the woods, take shelter in a cottage. 'Methinks, gammer', one of them suggests to their hostess, 'a merry winter's tale would drive away the time trimly.' Another begs for a story about a giant and a king's daughter. 'Well,' she responds, 'I am content to drive away the time with an old wives' winter's tale.'[4]

Evidently, winter's tales concern supernatural figures and magical events. They register the sources and occasions of dreams and anxieties, desires and fears, not truth. The youthful hero of John Lyly's boys' play, *Sappho and Phao* (1584), encounters the sibyl on his travels. It is late, and the shrivelled old woman offers him shelter for the night, adding, 'Now, for that these winter nights are long, and that children delight in nothing more than to hear old wives' tales, we will beguile the time with some story'.[5] The tale she recounts is her own. Apollo granted her long life, but she failed to ask for youth. The sibyl thus joins the list, from King Midas to the old couple in 'The Three Wishes', of people who should have taken more care in choosing magical gifts.[6]

The sibyl's story does not end 'in general joy'. It seems, then, that while a 'winter's tale' was more or less synonymous with an 'old wives' tale', such narratives are not always merry. Mamillius promises a story of sprites and goblins, on the grounds that 'A sad tale's best for winter', and begins ominously: 'There was a man ... / Dwelt by a churchyard' (*The Winter's Tale*, 2.1.25–30). Marlowe's Barabas remembers 'winter's tales' recounted by old women, who spoke of 'spirits and ghosts that glide by night'.[7] The supernatural component of such stories can be frightening, it seems, at least to the young or the gullible. When Macbeth freezes at the sight of Banquo's ghost, his wife derides his cowardice as childish. This terror, she tells him, 'would well become/ A woman's story at a winter's fire,/ Authoris'd by her grandam' (*Macbeth*, 3.4.63–5).

Meanwhile, a 'sad' tale can be a serious one, or it can 'send the hearers weeping to their beds'. Richard II, at the final parting from his queen, urges her to sit by the fire 'in winter's tedious nights', and tell his lamentable history (*King Richard II*, 5.1.40–5).

Realism?

Is Shakespeare's *Winter's Tale* predominantly merry, then, or sad? And does it, like the best fireside narratives of the period, involve the supernatural? Ben Jonson thought so. Believing, in true neoclassical fashion, that drama should obey the laws of probability, Jonson condemned the 'drolleries' of *The Winter's Tale* that 'make nature afraid'.[8] These are certainly there for all to see: a riddling oracle, a royal child saved against all odds and, perhaps, a resurrection from the dead. Modern critics have generally ignored the possibility of a magical ending, however, to follow instead the play's alternative hints that Paulina has kept the Queen's survival secret for sixteen years in order to create a fiction of her miraculous awakening in the chapel. A century after modernism first challenged the assumption that art must copy what the eye sees, it seems that nineteenth-century novels and twentieth-century soap operas still constrain the collective imagination to the point where fiction ought always to replicate what might happen in real life.

It could, of course, be argued that the idea of keeping a wife concealed and in isolation from her remorseful husband for sixteen years, then exhibiting her collusion in a fictitious revival as a basis for reconciliation, is no more realistic, in the strict sense of the term, than bringing her back from the dead. Is the play best understood as an imitation of life? Or, should we, as its title suggests, approach it in the first instance as an old wives' tale, although one with a considerable difference in the telling? And have critics since Schlegel been right to suppose that it culminates in general joy?

The first three acts are as mimetic as any of Shakespeare's court scenes. There is not much here that could be described as 'merry'. Indeed, the court of Leontes seems remote from fairy tale of any kind. Psychoanalysis would support the view that marital jealousy might well be as unheralded, inexplicable, and unyielding as it seems in Leontes. That unprompted jealousy, a kind of madness,

is specified with a bluntness that makes it live for the audience,
even though we know it has no grounds:

> many a man there is (even at this present,
> Now, while I speak this) holds his wife by th' arm,
> That little thinks she has been sluic'd in 's absence
> And his pond fish'd by his next neighbour, by
> Sir Smile, his neighbour. (1.2.192–6)

This bitter phrasing differs from the grand, cosmic metaphors that
characterize the tragedies. While the jealous Othello swings between
extremes, from the invocation of cisterns for toads to breed in to
the high poetic eloquence of 'the plumed troops and the big wars'
(4.2.62–3; 3.3.352), Leontes' account of the imagined adultery is
relentlessly ordinary. Here he visualizes it as an everyday occurrence,
executed by the ingratiating man next door, and baldly represents
it as sluicing, washing out, or flushing with (seminal) fluid. In the
analogy kings are reduced to fishermen poaching on each other's
property, and the comparison of wives to ponds shows how far the
forgeries of jealousy coarsen the sexual act.

There is nothing in the source text to suggest the physiological
revulsion of Shakespeare's protagonist. Robert Greene's *Pandosto* is
a romance, at that time an episodic story of extravagant emotion
and far-fetched adventure. While Greene's tale of tyranny in action
records Pandosto's mounting sexual jealousy, it does not anticipate
the play's brutal realism in depicting the king's disgust. There might,
Leontes maintains, in a variation on the proverbial wisdom of the
time, be a spider at the bottom of the cup, and it would be possible
to drink without consequences, as long as the drinker didn't know
it. But suppose a man were to see it there after drinking? At once,
'he cracks his gorge, his sides,/ With violent hefts.' And Leontes
concludes: 'I have drunk, and seen the spider' (2.1.44–5). That
terse final assertion is rendered the more shocking by the repulsive
parallel.

Florizel and Perdita

In between this opening dramatization of a love that turns to hate
and the closing scene of reunion in Paulina's chapel, however, a

story familiar from countless winter's tales, of a princess in exile and a prince who perceives her worth even in humble circumstances, constitutes an episode so distinct that we might treat it as a play-within-the-play, a self-contained narrative belonging to a different genre. Indeed, the eighteenth century did exactly that. The first performance of the whole play since the 1630s did not impress the audience in 1741. For the rest of that century the only available versions on the stage were romantic comedies: at Covent Garden Morgan Macnamara's *The Sheep-Shearing or, Florizel and Perdita*, based on Act 4; and at Drury Lane David Garrick's *Florizel and Perdita*, in effect an adaptation of Acts 4 and 5.

Thanks to the source text, *Pandosto*, Shakespeare's dramatization of Perdita's story is generally classified as pastoral romance, and so, in a sense, it is. But what if we were to take seriously the title's allusion to fairy tale, the genre romance itself draws on and recasts as literature? How far does the text authorize a reading that embraces improbability? How would the invocation of the fireside tradition affect our understanding of the genre of *The Winter's Tale*, and specifically of the statue that comes back to life?

Fairy gold

In *Pandosto* Greene narrates the unexpected discovery of a well-dressed baby with a great deal of circumstantial detail. Missing one of his flock, a shepherd looks for it in the ivy by the sea. Instead, he finds a little boat, with a child wrapped in scarlet and gold. He thinks of taking the infant to the authorities but, when the bundle also turns out to contain a full purse, he hesitates and finally succumbs to the lure of the gold. His wife is less enthusiastic at first: surely this baby must be an illegitimate child of her husband's? She too, however, is eventually persuaded by the money, and the couple resolve to treat both wealth and child as their own.[9]

The romance thus inventively echoes the father's story at the beginning of the daughter's in this momentary parody of the marital jealousy that motivated the exposure of the baby in the first place. At the same time, the provision of so much explanatory information ensures that *Pandosto* concentrates on verisimilitude at the most improbable point of the narrative, namely, the moment in the story that is most evidently derived from fairy tale. It is as if Greene's romance is eager to leave its folklore origins behind. Children abandoned to their fate and fostered by poor people had been a staple of both written fiction and oral narrative in Europe at least since Sophocles converted the legend of Oedipus into high tragedy.[10] If in the Greek tale Oedipus was exposed, but saved and brought up by a shepherd, Rome owed its foundation to Romulus and Remus, thrown into the Tiber but rescued and suckled by a wolf, until a herdsman discovered the boys and reared them as his own.

Romance took up the tradition. Daphnis and Chloe, whose Greek love story was popularized in England by Angel Day's translation in 1587, are both children of noblemen brought up by herdsmen.[11] By the 1590s, when Sir Calidore, knight of Book VI of *The Faerie Queene*, falls in love with a beautiful shepherdess, it must have come as no surprise to Spenser's readers that she turns out to be the long-lost daughter of the lord and lady of a nearby castle, found and fostered by a shepherd.[12]

Where Greene's romance sets out to distract attention from its folktale elements, however, Shakespeare's play draws attention to them. While the ivy survives in vestigial form, and illegitimacy (but with no implications for marital jealousy) strikes the Old Shepherd as a likely explanation of the baby's exposure (3.3.65–77), the text of *The Winter's Tale* explicitly introduces fairy tale at the high point of the rescue itself: 'So, let's see: it was told me I should be rich by the fairies. This is some changeling' (3.3.114–16). There is no mimetic moral or psychological deliberation here, and no surrender to the temptation of the gold. Instead, the wealth that comes with the child simply serves to confirm the supernatural prediction: 'This is fairy gold, boy, and 'twill prove so' (3.3.119). The idea of magical enrichment was a familiar one. Ben Jonson's Mab, queen of the fairies, leaves money in people's shoes.[13] Maids who keep the house spick and span may find the fairies have left silver in their shoes, their pockets, or some brightly polished vessel.[14] As late as 1881, the seventy-year-old James Napier recorded his own childhood belief that the fairies hid money in places where good people were sure to find it.[15]

Without abandoning its romance heritage, *The Winter's Tale* also emphasizes its resemblance to an old wives' tale. Moreover, like such stories, the play accommodates the passage of time without anxiety. 'Snow White' begins with a mother's wishes for her unborn daughter, and in no (narrative) time at all the mother dies and the daughter grows up to constitute a threat to her stepmother's pre-eminence as the fairest of them all. The Sleeping Beauty passes a hundred years of oblivion in the blink of a textual eye. By contrast, if *Pandosto* rationalizes the folktale elements that constitute the origin of romance, it also smoothes over the transition from one generation to the next by recording realistic details of the found-ling's childhood. *The Winter's Tale*, however, proclaims the power of Time – and fiction – to 'leave the growth untried/ Of that wide gap' (4.1.6–7). Verisimilitude, it seems, is not the main concern in this episode, at least, of Shakespeare's play.

The shepherds in *Pandosto* call their adopted daughter Fawnia, giving her an appropriately pastoral name. Perdita's name, instead, is conferred by her mother in a dream, and identifies her state: 'for the babe/ Is counted lost for ever, Perdita,/ I prithee call't' (3.3.32–4). Perdita, 'the lost girl' in Latin, thus represents the solution to the riddle posed by the oracle: '*the king shall live without an heir, if that which is lost be not found*' (3.2.134–6). Her name aligns her with all those other fairytale heroines called after their condition: Snow White with her pale skin; Cinderella, who sleeps among the ashes in the hearth; and Cap o' Rushes, disguised by a cloak and hood she weaves out of reeds.

Banishment

These young women are driven by cruelty or wickedness into exile, banished from their proper place, if only as far as the scullery. Like the Goose-Girl, ousted on her way to her own wedding by her perfidious maid and reduced to menial work, all of them bear their humiliation with patience, and all of them finally marry a rich husband when, by magical or other means, he sees them in the beautiful clothes appropriate to their true rank. Is there a trace of this familiar folktale pattern in Perdita's first appearance in the play, dressed up and garlanded as Flora, to the admiration of Prince Florizel?

Florizel, however, already loves the girl he believes to be a shepherd's daughter, and has sworn to marry her, despite the difference of rank. This difference presents a serious obstacle to Greene's
Prince Dorastus. Two contrary voices argue the case in his head, one
urging love and the other insisting on the disgrace of so unsuitable
a passion:

> Shamest not thou, Dorastus, to name one unfit for thy birth,
> thy dignities, thy kingdoms? Die, Dorastus; Dorastus, die.
> Better hadst thou perish with high desires than live in base
> thoughts.[16]

Happily, love prevails over considerations of status, but Fawnia
does not yield to her admirer until she has successfully held
out for marriage. *The Winter's Tale*, however, in true fairytale
manner, simply bypasses most of these issues. The anxiety of the
lovers centres not on the inappropriateness of their relationship
but mainly on the predictable anger of the King. Florizel himself
inhabits a realm of pure love, independent of social obstacles:

> Or I'll be thine, my fair,
> Or not my father's. For I cannot be
> Mine own, nor anything to any, if
> I be not thine. To this I am most constant,
> Though destiny say no. (4.4.42–6)

Although fine clothes are the key to Prince Charming's attention
in 'Cinderella' and its variants, the fireside tradition also supports
the possibility of love between a prince and a seeming pauper.
In Victorian Lincolnshire a little girl called Sally Brown told Mrs
M. C. Balfour, the folktale collector, a story she had heard from her
mother. A rich old lord, who lived in a palace by the sea, had only
one living relative, a little granddaughter. His favourite daughter
had died when her baby was born and the grandfather vowed never
to see the little girl's face. She grew up despised, her only friend
a gooseherd, whose merry piping could always make her dance.
Tattercoats, as she was mockingly known, lived on scraps and wore
torn clothes from the ragbag. One day, a prince asked Tattercoats
and the gooseherd the way to the palace. As the herd-boy played
a low, sweet tune, the prince fell in love with his companion. He

prevailed on her to come that night to the king's ball, where he was to select his bride. On the stroke of midnight, to the amazement of all the lords and ladies, Tattercoats and the gooseherd, with his flock of geese, walked the length of the ballroom to the throne. At once the prince stood up and presented the ragged girl to the assembled company as his chosen bride. Only then, when the gooseherd quietly played what sounded like birdsong in the distant woods, were her rags transformed to shining robes. (The gooseherd was never seen again.)[17]

In the highly stratified societies where such stories circulated, these tales clearly fulfilled in fantasy a desire to overcome social difference. At the same time, like the custom of choosing a May Queen, or a Summer King and Queen at Whitsun,[18] they commonly reproduce the hierarchy itself on which the longed-for accession to wealth and power depends: Tattercoats is *really* of noble birth. So too is Perdita, and if Florizel's insistence that all her acts are 'queens' both emphasizes the grace of her performance as mistress of the feast and represents a promise for the future (4.4.146), it also points to a perceived incongruity between the accomplished shepherdess and her rustic environment. Even Polixenes, in spite of himself, concedes that she seems 'Too noble for this place' (159). When in *Love's Labour's Lost* Shakespeare shows a courtier in love with a real country wench, the effect is comic, not romantic. Outside the folk tradition itself, with rare exceptions, it would be several centuries before the downtrodden heroine would successfully cross social boundaries in *My Fair Lady* or *Pretty Woman*. The issue was always class, rather than wealth. Jane Eyre belongs to Mr Rochester's own social class, even though the Reeds banish their orphaned relation, obliging her to earn her own living. Elizabeth Bennet's father is a gentleman, although he is so much poorer than Mr Darcy and Mr Bingley and lacks their aristocratic connections.

Unknown identity

Perdita's situation remains exceptional in one respect, however. While Snow White, Cinderella and Tattercoats know even in exile who they are, Perdita believes herself to be a shepherd's daughter. Like Oedipus, although with less catastrophic consequences, she does not know her real parentage. While this version of the tale of the exiled princess is less familiar to us now, it has an equally long history in Western culture. The author of the twelfth-century *Lais* attributed to Marie de France claims to have rewritten in verse for a courtly audience the Breton tales she had heard tell. Among them, 'Le Fresne' shows its folk roots clearly. This lay recounts the story of a mother who, to avoid the accusation of illegitimacy, exposes one of her newborn twins, with a length of rich brocade and a ring as tokens of her origins. The child is discovered by a convent porter, brought up by the abbess and named Le Fresne, after the ash tree where she was found. Years later, a noble lord falls in love with her. The two live together in his castle, but his knights persuade him that he needs a legitimate heir, born to a wife of his own station. They choose him a lady of suitable rank and, before she leaves, Le Fresne undertakes to make up the bridal bed in the way she knows her lover prefers. To honour him, she covers it with the brocade that was found with her so long ago. Seeing the fabric, and then the ring, the bride's mother recognizes her long-lost daughter, twin sister of the bride herself. The marriage is annulled, and Le Fresne marries her nobleman in due course.[19]

Sexuality

As 'Le Fresne' demonstrates, traditional stories are often sexually franker than our own Victorianized and Disneyfied versions might lead us to suppose. Le Fresne lives with her lover. In the seventeenth century such a liaison would ruin a princess, but a current of sexuality runs through Perdita's story, even so, possibly legitimized by her rural setting. She herself names her desire: she wants her lover 'quick, and in [her] arms' (4.4.132). At the same time, the danger of her situation is never far from the imagery of the play. Florizel expands on the source in *Pandosto* when he defends his disguise as a shepherd on the basis of divine example: 'Jupiter/ Became a bull, and bellow'd . . . ' (4.4.27–8). Jupiter, many in the audience would know, transformed himself into an animal in order to abduct and rape the terrified Europa.[20] Florizel's other mythological precedents are no more reassuring (4.4.28–30). The prince is quick to insist on the propriety of his own intent, but the parallels have been made. When Perdita appeals to Proserpina who, 'frighted', dropped her flowers from Dis's wagon, she invokes a young girl snatched up by the god of the underworld, and driven to his dark kingdom in a careering chariot (4.4.116–18).[21] The ideal pastoral world of Act 4 includes daffodils that 'take' the winds of March, and 'bold' oxlips. Like Florizel repudiating the explicitly sexual precedents he also invokes, Perdita, by contrast with the sexually assertive flowers she lists (119, 125),[22] refuses to cultivate 'nature's bastards' (4.4.83). But while the couple maintain the chaste relationship that befits royal love, sex remains in view in the margins of their exchanges.

Identifications

Ironically, Perdita has at this stage no way of knowing that her father had rejected her on the grounds that he too refused to cultivate a bastard. Perdita's ignorance of her birth helps to release her from the constraints of a fixed 'identity'. In the utopian world of the play's second half, she shows herself equally at home in a discontinuous series of subject positions, as diffident shepherdess, and courteous mistress of the feast, Princess of Sicilia, and future Queen of Bohemia; she is successively the obedient daughter of the Old Shepherd and the loving child of Hermione.

There are no identities, Jacques Derrida points out, only identifications. To put his proposition in Derrida's own words, which are more complicated, but also more nuanced, 'an identity is never given, received, or attained; only the interminable and indefinitely phantasmatic process of identification endures'.[23] His point in the context is that, in order to tell his own story as autobiography, he has to use a first-person pronoun, but this pronoun does not denote something fixed and given, a 'character' that precedes his story and accounts for his reaction to events. There is no prior, explanatory identity. Instead, the 'I' that speaks or writes forms itself for the purpose, in order to take up a position in a language that already exists and belongs to others. Identification thus occurs in a specific situation; it pertains to a particular time and place; and other identifications will succeed it, called forth by other situations.

The generic characters of winter's fireside tales are not expected to have explanatory identities, either. Except in so far as fairytale princesses are virtuous (or not), as well as beautiful (or not), there is very little else to know about them. Meanwhile, successive identifications come as standard in the tradition of popular narrative: woodcutter's sons gladly marry princesses and become kings; princesses reluctantly turn into goose-girls and scullery-maids without experiencing problems of adjustment. However welcome or unwelcome the change, there is no suggestion that they will find themselves psychologically incapable of sustaining their new role. On the contrary, rather than either gloat or repine, the stories require them simply to get on with it.

The Winter's Tale takes full advantage of the space this tradition allots to its generic characters. In the course of the action, Perdita moves with apparent equanimity from one situated subject-position to another. In a touch that seems to draw attention to the provisionality of all identifications, the play first introduces her to the audience as already other than she is, dressed up to represent a goddess: 'no shepherdess, but Flora' (4.4.2). With remarkable economy, the phrase evokes the duality of her situation, reminding the audience of Time's account of this new protagonist: at once a 'shepherd's daughter' and 'grown in grace/ Equal with wond'ring' (4.1.27, 24–5).

The audience, however, knows that neither identification is more accurate than the other. Perdita's true situation is not *there*: she is no more a shepherd's daughter than she is a goddess. At the same time, she is not yet a princess either, to the degree that the term implies another social situation. If in the first instance she has to be coaxed to put herself forward as mistress of the feast, she goes on to carry out this duty with perfect grace, engaging in courtly debate about the proper relationship between art and nature, and distributing flowers in a vocabulary that seamlessly blends the two (4.4.116–27). While the references in this eloquent and lyrical speech are literary (Proserpina, Juno, Cytherea), the wild flowers are closely observed, as we might expect from a keeper of sheep. Editors who worry over 'violets dim' have surely never seen a sweet violet growing in the wild. The earliest variety is barely perceptible at first glance, its short stem making the tiny purple flower especially hard to distinguish from the soil or the surrounding vegetation. Perdita's role invests her with a certain authority, but she also remains a shepherdess.

If 'Cinderella' and its variants, including 'Tattercoats', register social transformations as changes of dress, *The Winter's Tale* goes one better: here a changed identification becomes an *effect* of clothing. 'Methinks I play', Perdita comments, suddenly surprised by her own sexual explicitness, 'as I have seen them do/ In Whitsun pastorals: sure this robe of mine/ Does change my disposition' (4.4.133–5). An actor would recognize the plausibility of this claim: a different costume releases a different performance.

Meanwhile, just as his ballads parody the old tale that constitutes the plot of the play, Autolycus, the great impersonator, parodies Perdita's social versatility, as the courtier-turned-pickpocket-turned-victim-turned-pedlar. Autolycus, who has his own folk ancestry in the widespread tradition of tales about clever tricksters,[24] finally turns courtier again when he changes clothes with Florizel and peels off his pedlar's beard: 'Whether it like me or no, I am a courtier. Seest thou not the air of the court in these enfoldings? ... I am courtier *cap-a-pe*' (literally, from hat to foot) (4.4.732–8). Even the Clown is transformed by costume: 'You denied to fight with me this other day, because I was no gentleman born. See you these clothes? say you see them not and think me still no gentleman born' (5.2.130–1). The Clown's claim is absurd, of course, but not entirely so in a world where sumptuary laws governed the degree of finery legitimate for different social ranks. (In our own day, makeover shows often indicate the degree to which a change of appearance can still modify behaviour.)

Perdita's costume will continue to mark her changes of fortune. She accepts her demotion with remarkable resignation: 'this dream of mine— / Being now awake, I'll queen it no inch farther,/ But milk my ewes, and weep' (4.4.450–2). The vocabulary at this moment becomes appropriately simple and substantial, and 'queen it' is both condensed and colloquial. While the Folio text includes no stage direction, editors have tended to concur that the phrase incorporates both dream and costume: Perdita surrenders at once her fantasy of a royal marriage and her dress as Flora, perhaps removing her garlands in order to revert to her situation as a shepherd's daughter. To impersonate the Princess of Libya at the court of Leontes, however, she will in due course be 'habited' as becomes the wife of a prince (4.4.548–9). Leontes is perfectly convinced, until the message from Polixenes enlightens him.

Modern identity

By the eighteenth century, on the other hand, the processes of modernization had set in, and what passes for realism had begun to take hold, investing the protagonist with a fixed identity. Garrick's Perdita, who might well find a home in soap opera, is altogether more pallid, more properly 'feminine' than Shakespeare's, and much more consistent. She has, in other words, a 'character'.

But Garrick's rewritten text makes very clear how far this represents a loss of freedom. Virtuous 'character' tends to mean conformity to the prevailing stereotype. In accordance with eighteenth-century values, the virginal Perdita is now largely desexualized. Here she says nothing of her desire to hold Florizel in her arms. The raped Proserpina disappears from her utterances, too, while the bold oxlips in the catalogue of sexualized flowers become 'gold oxlips', and thus purely decorative.[25] Moreover, Garrick deletes Shakespeare's moment of egalitarian independence ('I was not much afeard', 4.4.444): instead, when Polixenes forbids their marriage, Garrick's insipid heroine begs Florizel to forget her – with the predictable effect of urging him on to still greater protest-ations of love. Overcome with emotion as the statue of her mother comes to life, she leans against Florizel for support, prompting him to exclaim, 'This is too much for hearts of thy soft mold'.[26]

Modern 'character' depends on consistency, and thus restricts the bearer: conceived as innate, disposition is more difficult to alter. At the end of the play Garrick's Perdita, unlike Shakespeare's, exper-iences considerable anxiety about the transition to her new social status. But the identity that modernity confers, it turns out, is partly socially produced after all, as acquired patterns of behaviour map onto disposition. To the degree that it is the effect of socialization, modern identity is not wholly fixed. It is capable of change, but only by a process of hard work. Perdita is a princess by birth but, brought up beyond the pale of civil society, she will have to learn how to conduct herself like one. Here is the eighteenth-century Perdita's final speech:

> I am all shame
> And ignorance itself, how to put on
> This novel garment of gentility,
> And yield a patch'd behaviour, between
> My country-level, and my present fortunes,
> That ill becomes this presence. I shall learn,
> I trust I shall with meekness.

In Garrick's version the 'novel garment' that will release Perdita from her country background is purely metaphorical. Evidently, she has to acquire the manners appropriate to her new station, and a virtuous meekness, understood as innate (and feminine) will enable her to submit to the necessary discipline.

It must be clear which of these Perditas has more in common with our own postmodern moment, and also which has more appeal for anyone who would welcome a more equal relationship between men and women. Like any fairytale princess, Shakespeare's figure has no identity, only a succession of identifications, and she inhabits each of them without indications of serious anxiety. Garrick's has a single, continuous character; this is feminine, innocent, vulnerable and demure; his Perdita can change only as a result of resocialization, in submission to others who know what's good for her.

Morgan Macnamara's *The Sheep-Shearing or, Florizel and Perdita*, meanwhile, the rival production at Covent Garden, evades the problem of adjustment with some ingenuity. Here the Old Shepherd is really Antigonus in disguise, and he has kept a close eye on the courtship. We can be sure, therefore, that this Perdita has been brought up with the manners appropriate to her birth.

Resurrection?

If we see Hermione's story as predominantly mimetic, with elements of folk tale (the slandered queen, the riddling oracle) and Perdita's story as predominantly a fireside tale, with elements of realism (the Clown's shopping list, the pedlar's wares, for instance), what are we to make of the moment when the two stories converge? Which of the two narrative logics prevails when the statue moves and speaks in Paulina's chapel? Does Act 5 revert to the realism of the first three acts, leaving the traditional story of the exiled princess as an interlude in an otherwise mimetic play, or does the fairy tale carry over? Should we assume that Hermione has been living in seclusion all along, or is her resurrection legitimately seen as magical?

Much of the motive for insisting on the realist option seems to be a critical reluctance to allow Shakespeare to have written an old wives' tale. The supporting textual evidence centres on the now wrinkled Hermione's own claim to have 'preserv'd' herself (5.3.127), in conjunction with the Second Gentleman's affirmation of Paulina's regular visits to the 'removed house' where the statue has been 'many years in doing' (5.2.107–8, 97). In this light, several of the earlier exchanges in Act 5 now take on new meanings, among them Paulina's reluctance to let Leontes marry again, unless she herself chooses a new bride, 'As like Hermione as is her picture' (5.1.74), as well as her assertion that this will be when 'your first queen's again in breath' (83). Intelligible at the time as a poetic negative, or the folk locution for 'never', like Florizel's 'The stars, I see, will kiss the valleys first' (5.1.205), that insistence now turns in retrospect from a prohibition to a veiled promise.

But precisely as realism, this account is not without its problems. Leontes saw Hermione, as he thought, dead (5.3.139–40). At the time, this carried absolute conviction for the audience. Paulina insists, 'I say she's dead: I'll swear 't.' Is this a wilful lie? She goes on to challenge Leontes to test the evidence for himself: 'If word nor oath/ Prevail not, go and see' (3.2.201–2). At the end of the scene the King accepts her invitation, although not in disbelief: 'bring me/ To the dead bodies of my queen and son' (232–3). Moreover, he vows to visit daily the chapel where they lie (238–9). If this has been a charade, he has prayed on her grave 'in vain' (5.3.140). In vain, too, is Perdita reduced to tears by the story of her mother's death (5.2.81–9). What is more, Hermione seems not to have been told of Perdita's return (5.3.121–5). (Just how assiduous have Paulina's visits been?)

If we interpret the play as realism, Hermione's 'death' must have been an ingenious illusion created by Paulina to sustain the punishment of a remorseful Leontes over sixteen years. But if we allow the title, as well as Ben Jonson's contemptuous reference to its 'drolleries', to prevail, the play is a fairy tale. And in this genre regeneration is not unusual, while recovery once enchantment runs out is common. The Sleeping Beauty, who wakes after a hundred years, shares a deathlike trance with Snow White, whose tale was evidently familiar to Shakespeare, since he rewrote it with some fidelity as the story of Imogen in *Cymbeline*, within a year or two of *The Winter's Tale*. Both Snow White and Imogen fall into a sleep so deep that it is taken for death. Imogen's brothers conduct her funeral; Snow White is encased in a glass coffin, until a prince falls in love with her beauty and brings her back to life.

Obsequies, then, can be reversed in fairy tales. The two brothers of Child Rowland, who is invoked in *King Lear* (3.4.178–80), are entombed by the Elfin King as if they are dead, but when Rowland defeats him, the brothers are magically released and spring to life, declaring that their souls have been away, but are now returned.[27] Moreover, stone can be revived. The triple-headed Red Ettin turns two lads to stone pillars. When their friend seeks them out and defeats the Ettin, he has only to touch the pillars with his wand and they come alive. 'The Red Ettin' was well known in Scotland in the mid-sixteenth century, and Sir David Lyndsay used to tell the tale to cheer up the young James V.[28] One of Straparola's sixteenth-century Italian tales includes a green bird that turns men to marble. A young woman captures the bird, however, and with one of its feathers restores her two brothers to life.[29]

Full-scale resurrection is not uncommon in the oral tradition. 'The Three Snake Leaves', well known in medieval Europe, brings a wife and then a husband back to life.[30] Perhaps more familiar to modern readers, thanks to the huge Victorian popularity of Blue-beard, the serial-killer husband who features in Charles Perrault's late seventeenth-century version, the story of the bloody chamber includes a resurrection. In 'Fitcher's Bird', an older variant of this tale, the third daughter to be abducted from her father's house finds the bodies of her sisters dead and dismembered in the forbidden room. But she loyally reassembles the pieces, and the women come back to life.[31]

When Paulina calls for music (5.3.98), she aligns her own process of resuscitation with one strand of the folk tradition. A story from Lorraine tells how a rascally French deserter becomes king of

England by means of a magic violin that has the power to raise the dead. A Flemish tale of regeneration also involves a violin, a Sicilian one a guitar and a Breton narrative a magic flute.[32] There is no reason to suppose that Shakespeare was familiar with any of these specific stories, but he might well have seen the slapstick resurrections characteristic of the mummers' plays.[33]

What, then, really happened in the sixteen years of Hermione's absence from the play? But perhaps this is the wrong question. Perhaps, instead, what should concern us is the theatrical experience of watching the statue come to life. In the theatre the moment is more magical than likely, and the play allows us to interpret it either way. At the time, the statue scene is presented without any distancing dramatic ironies to an audience that shares unprepared the amazement of the figures on stage.

We now live in a world so burdened by interpretations of Shakespeare that it is hard to remember what it was like to encounter the play for the first time and without expectations. I once saw *The Winter's Tale* in a provincial theatre, sitting in front of two women who talked all the way through, evidently behaving much as they did when they watched television. I was tempted to tut and shush but, mercifully, embarrassment restrained me, and I was rewarded by the direct experience of their raw reactions to a play they evidently did not know. As the statue scene began, one said, 'It's his wife!'

> 'No!', was the reply, but in a tone that did not contradict
>   her friend.
> 'It is.'
> 'It is!'

And, a little later, 'I think she moved.' Then they were silent, caught up, exactly like Leontes, in the miracle they were witnessing.

The play that calls itself a winter's tale celebrates the improbability of its own plot. Perdita's return to fulfil the oracle is so unlikely 'that ballad-makers cannot be able to express it' (5.2.25–6). We already know from the selection Autolycus offers that ballads commonly break the bounds of plausibility. The death of Antigonus is also beyond belief: 'Like an old tale still, which will have matter to rehearse, though credit be asleep and not an ear open' (5.2.62–4).

As Hermione embraces her husband, Camillo poses the question that surely puzzles the audience as well: is she a ghost, a revenant, or a living being? 'If she pertain to life, let her speak too!' Polixenes adds the uncertainty concerning the lost sixteen years: 'Ay, and make manifest where she has liv'd,/ Or how stolen from the dead!' (5.3.113–15). Hermione must surely know? But Hermione speaks only once and to Perdita:

> thou shalt hear that I,
> Knowing by Paulina that the Oracle
> Gave hope thou wast in being, have preserv'd
> Myself to see the issue. (125–8)

This hardly helps us to make retrospective sense of the plot. The Queen had no need to learn from Paulina what the oracle said: she was there. Nor does Hermione gratify the curiosity of Polixenes – and the audience – with details concerning the interim. She has preserved herself, she says. What does this mean? That she pretended to be dead, while concealed in a remote house for sixteen years, her secret existence known only to Paulina, who visited her several times a day? Or that she survived in an enchanted sleep, like Snow White, to be awakened by Paulina's magic, sixteen years older? Was she preserved entombed, like Child Rowland's brothers, or turned to stone, like the Ettin's victims, to be started into life by a friend? Was she stolen at last from the death inflicted by a cruel husband, like Bluebeard's wives, as a result of Paulina's loyalty? Leontes has the play's final word on the matter and he leaves us with an enigma. Paulina, he says, has 'found' his wife, but 'how is to be questioned; for I saw her,/ As I thought, dead' (5.3.138–40).

A sad tale for winter?

Possibly, after all, the statue scene is undecidable, and we do it an injustice to settle on either one of the options the play leaves open. In my view, no amount of critical discussion, no degree of textual analysis, will resolve the nature of Hermione's preservation. Readers poring over a written text long for closure, but in the theatre the play seems to sustain its own mystery, which is not so much narrative as generic: 'That she is living,/ Were it but told you, should be hooted at/ Like an old tale: but it appears she lives' (5.3.115–17).

A generic undecidability, however, leaves in question the extent of the play's happy ending, the resolution in general joy that critics have claimed for it. If we interpret *The Winter's Tale* as realism, the 'wide gap of time' (154) that has divided the family is lost irretrievably, but the survivors are finally reconciled; if we regard it as fairy tale, on the other hand, the magic holds only for the theatrical moment, for fiction, and the improbability of such a reunion remains. On such a reading, the play makes no promises that the damage done by marital cruelty can be forgiven, or that penitence is eventually rewarded.

'This news, which is called true, is so like an old tale that the verity of it is in strong suspicion' (5.2.28–30). Fairytale endings fulfil a wish, but they do not guarantee to tell the truth about life. Instead, the manifest gap between the imaginary possibilities that fiction allows and the actual limits imposed by reality may invest the conclusions of old wives' tales with a unique kind of melancholy for their hearers. Perhaps, in the event, even when it has a happy ending, 'A sad tale's best for winter'.

5

Fairy Tales for Grown-ups in *A Midsummer Night's Dream*

Scepticism

Theseus, Duke of Athens, has no time for old wives' tales: 'I never may believe/ These antique fables, nor these fairy toys', he insists, in response to the stories the lovers tell of their night in the forest (*A Midsummer Night's Dream*, 5.1.2–3). 'Toys' are trifles; fables are improbable stories, tales of magic and marvels. And such fables are 'antique' in two senses: ancient, in so far as they generally record events that took place once upon a time, in a genre belonging to the vanished world it records; and 'antic', absurd, laughable, unlikely. The effects of Puck's antics in the wood have indeed been laughable, as well as incredible: lovers have switched partners more than once; the fairy queen has spent the night with a donkey. If realism is our criterion of artistic success, *A Midsummer Night's Dream* scarcely passes muster. Even one of the figures in the play does not believe the lovers' fairy tales.

Most of Shakespeare's audience would probably not have believed them either, if they had been asked to take the events of the play literally. Magic, fairy ointment, and little people invisible to mortal eyes were the fabrications of Old Mother Hubbard, English equivalent of the French Mother Goose. Then, as now, they belonged to childhood. 'We hear from our nurses and old women tales of hobgoblins and deluding spirits that abuse travellers and carry them out of their way', William Cornwallis noted in 1601. 'We hear this when we are children and laugh at it when we are men.' It is fear that transforms bushes into men and bulrushes into spears, he added.[1] Meanwhile, Protestant divines condemned such beliefs as delusions of the devil, not least because fairy tales affirmed a world of the supernatural that rivalled their own religious account

of the cosmos. Educated adults had left such 'toys' behind; orthodoxy rejected them out of hand. The sceptical Reginald Scot and the
devout James VI and I both repudiated the fairy world with equal
vigour.

What about the old wives themselves? Did they believe in fairies?
We shall probably never know. Perhaps they didn't know for
certain, either. It is possible to be in two minds at once. I myself, for
example, cannot imagine how anyone in the twenty-first century
can take any version of the supernatural seriously, or live life in
obedience to a set of commands issued centuries ago on the basis
of special access to a superhuman deity. And yet I find I rarely omit
certain ceremonies designed to protect or propitiate when it comes
to ladders, black cats, magpies, and the full moon. To reconcile
myself to this inconsistency, I call it cognitive dissonance.

Many people and, indeed, many cultures practise cognitive
dissonance, believing and not believing at the same time. Three
hundred years after the play, Bridget Cleary was burnt to death in
rural Ireland on the grounds that she was a fairy changeling. Her
husband, Michael, was no illiterate and impoverished peasant. On
the contrary, he would have seen himself as a cut above his neigh-
bours; both he and Bridget could read and write. When his wife fell
ill, he tried the doctor first. It was only when medical science failed
him that he reinterpreted the situation in terms of another set of
beliefs and values. The old world of magic occupied the same social
and geographical space as modernity: it just represented the same
events differently.

In the present fairy tales live on, even if wholehearted belief in
them once again belongs to childhood. This is not as surprising
as we might think, since the supernatural makes for such good
stories. Four hundred years from now, literal-minded cultural historians may find themselves puzzling over whether we believed in
extraterrestrials and interplanetary body-snatchers, not to mention
demonic possession and revenants. Some of us do; most of us don't;
but Hollywood makes compelling narratives out of all of them, and
literal belief is not a condition of enjoyment.

Even so, Western culture continues to relegate fairy tales to
the nursery. Are we always right to do so? I shall suggest that *A
Midsummer Night's Dream* takes its own world of magic seriously,

without asking its audience to believe in fairies. Instead, its creatures of fantasy have the effect of deconstructing the conventional opposition between fact and fiction, reality and dream.

Bottom's dream

Bottom is not the first mortal man to have been loved by the queen of the fairies. The ballad of Thomas the Rhymer recounts how, as Thomas lies on a grassy bank, he sees a beautiful woman riding towards him, dressed in green silk and a velvet mantle, while silver bells ring out from her horse's mane. Such a fine lady, Thomas supposes, must be the Queen of Heaven, but she soon corrects him. Instead, she reigns in Elfland, and Thomas is to spend seven years with her there, before he returns to his own world.[2]

The ballad of Thomas the Rhymer is derived from the fifteenth-century romance of Thomas of Erceldoune, a Scottish story that survives in four English manuscripts. This tale of Thomas's encounter with the fairy lady exercised a considerable hold over the imagination of the period, on both sides of the border, as the prelude to the prophecies of the poet and prophet, 'true Thomas'. In a mainly first-person narrative, the medieval romance records Thomas's longing for love when he hears the birds sing one May morning. Many precious jewels adorn the lady's harness as she rides towards him. He makes love to her seven times there and then, until he is compelled to accompany her to her own country under the hill, where all is joy and revelry. Thomas is happier than words can say, and when the time comes for him to return to his own world, he laments that he has been in fairyland no more than three days. But it has been three years: fairy chronology does not match mortal time.

The elf queen bears some resemblance to a long line of enchantresses from Circe and Lamia to Morgan le Fay and Mélusine, as well as Edmund Spenser's Acrasia, who transforms men into beasts in her Bower of Bliss. But, unlike all these, the queen of the fairies does her mortal lover no harm, while introducing him to an earthly paradise. In *A Midsummer Night's Dream*, too, Titania promises Bottom, the weaver, not only a sexual encounter, but a way of life that is rich

and romantic beyond the dreams of a working man, and to match
it an identity that exceeds the limitations of human life itself:

> I am a spirit of no common rate;
> The summer still doth tend upon my state;
> And I do love thee; therefore go with me.
> I'll give thee fairies to attend on thee;
> And they shall fetch thee jewels from the deep,
> And sing while thou on pressed flowers dost sleep.
> And I will purge thy mortal grossness so,
> That thou shalt like an aery spirit go. (3.1.154–61)

The diction of these elegant pentameter couplets catches something
of the elusiveness that also characterizes the deceptive simplicity of
the romance, as well as the ballad. Like Titania's promise, both narratives are haunting, elliptical; they suggest more than they specify.

Similarly, whatever takes place in Titania's bower does so off-
stage. The play tactfully leaves that question to the imagination
of the audience. When they reappear, Bottom is more interested
in food and sleep. It is not until he wakes in his own world that
the weaver retrospectively invests his 'rare vision' with a more
than mortal quality (4.1.203). Like Thomas, he associates the fairy
queen with divinity. In search of words to do justice to his experience, Bottom reaches for the biblical account of the kingdom of
heaven:

> The eye of man hath not heard, the ear of man hath not seen,
> man's hand is not able to taste, his tongue to conceive, nor his
> heart to report, what my dream was. (4.1.209–12)[3]

And if his senses are comically confused here, perhaps that too is
part of the tribute mortality pays to enchantment.

The Faerie Queene

Five or six years before the play, Spenser had ascribed a similar
vision to Prince Arthur, hero of *The Faerie Queene*. As the prince slept
it seemed to him that a royal maiden lay down beside him. 'Most
goodly glee and lovely blandishment/ She to me made', he recalls.[4]

She loved him and sought his love in return, and only as they parted did she reveal that the figure who had so ravished his heart with delight was the queen of the fairies. Here too, it is not entirely clear exactly what took place, nor even whether the episode was a dream or reality. But this is as discretion requires. Spenser's fairy queen, Gloriana, personifies glory, but she also represents Elizabeth I, the Virgin Queen.[5]

Titania, in my view, does not represent Elizabeth.[6] Instead, Spenser's royal allusion is transferred to another part of the play, where, according to a tale told in the manner of Ovid, Cupid's arrow misses the 'fair vestal, throned by the west', and falls instead on a little flower. In consequence, 'the maiden meditation' of Oberon's 'imperial votress', or, in other words, the Queen's indifference to desire, mythologically causes the magic properties of the wild pansy known as love-in-idleness (2.1.155–72). Oberon's story of Cupid's shaft explains the origins of the magic ointment.

The vision of Spenser's Prince Arthur is depicted with intensity in a poem characterized by high seriousness throughout. This encounter represents the origin of his quest for Gloriana, the central theme of Spenser's national epic. Bottom's love affair, meanwhile, is dramatized in a very different key. And yet there was a precedent for treating supernatural passion comically. *The Tale of Sir Thopas* constitutes the pilgrim Chaucer's first fictitious contribution to his *Canterbury Tales*. Ironically, the author of this wide-ranging anthology of styles and genres portrays himself within it as unable to compete in storytelling with the other pilgrims. He knows only one tale, he claims, and that is a ballad he learned long ago. In this humblest of genres, the pilgrim Chaucer tells the story of Sir Thopas, who falls into love-longing as he hears the birds sing, and resolves to make the elf queen his mistress, since no mortal woman is worthy of him. Sir Thopas is about to do battle with a fearsome giant, when the Host interrupts the story to say that he has heard quite enough of this doggerel, and the tale is left incomplete.

Sadly, too, by the late sixteenth century, human relations with the queen of the fairies were open to exploitation by confidence tricksters. Judith Phillips, for one, was publicly whipped in 1595 for extracting large sums of money from gullible Londoners in exchange for extending them this privilege.[7] Is it possible that

Bottom's encounter with Titania playfully rewrites Arthur's with Gloriana in the light of such comic precedents? If so, *A Midsummer Night's Dream* makes exceptionally sophisticated capital out of its folktale materials, while still offering excellent value as comedy to any members of the audience indifferent to either literary or topical allusions.

Poetry

However this may be, even Bottom perceives that only poetry can hope to do justice to the wonder of his mortal experience of immortal love. Since the heart cannot conceive and the tongue cannot report what has taken place, 'I will get Peter Quince to write a ballad of this dream: it shall be called "Bottom's Dream", because it hath no bottom' (4.1.212–14). Poetry alone can make intelligible mysteries beyond the reach of prose. Bottom thus implicitly anticipates the view that Theseus will shortly spell out. The poet, moving easily between nature and the supernatural, invests visions with substance:

> And as imagination bodies forth
> The forms of things unknown, the poet's pen
> Turns them to shapes, and gives to airy nothing
> A local habitation and a name. (5.1.14–17)

If his encounter with the fairy queen stirs Bottom's poetic impulse, it also underwrites the truth of Thomas's rhyming powers. Bottom does not trust himself to write a poem; he will leave the task of versifying his dream to Peter Quince. But Thomas of Erceldoune, first-person author of his own romance, is already a poet. Thomas parts from the pleasures of fairyland and from his lovely lady with heavy cheer. When she finally returns him to the bank where she found him, he does his best to detain her. First, he asks for a token, and she promises him that as a poet he will always tell the truth. Then he begs her to tell him something magical, and in return she utters the figurative prophecies that were to spread his reputation throughout both Scotland and England. Thomas's fame would reach its height in 1603, when his final verse prophecy of the union of the two realms was fulfilled on the accession of James VI of Scotland as James I of England.[8]

The story of Thomas's encounter with the fairy queen thus constitutes a myth of origins: his poetry is true because the gift comes from elsewhere; Thomas has touched 'the forms of things unknown', which guarantee a special knowledge. He has moved between distinct worlds, seen beings invisible to ordinary human eyes, experienced the secret, unnameable otherness of fairyland.

Bottom will get Peter Quince to record *his* ineffable experience in a ballad. He probably has in mind a song, or a street ballad on the lines of those Autolycus sells to the gullible shepherds (*The Winter's Tale*, 4.4.260–315). The genre is appropriate, of course: this was poetry in its popular form, at the *bottom*, in fact, of a scale where epic occupied the highest pinnacle. Ironically, nowadays we might prefer a traditional folk ballad, so-named from the eighteenth century onwards, in the manner of 'Thomas the Rhymer'. The austerity of the traditional ballad form, the haunting suggestiveness of its characteristic ellipses, allows it a special relationship with the unknown and unutterable, permits it to indicate the existence of secrets it does not reveal. Perhaps this is why something very close to the ballad form seems right for Keats's poem about an encounter between a mortal knight and a fairy lady, 'La Belle Dame Sans Merci'. The genre leaves so much unsaid. Perhaps, too, it accounts for the elusiveness of Coleridge's 'Ancient Mariner', as the story of another human being who has experienced an alien realm and returns with a compulsion to tell his strange tale in verse.

Aetiologies

The ballad of 'true Thomas' constitutes a fable of origins, an aetiology. In other words, it assigns a cause to his poetic and prophetic powers. Peter Quince is not shown to have written the ballad of Bottom's dream, but he appears as the author of *Pyramus and Thisbe*, and poetic powers are what the author of the play-within-the-play conspicuously lacks. As Shakespeare's fictional surrogate, he is no more competent than the fictitious pilgrim Chaucer. Even so, he chooses for the theme of his drama another aetiology, taken, this time, directly from Ovid.

The fruits of the mulberry are deep purple, almost black, but their juice runs blood-red. Why is this? Because, as Ovid records in the *Metamorphoses*, long, long ago, young lovers, forbidden to marry by their parents, agreed to leave the city and meet in the woods. When Pyramus misinterpreted Thisbe's blood-stained cloak, he killed himself, and his own red blood, the mark of true love, fell upon the mulberry. At once, its snow-white berries changed to purple. Seeing the effects of this transformation, Thisbe appealed to the mulberry, as she fell upon her lover's sword, to keep its mourning colour in memory of a couple who died for love.[9] The fable assigns a cause to both red juice and near-black berries.

Despite the difference between Ovid's elegant Latin verse and the unassuming prose of most fireside stories, there are affinities between the *Metamorphoses* and old wives' tales. If a classical love story is not the most natural vehicle for Quince and his fellow craftsmen, their choice of plot is by no means inappropriate in other respects. Aetiologies are also the stuff of popular narrative. A Scottish folk tale records how the wolf lost his long tail. (A fox tricked him into letting it get stuck to the ice.)[10] Any number of traditional legends are designed to explain the existence of place names or geographical features. Crawl Meadow, Bromfield, in Shropshire owes its name to the story of an heiress forbidden by her father to marry the knight she loved. When she insisted on going ahead with the wedding, her father told her she would inherit no more land from him than she could crawl round in one night. Undeterred, the young woman set out on her knees, and had covered a good-sized area by morning.[11]

In the same county, the Wrekin dominates the surrounding landscape. This hill was formed, it seems, when a vengeful Welsh giant set out to flood Shrewsbury by damming the River Severn. The giant asked a passing cobbler how far it was to the town. Seeing that the giant was carrying a huge spadeful of earth, the quick-witted cobbler told him Shrewsbury was a great distance away. In evidence he produced the sack of old shoes he was taking home to mend. He had worn them all out on the road, he claimed. Thus discouraged, the giant dropped the earth where he stood, and went back to Wales. The story remains current in the new town of Telford close by. Aetiologies keep their charm. Rudyard Kipling's *Just So Stories* for children, which tell how the elephant got its trunk and the camel its hump, are still in print over a century after they were first published in 1902.

Ovid's *Metamorphoses* are also a repository of aetiologies. Why are poets crowned with laurel wreaths? Because, when Daphne fled from the embraces of Apollo, god of poetry, she was transformed into a tree, and Apollo was left embracing a laurel. When the young Adonis died, Venus turned him into the delicate anemone so that he would live again every spring.

Meanwhile, spanning the centuries and the genres, Aesop's fables, too, include a good many aetiologies. Jupiter invited the animals to his wedding, and only the tortoise preferred to stay at home. As a punishment, Jupiter ordered the tortoise to carry her house with her wherever she went.[12] This story does not appear in the selection of Aesop's fables published in English by Caxton in 1483, and reissued at intervals in the course of the following century. But Caxton does include a sad tale about the camel. The animal envied the horns sported by other beasts and asked for protuberances of its own. Jupiter was so annoyed by this presumption that he took away the camel's ears.[13]

Aesop's moralizing tales, conventionally attributed to the Greek storyteller, were written down in the classical period and beyond. Their educational value meant that they were recycled and emulated in primers and sermons throughout the Middle Ages and the early modern period. From there they sometimes re-entered the folk tradition itself.

What is the appeal of such aetiologies, the reason for their long survival at all levels of European culture? Is it that they explain what seems arbitrary? Not necessarily, in my view. Theseus is not alone in his disbelief. Aren't fables by definition always what *other* people believe? Then, as now, such myths of origin were old wives' tales, stories for children, fit for the nursery. The pleasure they give comes from their inventiveness *as stories*. Pretending to explain, they draw attention, by the ingenuity of their very improbability, to the curiosities they identify: the elephant's trunk, the tortoise's shell, the surprising, blood-red juice of the purple mulberry. Mimicking the assignment of causes and effects, in practice these aetiologies proclaim themselves as fiction, and in the process invest what we know with mystery, reduce the familiarity of things to emphasize the strangeness of the landscape, say, or the eccentricity of its place names. Fables of origin are a way of alluding to oddity, paradoxically rendering the world more *un*accountable in the process. To that degree, they have something to offer grown-ups, as well as children.

A Midsummer Night's Dream ascribes the capriciousness of love to a little western flower. At the same time, it associates desire with danger. When Theseus refuses the proffered epilogue to the mechanicals' play (5.1.350), he no doubt suppresses Ovid's account of the origins of the strange discrepancy between the funereal near-black of the mulberry and its blood-red juice. But Shakespeare lets nothing go to waste. The change of colour is transferred to Oberon's aetiology, this time delivered with an eloquence to match Ovid's own, of the wild pansy, accidental butt of Cupid's arrow, 'before milk-white, now purple with love's wound' (2.1.167). The transfer links that wound, as the origin of the juice that will cause so much trouble, with the violent deaths of Pyramus and Thisbe. In the *Metamorphoses* there is one tale; *A Midsummer Night's Dream* tells two. Shakespeare's division of Ovid's aetiology gives 'a local habitation and a name' to the source of all that is unaccountable and arbitrary in the story of the lovers' night in the woods, and at the same time connects Cupid with tragedy. Ovid's story of forbidden passion is rendered comic by the well-meaning ineptitude of Peter Quince and his troupe, but it offers a reminder, none the less, in the margins of *A Midsummer Night's Dream* itself, of another possible outcome for the story of the play's own young lovers who, in order to escape parental prohibition, also agreed, long, long ago in ancient Athens, to leave the city and meet in the woods.

The fairies

What makes the seasons grow topsy-turvy, generating the wrong weather for the time of year? Quarrels between the king and queen of the fairies (2.1.88–117). Why does the cream sometimes not produce butter, however hard the housewife churns? Why does the beer not always ferment? Why do travellers get lost in the dark? And why do old wives suddenly fall off their stools in mid-tale? These unexpected occurrences are ascribed to the anarchic Puck,

Robin Goodfellow, the hobgoblin of folklore, 'shrewd', 'knavish', lawless (2.1.32–57). In this sense, Puck offers a name for the sheer unpredictability of events, and like the improbable aetiologies, his existence has the effect of foregrounding freak happenings, and the apparent unaccountability of the world to the laws of cause and effect.

Shakespeare's fairies are composed of many elements, among them native folk beliefs,[14] but also existing poetry, which both draws on these beliefs and combines them intertextually with literary sources. If Robin Goodfellow, the habit of dancing, and the hierarchic social order of the fairies belong to early modern folklore, Oberon also owes his name to romance and Titania hers to classical mythology. The fairies of *A Midsummer Night's Dream* derive characteristics from Spenser and Lyly, from medieval narrative and Chaucer. And in their construction, the sophisticated Latin poetry of Ovid meets vernacular fireside tales to compose a fairyland that is intelligible as not quite solid fact, nor yet pure fiction.

Ovid's landscapes are peopled with gods, nymphs and strange, magical hybrids, as well as with mortal human beings. His Medea, who practises witchcraft, summons to her aid the gods of the groves and the deities of the night.[15] When in 1567 Arthur Golding translates this passage into English, he calls Ovid's gods 'elves', as does Shakespeare in ascribing magic powers to Prospero (*The Tempest*, 5.1.33). In 1594 Thomas Nashe affirmed that the figures of pagan mythology were no more than English spirits under Greek names.[16] These classical creatures certainly took readily to the native English countryside. Dismissing old wives' tales, the sceptical Reginald Scot affirms in 1584 that 'our mothers' maids' have frightened us with lists of bogeys, including 'urchins, elves, hags, fairies, satyrs, pans, fauns', as well as 'tritons, centaurs, dwarfs, imps, calkers [astrologers], conjurers [wizards], nymphs, changelings . . . '.[17] Here the classical satyrs, pans, fauns, tritons, centaurs and nymphs mingle apparently at random with native figures from the oral tradition. In the popular chapbook, Richard Johnson's fairy queen assists at the birth of Tom Thumb, accompanied by 'her attendants, the elves and dryads'.[18]

If these composite fairies occupy the same space as early modern mortals, they commonly seem, paradoxically, to belong to a vanished past, 'once upon a time', long-lost and never to be recovered. Ovid's stories are set in a distant epoch when the world was new, cleansed by the great flood and now in the process of reconstruction. *The Faerie Queene* records in archaic manner a world of giants and dragons, as well as the deeds of knights and ladies whose praise has 'slept in silence long'.[19] Spenser's Mother Hubberd sets her tale of the fox and the ape in a time 'before the world was civill'.[20] In 1613 Samuel Rowlands confined the fairies to 'old wives' days, that in old time did live/ (To whose old tales much credit men did give').[21] This antique world was always beyond recovery, it seems. Chaucer's Wife of Bath, who is old enough to have married five husbands and lost some teeth, locates her fairy tale in a period many hundreds of years ago, when the elf queen 'Daunced ful ofte in many a grene mede'. Since then, the fairies have been driven out by the preaching friars. This old wife, whose own wayward desires are condemned by religious orthodoxy, looks back nostalgically to a time when the paths now patrolled by the clergy belonged to the elves.[22] In the late seventeenth century John Aubrey also laments their disappearance, brought about this time by the inventions of science: 'the divine art of printing and gunpowder have frighted away Robin Goodfellow and the fairies'.[23]

If not entirely imaginary, the fairies are not seen as a current presence, either. Real, but long-gone, lost and yet immortal, believed in, but by other people, denominated from both English lore and classical literature, they subsist between fact and fiction. At once 'airy nothing' and the denizens of a 'local habitation', Shakespeare's fairies come close to naming what is unnameable and inexplicable in the world we think we know.

'Spirits of another sort'

Intertextual composites they may be, but Shakespeare's fairies talk like no others. Long-departed or not, their voices, unique in the play itself, assume a direct access to a more vital world. Where Lysander names the 'grey light' of dawn, Oberon's sun rises over the sea and 'Turns into yellow gold his salt green streams' (3.2.419, 393). Since the diction here is exceptionally simple, it seems that the world of the fairies is not only more vivid and more sensuous, but also more immediate than the realm of everyday experience.

Moreover, fairyland is oddly non-judgemental. The paradoxically lyrical quarrel takes place in this same unassuming but allusive vocabulary, with the minimum of self-consciously 'poetic' inversions. She never meets the fairy king, his queen insists, when the fairies assemble

> on hill, in dale, forest or mead,
> By paved fountain, or by rushy brook,
> Or in the beached margent of the sea,
> To dance our ringlets to the whistling wind,
> But with thy brawls thou has disturbed our sport. (2.1.83–7)

After the seductive list of settings for the fairy dances, none described, each prompting the audience to supply the details from their own imagination, the negative mention of Oberon's 'brawls', which are, after all, the thematic point at issue, seems oddly intrusive, unexpected. Apprehension of the natural world seems to deflect such condemnation. The disruption of the seasons, too, is often more pleasurable than distressing:

> hoary-headed frosts
> Fall in the fresh lap of the crimson rose;
> And on old Hiems' thin and icy crown,
> An odorous chaplet of sweet summer buds
> Is, as in mockery, set. (2.1.107–11)

It is hard to feel anything but delight as the rime sparkles among the rose petals. And despite his Latin name, old Winter seems more comic than threatening, his thin white hair incongruously wreathed with a coronet of flowers too young to be fully open.

Surely, spirits who speak so lyrically ought to be benevolent? But the same deferral of moral questions attends their relations with humanity. In the end, for the sake of 'peace' (3.2.377), Oberon sorts out the misunderstandings fairy magic has brought about. But his initial interest in the mortals is no more than incidental, a by-product of his plan to 'torment' Titania for withholding the child he wants (2.1.147). Oberon's first instructions to Puck are designed to turn the tables on the ungracious Demetrius, rather than to resolve the human conflict (2.1.246, 266). Meanwhile, his tactics for wresting the little Indian boy from Titania's care are hardly sympathetic. In view of the play's delicate treatment of her absurd passion for a donkey, any impulse towards feminist moral outrage seems humourless; at the same time, the play hardly characterizes the fairy king as a providential force. The mischievous Puck, who relishes what falls out preposterously (3.2.120–1), seems not so very different from his master.

The fairies inhabit an independent realm, where they are preoccupied by their own affairs. They seem indifferent to the ethical codes and emotional sympathies that bother mortal beings, wayward, beyond the reach of morality or law. Perhaps *The Tempest* offers a commentary. Describing the pitiful plight of the shipwrecked victims, Ariel tells Prospero that, if he saw their tears, his heart would relent. And to reinforce the point, Ariel assures him, 'Mine would, sir, were I human' (5.1.20). But he is not, and neither are the spirits in *A Midsummer Night's Dream*. They are without humanity – in both senses of that term. Possessed instead by an anarchic energy, they make merry by night:

> And we fairies, that do run
> By the triple Hecate's team
> From the presence of the sun,
> Following darkness like a dream,
> Now are frolic. (5.1.377–81)

Hecate is the goddess above all of witchcraft.

And yet, if Shakespeare's fairies are not tender-hearted, they are not consistently malevolent, either. It is as if our ethical categories do not obtain in the fairy world. Puck reminds Oberon that their work must be complete by morning, when the ghosts of the damned are compelled to hide from daylight. Oberon, however, insists on their difference from these evil phantoms: 'But we are spirits of another sort' (3.2.388). What sort is never exactly specified, but in evidence, Titania's husband shamelessly adduces that he has often 'made sport' 'with the Morning's love', Aurora (389). Fairyland gives a 'habitation and a name' to desire, a force outside conventional morality, unconstrained by the obligations, prohibitions, and restrictions of human society.

Even reciprocal love is not always benign. At the end of the play the newly married couples go to bed. Theseus makes the point twice, in case the audience missed it the first time (5.1.358, 362). It is midnight, and the fairies, who belong in the woods, now enter the palace to carry out their traditional check that the house has been properly swept. Their king and queen have come to bless the three bridal beds, but not before Puck has listed the terrors of the night: the screech owl, death, and the graves that open in darkness to release their ghosts (365–76). This is not quite like the lullaby for Titania in the imperative mood, designed to keep such perils at bay (2.2.9–23), or the parallel exorcism in the subjunctive of Spenser's contemporary marriage poem, *Epithalamion*.[24] The mood of Puck's speech is indicative, and each quatrain begins, 'Now . . . ': 'Now the hungry lion roars,/ And the wolf behowls the moon'. It is as if the play acknowledges, by displacing them onto these traditional bugbears, the anxieties that accompany the joys of the wedding night. Hobgoblin is another name for threat; enchantment in the play points to drives reason cannot master. As Angela Bourke puts it in her brilliant book about the death of Bridget Cleary, burned as a changeling in 1895, tales of encounters with the fairies can remind their audiences of 'everything in life that is outside human control'.[25]

Anarchic, unpredictable, now dangerous, now beneficent, Shakespeare's fairies offer a way of naming otherwise unnameable desires and fears. Love is irrational, as the play repeatedly insists (1.1.236; 3.1.136–8). Lysander is as eligible as Demetrius (1.1.99–102), Helena as fair as Hermia (1.1.227). Puck plays Cupid, the blind god of love, whose arrows strike suddenly and at random. And in this condition, subject to desire, beyond the reach of reason or law, lies the possibility of pain, as well as joy. Moreover, the 'goblin' Puck (3.2.399), 'mad spirit' whose 'night-rule' does so much mischief (3.2.4–5), also personifies something earthier than the classical god of love, if just as uncontrollable. Like so many lovers, the victims of the magic juice hasten to rationalize their feelings: Titania claims to be moved by Bottom's 'virtue', and adds, 'Thou art as wise as thou art beautiful' (3.1.134, 141); Lysander absurdly insists that he has grown up overnight, and 'reason' calls Helena 'the worthier maid'

(2.2.114–19). But we know better. Desire, sudden, unruly, intract-able, inhabits a world outside the processes of selection by virtue or worth. In *A Midsummer Night's Dream* love is the work of the fairies.

Shadows

Oberon, meanwhile, is 'king of shadows' (3.2.347). Unlike the daylight world, his realm is peopled by creatures of the moonlight, fleeting shapes, of questionable reality. As shadows, the fairies are only undecidably there, perhaps illusory, no more than figments of the imagination. The spirits conjured up by the tales of 'our mothers' maids' keep us in such awe, Reginald Scot insists, 'that we are afraid of our own shadows'.[26] The phrase is proverbial, and it registers Scot's scepticism perfectly. Our own shadows, after all, are what we ourselves bring into being, as we project onto another surface what is no more than an image of ourselves.

No wonder, then, that the lovers will forget the details of their night in a moonlit wood populated by shadows, remembering its events 'But as the fierce vexation of a dream' (4.1.68). And no wonder that Bottom cannot be sure, in retrospect, of his unearthly encounter with the fairy queen. After all, 'A dream itself is but a shadow' (*Hamlet*, 2.2.261). And yet the happy ending of the play will depend on the changes the fairies have brought about. As he marries Helena, Demetrius is still under the spell of the magic oint-ment that has miraculously restored him to his first love.

Imagination, Theseus declares, 'bodies forth/ The forms of things unknown' (5.1.14–15). But need 'unknown' mean 'untrue'? As Hippolita urges,

> all the story of the night told over,
> And all their minds transfigur'd so together,
> More witnesseth than fancy's images,
> And grows to something of great constancy;
> But howsoever, strange and admirable. (5.1.23–7)

The story of the night is strange, certainly, and admirable (a cause of wonder), but not, she indicates, easily dismissed. Like Bottom's dream, the fairy tale we have witnessed 'hath no bottom' in two alternative senses (4.1.214): either it is groundless, or it is unfathomably profound, and there seems no way to be sure which.

Puck's epilogue neatly turns the undecidable status of the fairies into an appeal to the audience:

> If we shadows have offended,
> Think but this, and all is mended,
> That you have but slumber'd here
> While these visions did appear.
> And this weak and idle theme,
> No more yielding but a dream. (5.1.417–22)

When Puck speaks here for shadows, however, he also addresses the audience as an actor. The epilogue, hybrid form, at once inside and outside the play itself, begins to identify what has gone before as a performance. Hippolyta's disdain for the performance of *Pyramus and Thisbe* provokes Theseus to come out for the actors: 'The best in this kind are but shadows' (5.1.209).[27]

Plays

Like the fairies, in other words, actors are 'shadows'. Impersonating others, they are flesh and blood, certainly, but of the same doubtful status, mere shapes, shifting, changeable, other than they are. And like the fairies, actors body forth 'the forms of things unknown'. If *A Midsummer Night's Dream* probes the status of fairy tales, it also addresses the question of fiction. Can a play make truth claims? Or can it do so only on condition that it replicates reality, excluding improbabilities? Shakespeare's play suggests not.

As the actors present it, *Pyramus and Thisbe* is laughable in the first instance to the degree that it departs from reality. Its personified Wall, its Man in the Moon, the jigging verse forms and the heroics alternating with bathos all divorce it from anything that might actually happen in a real world. Tragic events are here rendered comic by the lack of realism in their dramatization. And yet the rehearsals, absurd as they are, have the serious effect of calling into question the criterion of realism itself. The lion will frighten the ladies (1.2.70–1) only on the assumption that they take it for real;

the ladies will be upset by the death of Pyramus (3.1.10–11) only if they think he really dies. The solution, therefore, is to explain in a prologue that Pyramus is not Pyramus, but Bottom the weaver (3.1.15–20) and that the lion is a man, and Snug the joiner (40–3).

Why is this funny? Because, of course, the on-stage audience already know that the play is fiction, performed by actors. 'Well roared, Lion!'; 'Well run, Thisbe!'; 'Well shone, Moon!' (5.1.259–61). The praise is for a job well done, an impersonation effectively executed. Like the Athenian audience in the play, we too know while we watch that we are witnessing a performance, or that plays are fiction.

What impels us, then, to confine them to realism? Realism is no more than one mode, and by no means the only one. Historically, it represented the highest aspiration of Victorian fiction; it still prevails in soap opera; it has the virtue of familiarity. But for decades, in the hands of Pirandello, Bertolt Brecht, and Samuel Beckett, among others, theatre has experimented with other modes. These dramatists demand more from their audiences than the easy recognition of everyday reality. Their actors, like Shakespeare's fairies, are required to body forth 'the forms of things *un*known'. *A Midsummer Night's Dream* preceded the epoch of high realism: was it too, in its own way, experimental? Did Shakespeare, on a hint from Chaucer's *Tale of Sir Thopas*, make his own art a theme of the play, in anticipation of *As You Like It*?

Parody

Pyramus and Thisbe tells the story of young lovers, forbidden to marry, who arrange to meet in the woods by moonlight, beyond the reach of parental prohibition. The production parodies mummers' plays and English Seneca, previous poetry and the excesses of the earlier drama. But it also parodies *A Midsummer Night's Dream*'s own depiction of lovers who meet in the woods by moonlight, in defiance of parental prohibition. How great, for example, is the distance from Helena's 'O weary night, O long and tedious night' (3.2.431) to Pyramus's '*O grim-look'd night! O night with hue so black!/ O night, which ever art when day is not!/ O night, O night, alack, alack,*

alack' (5.1.168–70)? Here is Demetrius, waking to discover he is now
in love with Helena:

O Helen, goddess, nymph, perfect, divine!
To what, my love, shall I compare thine eyne?
Crystal is muddy. O how ripe in show
Thy lips, those kissing cherries, tempting grow! (3.2.137–40)

And here is Thisbe, discovering the dead body of *her* lover:

These lily lips,
This cherry nose,
These yellow cowslip cheeks,
Are gone, are gone!
Lovers, make moan;
His eyes were green as leeks. (5.1.325–30)

Demetrius adheres to iambic pentameters and traditional poetic allusions; Thisbe's jingle could be rewritten as old-fashioned fourteeners,
the flowers and vegetables she invokes break with courtly decorum,
and she confuses their colours. But in the first passage, the archaism
of 'eyne' draws attention to the artifice of the verse; and eyes that
make crystal look 'muddy' is a clear case of poetic licence. Demetrius
does not know his sudden and total change of heart is comic from
the point of view of the theatre audience; Thisbe has no sense that
her grief will make the on-stage spectators laugh. Despite the differences, there are also enough resemblances between them to throw
into relief the degree to which the utterance of Demetrius is already
scripted by the same poetic conventions that Thisbe travesties.

The Athenian Lovers

Is it possible that the romantic plot is already scripted by convention, too? In the first scene the exchanges of the lovers make a
striking contrast with the dialogue between Theseus and Hippolyta
that opens the play:

Now, fair Hippolyta, our nuptial hour
Draws on apace; four happy days bring in
Another moon: but O, methinks, how slow

> This old moon wanes! She lingers my desires,
> Like to a stepdame or a dowager
> Long withering out a young man's revenue. (1.1.1–6)

There is a good deal of information for the audience here, and it is delivered in pentameters that come remarkably close to the rhythms of speech. The moon, conventional symbol of romantic love, is rejected as a nuisance. Theseus has 'desires', and he compares them, in a singularly unconventional image, with money: the moon that delays his wedding is like an old woman who won't die and leave her wealth to her heir while he is still young enough to enjoy it. The 'unpoetic' simile establishes his intense impatience for this marriage. Meanwhile, as so consistently in the conversations between them, Hipppolyta addresses the issue from a different angle, in this instance more lyrical, more romantic, consolatory, and yet just as eager:

> Four days will quickly steep themselves in night;
> Four nights will quickly dream away the time;
> And then the moon, like to a silver bow
> New bent in heaven, shall behold the night
> Of our solemnities. (7–11)

Appropriately, the Amazon compares the new moon with a bow but, without further elaboration, 'silver' lifts it from the world of warfare into a precious and beautiful object.

When Lysander and Hermia are left alone together, by contrast, their exchanges are delivered in a very different register:

> How now, my love? Why is your cheek so pale?
> How chance the roses there do fade so fast? (1.1.128–9)

Here is a familiar reference to the rosy cheeks of conventional beauty. And doesn't Lysander already know why they are suddenly pale? He has, after all, just seen Hermia threatened with death or the convent if she will not marry his rival. But it is almost as if he asks the question in order to prepare the ground for the conceit that constitutes her reply:

> Belike for want of rain, which I could well
> Beteem them from the tempest of mine eyes. (130–1)

Hermia will water the fading roses with her tears. This is inventive and witty, and it has the effect of distancing the audience from any serious anxiety on behalf of these young people, who are disarmingly ready to acknowledge that all they know about love comes from stories:

> Ay me! For aught that I could ever read,
> Could ever hear by tale or history,
> The course of true love never did run smooth. (132–4)

Theseus and Hippolyta break with the poetic conventions that the lovers reproduce and Pyramus and Thisbe burlesque. There are different levels of conventionality here. Are there also different levels of realism?

Fiction and reality

Pyramus and Thisbe is self-evidently a play-within-a-play. Could *The Athenian Lovers* possibly be another? Time hangs heavy on the hands of Theseus and Hippolyta while they wait for their wedding day, and the Duke sends the Master of the Revels off to find entertainment. At Queen Elizabeth's court it was the Master of the Revels who took responsibility for licensing plays for performance. Exit Philostrate, and enter, pat, an old man with his daughter and two rival suitors. The Athenian setting, the heavy father, and the arranged marriage against the will of the young people all evoke the Roman comedy of Terence, familiar from the school curriculum. As Egeus speaks, the manner becomes formalized, stagey: 'Stand forth Demetrius'; 'Stand forth Lysander'; 'This man ... ' and 'This ... ' (1.1.24–7). Perhaps the promised 'revelling' has begun (1.1.19).

The verse that defines the passions of the lovers owes nothing to Terence, however, but draws on the lyric tradition. Meanwhile, in no time at all, this Roman-comedy-in-conjunction-with-love-poetry has turned into a fairy tale, complete with magical transformations and a nursery rhyme ending: 'Jack shall have Jill,/Nought shall go ill' (3.2.461–2). It seems that Shakespeare experiments with the genres, mixing them to see how they blend, all the while isolating the result

as an entertainment for the fictional court of Athens. And when
the court audience is all but forgotten, this play-within-the-play
is apparently performed for the benefit of the fairies themselves:
'Shall we their fond pageant see?/ Lord, what fools these mortals
be!' (3.2.114–15). A pageant could be any kind of show but, in relation to the mystery cycles, it had come to be associated specifically
with drama. Shakespeare's Julia claims to have acted the part of
Ariadne in a Whitsun 'pageant' in *Two Gentlemen of Verona* (4.4.156);
a 'pageant' is synonymous with a play in *As You like It* (2.7.138;
3.4.49–56).

Puck and Oberon remain as a silent audience to the lovers' quarrel
that follows; Oberon has already taken advantage of his invisib-
ility to overhear the exchanges between Helena and Demetrius
(2.1.186–7). It is no bar to this reading that their on-stage audiences also take part in the drama devised to amuse them, or that
Theseus pronounces judgement on the lovers, while the fairies reor-
ganize them. Elizabeth herself was often directly addressed in plays
performed at court, and in her own person constituted the central
figure in the spectacles that greeted royal progresses to other house-
holds. Besides, when Puck promises to be an auditor at the rehearsals
of *Pyramus and Thisbe*, he adds, 'An actor too perhaps, if I see cause'
(3.1.75).

If *The Athenian Lovers* can be seen as framed in this way, as a
performance for on-stage spectators, *A Midsummer Night's Dream*
calls into question the boundary between fiction and reality. Or,
more precisely, in doing away with the clear distinction between
levels of reality within the play itself, Shakespeare's comedy poses
questions about the status of fiction. *Pyramus and Thisbe* is explicitly fictitious, and the contrast between Peter Quince's play and
Shakespeare's renders *A Midsummer Night's Dream* more apparently
'true': true to life, realistic. But that opposition, defined in those
stark terms, depends on a belief in fairy tales, which the play itself
does not seem to share wholeheartedly. To isolate *The Athenian
Lovers* as fictitious too, however, is to destabilize the opposition, and
at the same time to pose a question about the relationship of fiction
to reality – and realism. Thanks to the magic that drives the plot,
The Athenian Lovers does not establish a one-to-one correspondence
between the world it depicts and the one we (think we) know. Even

so, the story of the night in the woods seems to grow to 'something of great constancy'. Perhaps fiction is not the opposite of truth, nor the repository of it either, but a way of giving form to 'things unknown' that is distinct from either.

A Midsummer Night's Dream, however, does not explicitly identify any part of itself as what I have called *The Athenian Lovers*. Is this suggestion that there are different levels of fiction in the play just my reading, then, or the effect of my imagination? Possibly. But perhaps that's the point. When Theseus says, 'The best in this kind are but shadows; and the worst are no worse, if imagination amend them', Hippolyta replies, 'It must be your imagination then, and not theirs' (5.1.209–12). Shakespeare's play invites a range of different interpretations. By withholding answers to the questions it poses about the imperatives of desire and the capabilities of fiction, the play creates a space for the audience to exercise its own imagination. Intelligible as a fairy tale for children, or, alternatively, as a charming diversion for their parents, *A Midsummer Night's Dream* can also be seen as exploring the limits of fiction itself, assessing the capacity of a story, however improbable, to name what in daylight seems both unaccountable and irresistible in the nature of desire.

6

Hamlet and the Reluctant Hero

The decision

At school I was asked to write an essay on the question, 'Why Does Hamlet Delay?' The reason seemed obvious to me: if he hadn't, the play would have ended early in Act 2. But I sensed that this was not the answer the teacher was looking for. In quest of an alternative way of completing the assignment, I read *Hamlet* with some attention and decided that in practice the hero didn't delay all that much. On the contrary, while telling himself that he ought simply to get on and avenge his father, Hamlet struck me as behaving more rationally than that, checking the facts, assessing the damage, and selecting the right moment. This argument elicited a mark of C+.

Always inclined to be suspicious of authority, I still think I had a point, though I can now concede that the play is a little more complicated than I realized then. *The Tragical History of Hamlet Prince of Denmark* could well have been subtitled *The Decision*. Each of Shakespeare's tragic heroes can be seen to make a decision, of course: Lear decides at the beginning, with devastating consequences; Othello implements his decision at the end, equally catastrophically; Antony puts his off until it's too late; Macbeth takes action when he has more or less decided not to, and regrets it almost at once. But only *Hamlet* turns over a whole play to tracing the process of thinking through the implications of a passionate imperative that just might be ethically wrong.

The unlikely hero

Hamlet, he tells us, well before any specific task confronts him, is not like Hercules (1.2.152–3), the mighty hero whose twelve legendary labours included cleansing the filthy stables of Augeas. Allusions to this ultimate strong man, readily moved to anger, are common in the drama of the period. Antony must be Shakespeare's own most Herculean hero, while *Love's Labour's Lost* makes comedy out of little Moth's impersonation of the muscular protagonist in the Pageant of the Nine Worthies.[1] Any members of the original audience who did not know the details of the story could have made sense of Hamlet's comparison by reference to the sign of the Globe theatre, where Hercules was shown carrying the world on his shoulders (2.2.362–3). In so far as the present time is out of joint (1.5.196), Hercules would have been just the man to set it right.

Laertes, by contrast with Hamlet, displays an altogether more Herculean way of tackling problems (5.1.291). Hamlet is surrounded, both textually and dramatically, by figures who behave like the heroes of tradition. In fairy tales, as elsewhere, young men generally relish the opportunity to put right a wrong. Child Rowland, mentioned in *King Lear* (3.4.178–80), pleads with his mother until she reluctantly agrees to let him risk the perils of the Dark Tower to rescue his sister. Similarly, Child Wynd, hero of 'The Laidly Worm', like his equally intrepid analogue, Kemp Owyne, springs into action the moment he hears of *his* sister's transform-ation by her wicked stepmother.[2] The brave lad who defeats the triple-headed Red Ettin does not hesitate to embark on the adven-ture that will enable him to rescue his two friends.

At the beginning of *Hamlet* young Fortinbras, whose name ('strong-in-arm') aligns him with these popular champions, is already preparing to recover the land wrested from his father, killed in combat by old Hamlet (1.1.83–107). Diverted to Poland, he equally gladly exposes 'what is mortal and unsure/ To all that fortune, death, and danger dare' for the sake of honour (4.4.51–2, 56). (This episode appears in the second quarto edition of the play (Q2), printed in 1604, but not in the first quarto of 1603 (Q1) or the folio text (F) of 1623. Possibly, it was cut in performance, on the grounds that it duplicates information available elsewhere in the play.) Meanwhile, Laertes himself breaks into the royal castle, where he willingly faces hell itself to avenge the murder of Polonius and the madness of his sister. 'I dare damnation. To this point I stand', he insists, 'That both the worlds I give to negligence,/ Let comes what comes, only I'll be reveng'd' (4.5.133–5). And in a play whose common theme, like nature's, seems at times to be the death of fathers (1.2.103–4), *'The rugged Pyrrhus'*, son of Achilles, makes his furious way through the streets to avenge the slaughter of *his* father. If Pyrrhus hesitates when Priam falls to the floor, it is only for a moment. *'Aroused vengeance sets him new awork'*, as his remorseless sword puts paid to the life of the Trojan King (2.2.451, 489). Among so many avenging sons, only Hamlet hangs back. Why?

The answer I was expected to give in my school essay, and centuries of criticism have almost cemented as truth, is that Hamlet finds himself incapacitated by his own psyche. Unable to overcome his grief, at odds with the world, indecisive to the point of madness, the hero perceives his duty clearly enough but fails to take the action he should. Hamlet is rendered unaccountably ineffectual by a fatal 'soul sickness'. The phrase is Stephen Greenblatt's,[3] but it accords with a diagnosis made and repeated by Romantics and Victorians alike. So inadequate did Hamlet seem to his manly task, so effete indeed, that the part was commonly played by women in the nineteenth century. When Eugène Delacroix came to paint him (again and again), he used a woman as his model.

There can be no doubt that Hamlet is reluctant to act, and that he is alienated from a social framework he perceives as out of joint, and no question that he condemns himself for his own inaction. But the drawback of attributing his delay entirely to the protagonist's character is, in my view, twofold. First, it reduces the play to a psychiatric case history. Two hundred years ago fiction was the main source of a mounting interest in individual psychology, but if *Hamlet* is no more than a study in bipolar disorder, there are now good, up-to-date, professional accounts of manic depression. And second, explanation at the level of character effaces the question Hamlet so insistently confronts: what *ought* he to do?

'To be, or not to be'

Two very different approaches to the play find a focus in their respective readings of the 'To be, or not to be' speech (3.1.56–88). Is Hamlet contemplating his own death or his uncle's? For the character critics, the melancholy prince, who had begun his first soliloquy with an acknowledgement that God prohibits suicide, now reverts to the idea as a way out, but cannot make up his mind even to that. For the rest of us, this speech represents one of Hamlet's most rational attempts to come to terms with the obligation to respond to the Ghost's appeal. The first account generally prevailed in the nineteenth century, and still does in some quarters. The second reading, or something like it, follows Samuel Johnson's in the eighteenth century and, on the grounds that it restored attention from the author to the play, has gained increasing currency in our own time. Which does the textual evidence support?

The first line of the soliloquy can be wrenched to defend more or less any interpretation. Is 'it' (revenge, or suicide, according to preference) to be (to take place) or not? Am 'I' to be (exist or, alternatively, live to the full), or not? Dr Johnson thought the opening question concerned survival after death.[4] But the following lines, by contrast, seem remarkably clear and distinct:

> Whether 'tis nobler in the mind to suffer
> The slings and arrows of outrageous fortune,
> Or to take arms against a sea of troubles
> And by opposing end them. (57–60)

Is it 'nobler', more honourable, to suffer or to take arms, patiently enduring what fortune inflicts, however painful, or valiantly fighting back, however overwhelming the odds? To 'suffer' misfortune is to put up with it. To 'take arms', by contrast, is to become a warrior; the phrase has no relish of suicide in it; 'opposing' troubles does not mean 'evading' them, but tackling them resolutely, like Hercules, perhaps. These verbs register active resistance to fortune's arrows, and introduce the antithetical alternatives that will resurface later in the speech between submission and intervention. Who would 'bear' (70, 76, 81), Hamlet wonders, the oppressions inflicted on 'patient merit' (74), if it were not for the fear of what might come after death? This anxiety concerning an afterlife is the consideration that deflects 'resolution' (84), as well as 'enterprises of great pitch and moment' (86), and inhibits 'action' (88). 'Pitch' (Q2, as opposed to F's 'pith') is the height to which a falcon soars: these 'enterprises' hardly sound like taking the easy way out. Instead, the options the speech defines are passivity on the one hand, and combat on the other.

The problem of interpretation arises with the ellipsis in line 60: 'And by opposing end them. To die'. In order to make this the utterance of a suicidal prince, we should have to ignore the contrast running through the soliloquy between bearing troubles and taking arms against them. Alternatively, to confirm the reading that sees revenge as (Herculean?) intervention, we need to find a link between such opposition and death. My own view is that this resides in contemporary assumptions about the crime of regicide, confirmed in the conventions of revenge drama itself, which was by now well established on the early modern stage. When revenge entails murdering the ruler, with the exception of Marston's Antonio, who goes into a monastery, contemporary revengers do not survive their crimes. It is impossible to conceive of Kyd's Hieronimo or Shakespeare's own Titus Andronicus settling down to a peaceful old age. A few years later, *The Revenger's Tragedy* will show Vindice, who owes a good deal to Hamlet himself, so eager to proclaim his own part in the punishment of the old Duke that the new ruler promptly orders his execution: such men are dangerous to the stability of the regime. Where revenge was synonymous with regicide, traitors could expect to be executed, and damnation was thought sure to follow. This was quite a deterrent: no wonder monarchs felt sure they were specially protected. Despite the irony that heaven could not be relied on to protect usurping murderers, Claudius only reaffirms a commonplace of the period when he insists that he is secure against assassination: 'There's such divinity doth hedge a king/ That treason can but peep to what it would,/ Acts little of his will' (*Hamlet*, 4.5.123–5).

If we concede that conventional connection between revenge, regicide, death and damnation, Hamlet's reflections on dying in the rest of the soliloquy arise not from the desire to take his own life but, instead, from the fear of losing it. To die, he reassures himself, is 'to sleep,/ No more' (3.1.60–1), and this end to the suffering that life inflicts ought rationally to be welcome. Surely anyone who contemplated the miseries of human existence would be ready to commit suicide? Hamlet could have found exactly the same argument in *The Praise of Folly*, where Erasmus makes the goddess Folly claim dominion over the world in very much these terms. Anybody with any sense, Folly argues, would forestall the advent of death, when life involves so many troubles, including 'the injuries which one of you scourgeth another withal, as poverty, imprisonment, worldly shame, rebuking, racking, guile, treason, slander, dissension, deceit . . . '. Folly has no personal plan to do away with herself. On the contrary, her point is that, since most people *don't* kill themselves in spite of life's calamities, the majority must be fools and this proves her case that she rules over human beings.[5]

Shakespeare would probably have known this influential work. The Latin original was a grammar school text;[6] an English translation of 1549 was reissued in about 1560, and again in 1577. It is possible that Hamlet knew it, too. In the first quarto of 1603, 'To be, or not to be' comes only five lines after the protagonist enters reading: 'See where he comes, poring upon a book'. In Erasmus, Folly goes on almost at once to 'slander' old men, as does Hamlet's book (2.2.196–200). In Q1 this allusion to the 'satirical' work in question comes soon after the soliloquy, and in the same scene.[7]

If Hamlet appropriated the outline of Folly's case in his own meditation, however, he did so for different ends. In the event, Hamlet's point is not the same as Folly's. Instead, he takes the argument a stage further. What stops us looking forward to escaping life's ills, Hamlet reasons, is 'the dread of something after death' (3.1.78), the unknown consequences of our 'sins' (90) here and now. It is the fear of hell that prompts 'conscience' to inhibit action, resolution, undertakings of great pitch and moment – such as regicide, perhaps. It makes us 'cowards' (83).

In a Christian framework conscience is surely right to instil a fear of punishment in the life to come. *Richard III* includes a moment of gallows humour, when the Second Murderer sent to kill the Duke of Clarence has an unexpected attack of conscience at the thought of the Last Judgement.

'What', challenges his comrade, 'art thou afraid?'
'Not to kill him—having a warrant—but to be damned for killing him, from the which no warrant can defend me'.
'I thought thou hadst been resolute', reasons the First Murderer (1.4.106–12).

The Second grapples with his scruples. When he remembers the promised fee, however, he banishes 'conscience': 'I'll not meddle with it, it makes a man a coward' (132–3). Even so, he does not take part in the killing, and the First Murderer dismisses him unpaid because of his cowardice (276).

Later, in an episode that bears no trace of comedy, the same play reaffirms the association between fear and the moral sense. Confronting death on the eve of battle, the villainous Richard himself remembers his crimes, 'O coward conscience, how dost thou afflict me!' (5.3.180).

If, as the Romantics assumed, revenge is a sacred duty, Hamlet's conscience ought to impel him to act. Instead, it urges him to fear damnation. Is conscience right?

Ghosts

Let us go back to the beginning of the play. It is just after midnight, a time out of time, neither ante meridian nor post meridian, but a turning point between them, and as far as can be from noon, the blaze of day. In an early modern world without electric light, the darkness of the earth on a moonless night must have been deep indeed. Even in the twenty-first century, when the night sky is barely visible for the light thrown up by our cities, the hour has not wholly lost its uncanny quality: midnight appears on our digital clocks as the moment when time is told by a row of zeros, as if the second after twelve o'clock is no time at all.

At the 'dead hour', between twelve and one, 'In the dead waste and middle of the night', two soldiers and a scholar sit down to wait for an 'apparition' (*Hamlet*, 1.1.68; 1.2.198; 1.1.31). One of the company does not believe that the dead walk but, as in all good ghost stories, he is doomed to be proved wrong. 'The Men in the Turnip Field' neatly exploits this convention. Two men were hoeing turnips. One said, 'Yur – I don't believe in these yur ghosteses.' 'Don't ee?', answered his companion – and vanished.[8]

The soldiers have seen this 'thing' (24), they insist. Barnardo has no sooner begun his narrative than the Ghost appears again in the guise of the late King Hamlet. Can this armed figure be an omen of disaster, they wonder: there are threats of war with Norway. But the three misread the spectre's meaning in this particular: the apparition is a family matter, and the Ghost will speak to no one but young

Hamlet, the prince in mourning for a dead father supplanted by an unctuous stepfather.

Elizabethan stage ghosts are conventionally ascribed to the influence of Seneca. But they often owe at least as much to old wives' tales. Macbeth's terror at the sight of Banquo's ghost, his wife tells him, 'would well become/ A woman's story at a winter's fire,/ Authoris'd by her grandam' (Macbeth, 3.4.63–5). In 1661 Thomas Ady complained that, rather than attend to the Scriptures, people listened to old wives' fables about witches and fairies, and 'walking spirits, and the dead walking again'.[9] According to the folklorist Katharine Briggs, 'Almost every village in England has several ghost stories attached to it.'[10] In the twenty-first century we tend to associate ghosts with the Victorians, who invented a great many in their fiction, and went on to make a habit, as the period wore on, of consulting others in spiritualist seances. But the nineteenth-century interest in supernatural revenants runs parallel with the folk revival in the same epoch, and the genre itself is much older. There are many ghost stories among the ballads.[11]

The dead cannot rest in their graves, perhaps recalled by the grief of those they have left behind. Or they may be anxious in the knowledge of something hidden before death, especially money.[12] The old wives' tales Marlowe's Jew of Malta remembers were 'of spirits and ghosts that glide by night/ About the place where treasure hath been hid'.[13] A story recorded in 1833, but set in a much earlier time, tells how a ghost revealed a great heap of gold and silver, and then faded at cock-crow, when such spirits are compelled to return to the other world.[14] Can anything be done to relieve the Ghost, Horatio asks it; or is there a treasure hoard the spectre wants to tell them about (1.1.133–4, 139–42)? Or does it foreshadow political turmoil? It seems that the scholar knows his folklore, as well as the Roman history he invokes as precedent (116–23). So, indeed, does Hamlet. The commonest oral tales of all concern victims of violence, unquiet in the tomb until the wrong is avenged and the perpetrator called to account. 'My father's spirit—in arms! All is not well./ I doubt some foul play' (1.2.255–6).

Horatio views the apparition that controverts his former scepticism with an understandable terror: 'It harrows me with fear and wonder' (1.1.47). Why are people afraid of ghosts? In the first place, perhaps, because they defy the oppositions we take for granted. What is a ghost? How should we classify it? An emanation from another world, encountered in our own, returned from beyond the grave, and thus at once both living and dead, the spectre calls into question the distinctions that structure human knowledge.[15] Material, visible, capable of speech, and at the same time insubstantial, able to 'fade' at will (1.1.162), a ghost is a 'thing' that is not a thing. There, but unknowable, simultaneously present and absent, ghosts represent the uncanny incursion of the other into the selfsame, a trace of the impossible in what we know as reality.

In the second place, ghosts are frightening because their effects can be malign. Their purposes may be to do us harm. Recent films have sometimes represented ghosts as guardian angels, watching over their loved ones in this life. This treatment is out of line with centuries of popular tradition, where supernatural revenants are generally objects of dread. Sometimes a spectre can be laid once a wrong has been put right: there are stories of legal proceedings initiated on the evidence of ghosts.[16] But more commonly apparitions predict disaster. Horatio rightly remembers that manifestations of 'the sheeted dead' heralded the murder of Julius Caesar (1.1.118). The spirit of a former Lady Dedlock walks when calamity or disgrace threatens the family in *Bleak House*.

Contact with a ghost can incur death. The departed spirit in the ballad of 'The Unquiet Grave' tells the lover, 'If you have one kiss of my clay-cold lips,/ Your time will not be long'.[17] Moreover, the victims of crime who seek restitution are frequently vindictive. An ancestor of the man he had wronged appeared to Ezekiel Grosse. Even though Grosse eventually did what he could to put right the injustice, it was rumoured that his body was borne away by devils after a violent death. A farmer who had just buried his wife went out courting on the evening of the funeral. He saw his wife looking in at him through the window, and died of a brain fever two weeks later. Sometimes avenging spectres appear to those who have played no part in the crimes against them. Their terrified victims may well die even so.[18]

Briggs records that a man passing though Devil's Batch in Somerset asked a dark figure the time. ' "Past midnight, and time you left this place to Those to Whom it Belongs", said a deep, cold voice. Then the vision clanked away, the starlight shining on his armour.' As this story suggests, spectres may be of devilish origin. Lured to the spot by a ghost, Ezra Peden, the Presbyterian pastor, comforted a young widow, who turned into a demon at the moment of his death.[19] When the Ghost of Caesar appears to Brutus, he questions its origins: 'Art thou some god, some angel, or some devil,/ That mak'st my blood cold, and my hair to stare?' (*Julius Caesar*, 4.3.276–8). In *Hamlet* the first observers associate the Ghost with what is 'guilty', 'erring', unwholesome (1.1.153, 159, 167). The hero is surely right to exclaim, 'Angels and ministers of grace defend us!' (1.4.39), and Horatio is equally right to fear that the Ghost may lure Hamlet to his death (69–78). In one sense, of course, it does.

The Ghost, forbidden to tell where it comes from, ends under the stage in the space known in the theatre as 'hell'. Although the recognition of its uncertain origin and designs does not deflect Hamlet's determination to confront it, from the moment of his first encounter with the Ghost the prince recognizes the ambiguity of its affiliation:

> Be thou a spirit of health or goblin damn'd,
> Bring with thee airs from heaven or blasts from hell,
> Be thy intents wicked or charitable . . .
> . . . I will speak to thee. (1.4.40–4)

Convinced in the heat of the moment that 'It is an honest ghost' (1.5.144), Hamlet subsequently keeps before him another possibility:

> The spirit that I have seen
> May be a devil, and the devil hath power
> T'assume a pleasing shape, yea, and perhaps,
> Out of my weakness and my melancholy,
> As he is very potent with such spirits,
> Abuses me to damn me. (2.2.600–5)

In such circumstances, 'Am I a coward?' (572). Is it cowardice to hesitate before obeying a visitant from another world, whose design may be damnation, or is it, instead, the proper response of any God-fearing hero?

The Ghost wants revenge, names it indeed, as a binding obligation (1.5.7). Hamlet's mission, should he choose to accept it, is
to murder his father's murderer. But *should* he choose to accept it?
What is the outcome of action for the revenger and regicide? Death,
almost certainly, and quite possibly eternal damnation.

Fools

Surrounded by the King's spies while he makes up his mind
on this issue, Hamlet sporadically assumes an 'antic disposition'
(1.5.180). He teases Polonius unmercifully, caricatures young love
in Ophelia's closet (2.1.87–100) and perhaps her grave (5.1.269–83),
parodies Osric, and performs a macabre routine on the corpse of
Polonius, with Claudius as his straight man (4.3.16–39). Critics
have complained that this mask of folly plays no significant part
in the plot, but it noticeably varies the pace of a long play, where
the conventional clowning is restricted to a single episode in the
churchyard, and the court jester is no more than a skull. Without
detailed stage directions, it is hard to tell in some instances where
Hamlet's assumed madness slides into passion or bitterness, though
Tiffany Stern puts the interesting case that Burbage would have
known which was which, since whenever he is fooling, Hamlet's
speeches turn from verse to prose.[20] Certainly, the Romantic treatment of all Hamlet's utterances as more or less transparent indications of his true state of mind gave the nineteenth century a truly
pathological prince.

His antic disposition is traceable to the earliest extant version of
Hamlet's story, Saxo's Danish retelling in twelfth-century Latin of a
Scandinavian legend. The Icelandic variant of Amleth's name means
'fool'. Amleth is very young when his uncle kills his father, and in
self-defence he pretends to be an imbecile, going about unkempt,
listless and dirty. Among his antics, Amleth rides his horse facing
its tail, and chops up the body of an eavesdropper, throwing the
pieces into a sewer. In practice, however, Amleth is anything but
mad: he is simply biding his time. The British King is so impressed
by the Prince of Denmark that he marries him to his own daughter.
In the end, Amleth gets the Danes drunk at what they suppose is

his funeral, and incinerates them in their own hall, killing his uncle in his bedchamber.

Amleth has a Roman analogue in Lucius Junius Brutus, whose story features in Shakespeare's early narrative poem, *The Rape of Lucrece*. Brutus, ancestor both of the Brut who founded Britain and of Marcus Brutus, who assassinated Caesar, feigned folly to escape the wrath of the Tarquin dynasty. Tarquin murdered his father and, when Lucius showed signs of resistance, killed his elder brother as a warning. After that, Lucius thought it politic to take cover in stupidity, and thus earned the new surname of Brutus (senseless, dull), which he proudly passed on to his descendants. One of these, Hamlet observes, would play a 'brute' part when he assassinated Caesar and his impersonator, Polonius (3.2.104–7); his comment proleptically aligns the prince with Brutus, since Hamlet will go on to kill Polonius himself. As soon as the death of Lucrece presented the opportunity to rouse Rome against the tyrannical Tarquins, Lucius Junius Brutus 'arm'd his long-hid wits advisedly' (*The Rape of Lucrece*, line 1816). He dropped the show of foolishness and persuaded the people to install the Republic, driving the entire royal family into exile. This story about an antic disposition evidently continued to resonate with Shakespeare. Prince Hal's youthful escapades in Eastcheap were, it turns out, 'but the outside of the Roman Brutus,/ Covering discretion with a coat of folly' (*Henry V*, 2.4.37–8). In *King Lear*, Edgar survives, like Hamlet, by feigning madness.

Saxo knew the story of Lucius Junius Brutus, just as Shakespeare did. But could there be a common folk origin for the story of a young man who adopts madness as a cover? One of Saxo's modern translators thinks so. William F. Hansen has found a number of Scandinavian tales of sons who pretend to be mad while they plan revenge for murdered fathers. Moreover, he has also traced an Iranian legend of a prince brought up by shepherds, who played the fool to avenge his dead father, and spoke in riddles.[21]

I have not found any stories quite like this in the native English tradition. Genuine fools abound in popular lore, of course, and 1 April is still their feast day. 'The Noodle family is strongly represented in English folk-tales', Joseph Jacobs notes,[22] and his own collection includes several instances. Fools often make good husbands, because they are kind-hearted: the lord's daughter gets a good bargain in Silly Jack; Dummling is generous to his mother and the little old grey man (see Chapter 2). Many of these figures are merely innocent, and a succession of Jacks allow themselves to be fleeced by landlords or pedlars because they are not given to suspicion. No less a work than Spenser's *Faerie Queene* draws on this tradition when it presents the naive protagonist of Book 1, who has never borne arms before. The Red Cross Knight, 'a tall, clownish young man', is prey to every kind of error, but he learns from each mistake, until a miraculous power enables him to defeat the dragon. The hero, it finally emerges, was a changeling, a prince reared by a ploughman.[23]

Folk fools are not always quite as silly as they seem.[24] On occasions, the mask of folly serves a useful purpose. One night long ago, Wiltshire villagers, trying to fish a keg of smuggled brandy out of a pond with hay rakes, told the excise man they were raking up the reflection of the moon, which they believed to be made of green cheese. Wiltshire people have been known as moonrakers ever since. Before it became the home of Batman, Gotham was known for its ludicrous antics. *The Merry Tales of the Mad Men of Gotham* may well go back to the early sixteenth century. Tradition has it, however, that the inhabitants of this Nottinghamshire village were only pretending to be fools in the hope that this would keep King John away from their neighbourhood. They believed that any path the king took would become a public right of way. When John's servants arrived in Gotham, they therefore found the people busily engaged in a range of absurd activities, among them trying to drown an eel in a pond.[25]

Indeed, fools may well be the wisest of us. 'If any man among you seemeth to be wise in this world, let him become a fool, that he may be wise. For the wisdom of this world is foolishness with God' (I Corinthians, 3.18–19). By an extension of this paradox, simpletons might possess a special kind of wisdom. Erasmus concludes *The Praise of Folly* by abandoning satire to celebrate the Christian contemplation of the things of God, which transports people out of their worldly wits. There is a divine folly, he affirms, that gives access to a truth that passes understanding.

Occupying a unique place in the social structure, Shakespeare's fools are licensed to tell the truth in courts where honesty may be dangerous. Combining wit with wisdom, Feste's riddle risks reminding Olivia that it is foolish to mourn her brother, when he is in heaven (*Twelfth Night*, 1.5.62–9). 'This fellow is wise enough to play the fool', Viola notes with approval (3.1.60). In a more secular key, the puns and paradoxes of Lear's Fool repeatedly draw attention to the King's folly, but without suffering the banishment Kent incurs.

In these circumstances, when Hamlet addresses Yorick's skull, does he confront his opposite, or his double? After all, the hero's antic disposition permits him to stand apart from the false courtesies of the new regime, exploiting the plurality of meaning to throw into relief for the audience the hypocrisy of Claudius:

> KING   But now, my cousin Hamlet, and my son—
> HAMLET   A little more than kin, and less than kind.
> KING   How is it that the clouds still hang on you?
> HAMLET   Not so, my lord, I am too much in the sun.
>   (1.2.64–7)

At such moments the play daringly incorporates the jester's role into the protagonist's, even before the hero has announced his plan. And yet all the while Hamlet knows only too well, with Sir Walter Raleigh, that though life may resemble a comedy, 'Only we die in earnest, that's no jest'.[26]

Violence

What the Ghost wants is a death to match his own. Revenge is violent, bloodthirsty, murderous. If it puts right a wrong, it does so outside the institutions of the law. Where the antic disposition is concerned, Hamlet's closest analogues in popular culture are probably to be found, ironically, in the private detectives and amateur sleuths of modern crime fiction, a genre which parallels the fairy tale, oddly enough, to the degree that it acknowledges the existence of evil, while gratifying the desire for poetic justice. Like old wives' tales, classic detective stories promise that wrongs will in the end be put right. Painful events occur, as we know; evil deeds take place; but the heroes of crime fiction track down their perpetrators and call them to account. This is a genre where questions are answered and problems resolved. Closure resides in the solution of the mystery and the appropriate allocation of punishment.

Many protagonists from the 'golden age' of British crime fiction adopt an antic disposition. In the period between the wars, Margery Allingham's Albert Campion, like Dorothy Sayers' Lord Peter Wimsey, mimics the vacuous demeanour of a upper-class buffoon, concealing an incisive intellect beneath a veneer of inanity. Both are descended from the romantic and exceptionally popular Scarlet Pimpernel. Frivolous, playful, apparently no threat to anyone, these detectives commonly dupe criminals and police alike, while behind their disguise they brilliantly and painstakingly assemble the truth. Agatha Christie constructs Miss Marple as another kind of figure of fun, a harmless old lady, perhaps a busybody, fluttery, ineffectual. Hercule Poirot, meanwhile, is fussy, self-indulgent, and absurd. At the same time, however, Christie's detectives pursue the logic of events without remorse, and implacably bring murderers to justice. The American tradition of the same period is slightly different. In the work of Dashiel Hammett and Raymond Chandler it is the prose itself that masquerades as indifferent to wickedness: sharp, witty, cool, the style of the narrative belies the determination of the private eye to challenge illicit power and the corruption that creates the underworld he so knowingly inhabits.

Part of the project of the detective's comic manner may be to delude the murderer, who will be caught off guard in consequence. But doesn't it also, perhaps, disarm the reader, catching *us* off guard at the same time? Working from outside the institutions of law, the amateur or private detective participates, however obliquely, and with less evident legitimacy than the police, in the violence that inhabits every operation of justice. Law is *enforced*, Jacques Derrida points out, and to that extent it resembles its apparent opposite.[27] Crime is committed against the will of the victim, of course; but law replicates that coercion when it arrests, interrogates, restrains the criminal. To recognize this is not to repudiate legality. On the contrary, constraint is a necessary component of justice, and incarceration by force protects society for the duration. But the inhumanity of crime finds a certain similitude in the necessary inhumanity of the law.

Justice seeks a degree of *equivalence*: an eye for an eye . . . . In so far as the punishment fits the crime, however, it also reproduces it. This resemblance between the wrong and the process that puts it right was most visible in legal systems where murderers were executed: a death for a death. In the golden age of British crime fiction, the killers tracked down by the detective could expect to be hanged. Capital punishment, now repealed in some but not all American states, was the norm in the epoch of Sam Spade and Philip Marlowe. The ultimate fate of the murderer adds a certain frisson to the narrative, though it is rarely discussed explicitly. *Busman's Honeymoon*, first published in 1937, is unusual in dwelling on the horror of execution and the anguish it causes the detective. Moreover, Lord Peter Wimsey exclaims, 'If there *is* a God or a judgement – what next? What have we done?'[28] When justice is at once benign and appalling, some of the success of classic crime fiction resides in the inscription of that ambiguity in the narrative itself. The rituals and procedures of the courts were one way of diverting attention from the violence that informs the exercise of justice; perhaps the characteristic flippancy or absurdity of the classic detective was another.

In a similar way, the comedy in *Hamlet*, the wit that distinguishes the hero from his mighty opposite, as well as from the King's various henchmen and spies, is arguably designed not so much to deceive Claudius as to distract the audience from the enormity of the Ghost's demand. Honest or not, the apparition implicitly asks Hamlet not only to believe his uncle guilty, but in effect to re-enact his offence. The revenge the Ghost expects is a repetition of the initial murder, which is also regicide, at the same time as violence against a close family member. The exorbitance of that demand clearly lies at the heart of Hamlet's dilemma. We are not invited to mistake the play for a comedy, but Hamlet's antic disposition permits us, as it allows him, a momentary escape from the question that resides at its heart, as if a break in our scrutiny enables us to refocus the issues. Each time Hamlet, and the audience, revert to the problem, the contradiction comes more sharply into view, while its resolution seems all the more pressing.

Revenge

Capital punishment meets violence with violence, but no one expects the classic detective to carry out the execution itself. Revenge, by contrast, is implemented personally. It allows no distancing apparatus of due process, trial and impartial sentence, in accordance with the impersonality of justice. On the contrary, when the ruler, as the source of law, is also the criminal, it is the individual responsibility of the revenger to enforce the outcome. Hamlet is called upon to act as judge, jury and executioner, but without their legal entitlement to act. Revenge meets lawlessness with lawlessness.

He knows that revenge must be brutal, and appalling: 'ere this/ I should ha' fatted all the region kites/ With this slave's offal' (2.2.580–2). And if the audience understandably has difficulty in associating such a grisly practice with the non-Herculean Hamlet, Pyrrhus is there to exemplify the proper condition of the revenger. Drenched in blood, which mixes with the dust of the hot city to encase him in a grotesque kind of pastry, this frenzied figure relentlessly hunts down the king he holds responsible for his father's death:

> Head to foot
> Now is he total gules, horridly trick'd
> With blood of fathers, mothers, daughters, sons,
> Bak'd and impasted with the parching streets,
> That lend a tyrannous and a damned light
> To their lord's murder. Roasted in wrath and fire,
> And thus o'ersized with coagulate gore,
> With eyes like carbuncles, the hellish Pyrrhus
> Old grandsire Priam seeks. (2.2.457–65)

The element of parody in Hamlet's recollection of an archaic speech should not blind us to the ethical judgements here. Priam's death is *'murder'*, the light in the streets is *'tyrannous'* and *'damned'*,

and Pyrrhus himself is unequivocally '*hellish*'. In this he resembles
Laertes, who might even be brought back to Denmark two acts later
to whet our almost blunted memory of the stock revenger:

> To hell, allegiance! Vows to the blackest devil!
> Conscience and grace, to the profoundest pit!
> I dare damnation. To this point I stand,
> That both the worlds I give to negligence,
> Let come what comes, only I'll be reveng'd
> Most throughly for my father. (4.5.131–6)

'A very noble youth', Hamlet calls him (5.1.222). But this readiness
to risk his immortal soul for the sake of revenge leads Laertes to
agree to challenge his opponent with an unbated sword. It is his
own plan to anoint the tip with a deadly venom, while Claudius
adds the poisoned chalice.

Even the most Herculean of revengers hesitates, however. Fortinbras allows himself to be deflected from the revenge he planned to
carry out with the 'lawless resolutes' 'Shark'd up' for the purpose
(1.1.101). At the end of the play Fortinbras and Hamlet endorse
each other as potential rulers (5.2.363, 404–5). Pyrrhus experiences an instant of paralysis over the unconscious body of Priam
(2.2.478–83). And Laertes momentarily recognizes the counter-
claims of conscience before he goes on to inflict Hamlet's death
wound (5.2.302). When all these conventional revengers hang back,
if only for a time, would we have more sympathy with a Hamlet
who did not?

Not that Hamlet ignores the principle of equivalence. On the
contrary, in the prayer scene he weighs his projected punishment
very precisely against his uncle's crime:

> A villain kills my father, and for that
> I, his sole son, do this same villain send
> To heaven.
> Why, this is hire and salary, not revenge. (3.3.76–9)

The point is not to reward Claudius for his action, but to repeat
it and damn him: 'Up, sword, and know thou a more horrid
hent' (88). F's 'foul son' may well be a misprint, but it would
reinforce the point. Dr Johnson thought this speech 'too horrible

to be read or to be uttered'.[29] Nineteenth-century commentators, unable to attribute such a remorseless intent to the sensitive prince, were compelled to assume that he didn't mean it: Hamlet, they concluded, was simply rationalizing his continued inability to do the right thing. Less squeamish now, perhaps, and more ready to trust the text, we can understand Hamlet's utterance as revealing revenge in its true light. If *that* is what the Ghost wants, no wonder the hero hesitates.

'Perfect conscience'?

At length, Hamlet comes close to a decision, but in the process the word 'revenge' is silently deleted from his reflections. With the evidence of the play scene and the letter designed to secure Hamlet's own death, Claudius has inculpated himself beyond all reasonable doubt. But the continuation of his original crime in the projected murder of Hamlet introduces the new question of prevention, as opposed to cure. Doesn't the obligation to protect society from future danger, Hamlet asks Horatio, necessitate the death of Claudius on other grounds?

> Does it not, think thee, stand me now upon—
> He that hath kill'd my king and whor'd my mother,
> Popp'd in between th'election and my hopes,
> Thrown out his angle for my proper life
> And with such coz'nage—is't not perfect conscience
> To quit him with this arm? And is't not to be damn'd
> To let this canker of our nature come
> In further evil? (5.2.63–70)

According to the last three lines (which appear only in F), damnation now seems to lie in doing nothing. At this stage it is no longer an option to suffer the slings and arrows, passively enduring what fortune brings. In these new circumstances, conscience seems to demand action.

But the speech still takes the form of a succession of questions, and before they can be satisfactorily answered, Hamlet is called upon to decide. The decision, Derrida points out in 'Force of Law', does not wait. However long we have to make it, he argues, the decision itself always *interrupts* the process of deliberation. The decision is necessarily finite, and in that sense it is of a different order from the infinite process of investigation and reflection needed to be sure what is right and just. Even though deliberation should precede it, action, including just action, is outside the process itself. But while the obligation to act leaves deliberation incomplete, this does not justify postponing action indefinitely: failure to act when the moment comes is also a kind of decision. 'That justice exceeds law and calculation . . . cannot and should not serve as an alibi for staying out of juridico-political battles.' At the same time, to rush in is folly: unreflecting action is even less likely to be just, or more open to appropriation by an unjust cause. 'And so incalculable justice *requires* us to calculate.'[30]

Hamlet 'calculates' his incalculable obligation for the duration of the play. But death interrupts the infinite process. Poisoned himself, with only minutes to live, the hero no longer hesitates: 'Then, venom, to thy work' (5.2.329).

Poison

And yet, even here, the play does not settle for an easy resolution of the question it has so minutely posed. Hamlet kills Claudius with the poisoned sword, the weapon of another noble youth transformed to a revenger. And to be doubly sure, he makes Claudius drink the poison the king has himself prepared, in something like a repetition of the original crime of poisoning Old Hamlet. This symmetry is at once satisfying and disconcerting: an eye for an eye; poison for poison. The equivalence foregrounds the element of criminality, as well as the inhumanity, in revenge.

Capable of successive identifications as revenger, fool, philosopher, and executioner, Hamlet eventually enforces a kind of rough justice. In the end, he does what most people would probably agree he must. And he uses the weapons that are to hand: he is not personally responsible for them. But we are invited to understand his reluctance not as a weakness of character but as a scrupulous apprehension of the problem he confronts. On the one hand, the Ghost of the father Hamlet loved has a case; on the other, obedience to the apparition bears more than a trace of the crime it is designed to put right. As Hamlet sees all too clearly, he is prompted to his revenge by both heaven *and* hell (2.2.586).

Although it draws on the tradition of popular narrative, the play is not a fairy tale, but a tragedy. Perhaps the main difference between the two genres lies in the refusal of tragedy to define clear oppositions between good and evil. The sure knowledge of what heroes ought to do commonly enables fairy tales to deliver a poetic justice we long for in fireside stories; we cannot, however, count on such certainty in tragedy – or in life.

7

Twelfth Night and the Riddle of Gender

Paradox

In disgrace for his unexplained absence from her court, Olivia's Fool restores his credit by a kind of riddle. Why, Feste asks his reclusive mistress, is it foolish to mourn for the brother you loved? Answer: because you believe he is in heaven (*Twelfth Night*, 1.5.63–71). Mourning is a requirement of the virtuous. In a more or less contemporary play, Hamlet finds the speed of Gertrude's remarriage scandalous: 'a beast that wants discourse of reason/ Would have mourn'd longer' (*Hamlet*, 1.2.150–1). And yet, paradoxically, good Christians grieve for those they suppose in a better place. The acknowledgement of their happiness in another world does not bring the dead back, or alleviate the pain of their loss to the living, but the answer to the Clown's riddle offers Olivia comfort, even so: 'What think you of this fool, Malvolio, doth he not mend?' (*Twelfth Night*, 1.5.70–1).

Shakespearean fools always include riddles in their repertoire of comic entertainment: *King Lear* is full of them; Touchstone knows a good few; the Gravedigger in *Hamlet*, called a 'Clown' in the stage directions, asks the one about who it is that builds stronger than the mason, the shipwright or the carpenter. Is it the gallows-maker? No, it's the gravedigger, whose work lasts till Doomsday (5.1.41–59).

Posing riddles was also a popular pastime, especially, no doubt, during the long Christmas holidays. As winter evenings lengthen, Thomas Campion affirms, the chimneys blaze and the wine flows, while some people 'knotted riddles tell' to 'shorten tedious nights'.[1] Robert Burton, too, names such verbal puzzles among the recreations of winter.[2] Sometimes these were derived from the printed collections in circulation in the period. The anonymous *Civil and*

Uncivil Life, which first appeared in 1579, lists the books that were typically read out on winter nights in the country, including *The Book of Riddles*.[3] This may well be the same *Book of Riddles* itemized in the library of Captain Cox, mason of Coventry, in 1575.[4] Is it also the volume Slender wishes he had to hand when it comes to courting Anne Page in *The Merry Wives of Windsor*? Simple thinks Slender lent it to Alice Shortcake sometime last autumn (1.1.186–90). If he did, perhaps she used it to entertain the young. In 1589 George Puttenham recalled enjoying such puzzles in his childhood: 'My mother had an old woman in her nursery, who in the winter nights would put us forth many pretty riddles.'[5]

It comes as no surprise, then, that riddles are also a staple ingredient of old wives' tales.[6] The three-headed Red Ettin, familiar in sixteenth-century Scotland, sets riddles for his victims: if they fail to guess the answer, he turns them to stone. Lives are commonly saved by asking or answering riddles.[7] Meanwhile, in stories of great antiquity, peasant boys surprise kings by responding to them in riddles and clever girls marry rich men by solving them. Their ingenuity exploits the plurality of meaning. After all, as Feste knows, 'A sentence is but a chev'ril glove to a good wit—how quickly the wrong side may be turned outward!' (*Twelfth Night*, 3.1.11–13).

A glove turned inside out is still a glove, but it fits the other hand; the answers to riddles fit the other question, the one we failed to spot in the words we took at face value. In George Peele's *Old Wives Tale* (1595) Erestus, gathering food at the crossroads, hands out advisory riddles to anyone who gives him alms. The play parodies a succession of fairy tales, loosely strung together, but the frame narrative, in so far as there is one, concerns a Wandering Knight, who seeks his long-lost love, imprisoned by an enchanter. No one can blow out the flame that keeps the wicked wizard alive, except 'she that's neither wife, widow nor maid' (line 449).[8] How, then, can the play end happily? Predictably, the story finds an elaborate and slightly absurd way to turn interpretation inside out. Erestus, it emerges, is transformed into a bear every night at sundown. His faithful wife is thus no wife at all for the time being and so embodies the paradox. She blows out the flame and the spell is lifted. This traditional riddle had other, more straightforward answers, of course. When in *Measure for Measure* Mariana claims to be neither maid, widow, nor wife, Lucio suggests that she may be a prostitute (5.1.172–81).

Paradox, which offers comfort to Olivia, is one of the most elementary forms of the riddle. In an American instance, 'what has a face, but no mouth?' 'A clock.' Or, in a Caribbean paradox, 'what has a neck, but no head?' 'A bottle.'[9] *The Demaundes Joyous* of 1511 asks, 'What thing is it the less it is, the more it is dreaded?' The answer is 'a bridge'. At the end of *All's Well That Ends Well*, Helena, supposedly dead, has met Bertram's challenge to secure his ring and become pregnant with his child by taking Diana's place in bed with him. It is Diana who proclaims the improbable outcome, with a pun on 'quick' (alive, pregnant): 'Dead though she be, she feels her young one kick./ So there's my riddle: one that's dead is quick'. And she adds, as Helena, the incarnation of this paradox, herself appears on stage, 'And now behold the meaning' (5.3.301–3).

Sometimes the conundrum draws attention to a surprising truth:

> What God never sees,
> What the king seldom sees;
> What we see every day;
> Read my riddle—I pray.[10]

In this case, commoners are uniquely privileged above kings and God himself: unlike them, we are surrounded by – our equals. At other times the paradoxical truth is one we ought to know, but easily forget: in *The Merchant of Venice* only Bassanio recognizes that to gain Portia, he must be prepared to lose all he has.

A fustian riddle

While Olivia finds relief in the wise Fool's riddle, to the 'Puritan' Malvolio (2.3.140) religion denies more than it cheers. Accordingly, the steward remains unimpressed by Feste's wit: 'I marvel your lady-ship takes delight in such a barren rascal: I saw him put down the other day with an ordinary fool, that has no more brain than a stone' (*Twelfth Night*, 1.5.80–2). Malvolio will in due course pay a high price for this dismissal, as the Fool does not scruple to remind him (5.1.367–9). With perfect symmetry, the play punishes the steward by subjecting him to another riddle, composed by Maria. This is one he is all too ready to solve:

> *I may command where I adore;*
> *But silence, like a Lucrece knife,*
> *With bloodless stroke my heart doth gore;*
> *M. O. A. I. doth sway my life.* (2.5.103–6)

Immense critical ingenuity has been devoted to finding esoteric explanations of this strange sequence of capital letters, in scholarly repetition of Malvolio's own desire to master it. But the best commentator is almost certainly Malvolio himself: 'If I could make that resemble something in me! Softly! "M. O. A. I." ... "M" — Malvolio! "M"! Why, that begins my name!' But now his laboured rumination encounters the obvious problem: ' "A" should follow, but "O" does ... And then "I" comes behind'. His enumeration of these letters generates a chorus of puns from his unseen on-stage audience, demonstrating the range of meanings each of them can be made to bear, while Malvolio forces out the answer he has wanted all along: 'and yet, to crush this a little, it would bow to me, for every one of those letters are in my name' (117–37).

Riddles are dangerous in so far as they invite the interpretation that suits their hearers best. Macbeth fatally misreads the prophecies that seem to promise him safety (*Macbeth*, 4.1.80–1, 93–4). He simply takes them at face value, while Malvolio, in contrast, 'crushes' Maria's riddle to fit his own fantasy. Without any help from the forged letter, he has already imagined himself married to the Countess: 'To be Count Malvolio!' (2.5.34). This scene is one of the high points of Shakespearean comedy: Malvolio postures and admires his own shadow (17), unaware of the hidden presence of the characters he imagines at his beck and call. Sir Toby, meanwhile, concealed in the box tree, but visible at intervals as he pops up behind the steward's back, can barely contain his outrage. When he threatens to betray their presence, Sir Toby is repeatedly tugged back by Fabian, who wants to hear more. Maria's trick is all the cleverer in that it allows Malvolio to entrap himself. 'A fustian riddle!', Fabian calls it (107). 'Fustian' was coarse cotton fabric, often used as a substitute for silk: it could thus mean worthless or false.[11]

A riddle of identity

The fallen letter incorporates a double riddle of identity. Who is the addressee? Malvolio settles that question to his own satisfaction. But who, it also implicitly asks, is the sender, the one who claims, '*I may command where I adore*'? This 'guess my identity on the basis of misleading clues' is another standard form of the riddle, which goes back at least to the Anglo-Saxons, and the answer is not always a person. The tenth-century *Exeter Book* includes a number of these ancient puzzles, among them one which begins, 'I am a strange creature, for I satisfy women'. As Viola points out, 'they that dally nicely with words may quickly make them wanton' (*Twelfth Night*, 3.1.14–15). The creature in the *Exeter Book* grows erect in a bed, can also make women cry, and turns out to be – an onion.[12] Unwary interlocutors are tempted into betraying a knowingness they might later want to disclaim. One of the riddles Puttenham heard from the old woman in the nursery went as follows:

> *I have a thing and rough it is,*
> *And in the midst a hole Iwis:*
> *There came a young man with his gin,*
> *And he put it a handful in.*

And Puttenham comments archly, 'The good old gentlewoman would tell us that were children how it was meant by a furred glove. Some other naughty body would peradventure have construed it not half so mannerly.'[13]

Maria's riddle implicating Olivia is entirely proper, however. The reference to Lucrece, who killed herself rather than live on disgraced by rape, confirms the indications of the handwriting: Lucrece is Olivia's device and appears on the seal of the letter itself (2.5.92–3). Malvolio easily solves Maria's riddle of the sender's identity: he takes the letter at face value – and gets the answer wrong.

And another

A deeper riddle of identity unexpectedly enlists the reclusive Olivia herself in desire. This time, the puzzle is put forward in the third person, and the speaker has no idea that he is propounding a riddle. Her curiosity aroused by the account of the young man at the gate, who will not take no for an answer, Olivia presses Malvolio for more details about him. How old is this insistent stranger, for example?

> Not yet old enough for a man, nor young enough for a boy ... 'Tis with him in standing water, between boy and man. He is very well-favoured, and he speaks very shrewishly. One would think his mother's milk were scarce out of him. (1.5.153–8)

Who is this figure defined by what he is not, not quite a man, not quite a boy, poised in the margin between these distinct and specifiable conditions? His shrill voice associates him with femininity (shrews were generally, though not invariably, women). So does his mother's milk. Is this just a hyperbolical reference to recent weaning, or are its implications wider? Aristocratic little boys wore petticoats in the early modern period and stayed with their mothers until they were 'breeched' at the age of six or seven, when they were taken away from the company of women to be trained in the manly arts of hunting, fencing and falconry. Allowing for a degree of exaggeration, is Malvolio's point that Cesario is barely separated from his mother, only just out of petticoats?

From the point of view of the audience, who think they know the answer to the gender riddle his identity poses, Cesario is just out of Viola's petticoats. But the enigma prompts Olivia, who doesn't, to change her mind: 'Let him approach' (159). Her motive, she affirms, is to 'wonder' at him (193). If Cesario embodies a riddle of identity, however, Olivia will confront him with another: she and her gentlewoman will appear veiled so that he does not know where to direct his embassy.

Knowledge is power; to know the answer to a puzzle is to take charge of the dialogue; riddles put their addressee at a disadvantage. What follows, as Cesario gains access to Olivia's house, is a contest of wit, which is also a miniature power struggle, conducted, of course, in the most courtly terms. But a veil, it turns out, is ultimately no match for a complete costume of the opposite sex. By the end of the scene Olivia has revealed her face, as well as her rank, and the cross-dressed Cesario is in control of the field – while Olivia, who is no closer to the answer *she* seeks, is in love.

Desire and power

In *The Merry Wives of Windsor* Slender thinks his *Book of Riddles* would help him court Anne Page. Is there a relationship between desire and knowledge-as-power? If so, it is a subtle one: most people probably do not experience humiliation as seductive. At the same time, an element of competition commonly enters into our court-ship rituals, as Shakespeare had already suggested in *Much Ado About Nothing*. This observation would also go on to inform William Congreve's *The Way of the World*, for instance, or Jane Austen's *Pride and Prejudice*, as well as the many popular romances that even now continue to draw on the tradition these works established. Love often begins as a game, and the victor may take more than the top score. Juliet imagines her wedding night itself as the process of learning 'how to lose a winning match/ Play'd for a pair of stainless maidenhoods' (*Romeo and Juliet*, 3.2.12–13).

Twelfth Night 1.5 places its antagonists with precision. Each is to a degree ambivalent: Olivia divided between an established commit-ment to seclusion and a newfound curiosity; Viola/Cesario torn between readiness to represent Orsino's interests and wanting to marry him herself (1.4.41–2). The courtly struggle is registered in distinct modalities of speech. To ask a question without knowing the answer is to invest an interlocutor with power. (No wonder men stereotypically find it hard to ask directions!) Meanwhile, the imperative, giving a command, claims authority for the speaker. In the exchanges between Cesario and Olivia, knowledge and power switch back and forth with the modes of address. At first it is Cesario who is at a disadvantage:

CESARIO The honourable lady of the house, which is she?
OLIVIA Speak to me, I shall answer for her. Your will?
(1.5.163–4)

After her initial imperative, Olivia's terse question rather resembles a command than a request for information. The Countess, it appears, defines the terms of the exchanges in her own house. But Cesario's reply does not follow the expected pattern. It begins with romantic hyperbole: 'Most radiant, exquisite and unmatchable beauty' (this, bear in mind, delivered by a speaker who has never seen the object of this address, and doesn't even know which one she is). Then the manner switches unpredictably to a disarming acknowledgement that the whole utterance is nothing more than a performance: 'I would be loath to cast away my speech: for besides that it is excellently well penned, I have taken great pains to con it' (165–9).

Olivia is puzzled, intrigued. Is this self-deprecation or mockery? What are the origins of this eloquent newcomer who, at the same time, whether diffidently or boldly, so evidently challenges convention? Olivia now becomes the questioner in earnest: 'Whence came you, sir?' (172). Cesario's reply, while still apparently also pressing for information, withholds more than it delivers, and at the same time sustains the ambiguity concerning the speaker's attitude. Is it deferential, or cheeky?

> I can say little more than I have studied, and that question's out of my part. Good gentle one, give me modest assurance if you be the lady of the house, that I may proceed in my speech. (173–6)

Olivia's curiosity deepens. Preserving a witty distance, however, she seizes on the references to 'part' and 'speech' to ask, 'Are you a comedian [an actor]?' Again, the reply, while ostensibly answering the question, only intensifies the enigma:

> CESARIO   No, my profound heart: and yet, by the very fangs
>   of malice I swear, I am not that I play. Are you the
>   lady of the house?
>   OLIVIA   If I do not usurp myself, I am. (177–80)

Each of the participants in this dialogue seeks confirmation of the other's identity, but while Cesario's question is straightforward (are you indeed the Countess?), Olivia is unable to formulate the issue in such a way that a simple yes or no will reveal what she increasingly wants to find out: who or *what* is this stranger? Perhaps surprisingly, it is the Countess who gives way, and the play awards the first round of the game unhesitatingly to Cesario.

As far as wit is concerned, the two are well matched: Olivia effectively counters all overtures on behalf of Orsino. But the riddle of
his messenger's identity remains unsolved: 'What are you? What
would you?' (206–7). As the scene goes on, Olivia's imperatives bear
less and less fruit: 'If you be mad, be gone: if you have reason, be
brief' (194–5). Cesario does neither. Instead, he gradually induces
Olivia to dismiss her attendants and to show her face, until eventually the lady who refused to hear Orsino's embassy presses his
messenger to speak of love in his own voice ('what would *you*?',
emphasis added, 262). The final shift of mood to the outright lyri-
cism of the 'willow cabin' speech prompts Olivia to acknowledge,
'You might do much', and she follows up this concession with yet
another question designed to cast light on the identity of the enig-
matic figure who has so unexpectedly enlisted her desire: 'What is
your parentage?' (283).

Gender

Who is it, then, that Olivia falls in love with here? Is the audience in possession of the knowledge Olivia seeks, the answer to
the riddle of Cesario's identity? Yes and no. And the conditions
of early modern stage performance would surely have emphasized
the element of undecidability. We are accustomed to watching this
scene enacted by women and, in consequence, the sharp eye that
we develop at an early age for the signifiers of sexual difference
keeps the femininity of Viola before us, beyond the disguise of
Cesario. Moreover, the written text insists on her identification as
a woman in the consistent speech prefixes. I have changed them in
my account of 1.5 in order to bring out the sequence of events from
Olivia's perspective – and the audience's, perhaps. In performance
Viola is not named, except as Cesario, until Sebastian recognizes
her (5.1.237). On the early modern stage, where the speech prefixes
were not heard, of course, and the actors were both boys, the identity of Viola/Cesario would have appeared much more ambiguous.
Beyond the fictional woman cross-dressed as a boy was a boy-player.

What would the spectators see? Two boys, one playing a character
who remains unequivocally a woman throughout, but the other a
woman playing a figure who is 'in standing water' not only between

boy and man, but also, perhaps, between man and woman. What, meanwhile, does the audience hear? If we ignore the speech prefixes yet again, the irreverence of the speaker who addresses fulsome compliments to a veiled lady, and then breaks off to point out just how much work has gone into learning the speech, might easily come from a boy. Then as now, boys occupy a liminal space, where cheekiness seems disarming, and to be 'saucy' (192) is to invite adult indulgence. When Olivia draws the 'curtain' that conceals the 'picture' of her face with 'Is't not well done?', her interlocutor replies mischievously, 'Excellently done, if God did all' (227–30). 'Painting' was appropriate to whores in the period; such teasing of the lady of the house, engagingly precocious in the mouth of a boy, would be downright offensive from another woman. Shakespeare's comedies consistently exploit the playfulness permitted to boys and, for obvious reasons, easily mimicked by boy-actors.

In 1929, when Joan Riviere affirmed that femininity was no more than a masquerade, a learnt mode of behaviour, she implicitly opened up the possibility that masculinity was equally acquired. Judith Butler developed this idea in the 1990s, arguing that gender was purely performative, the effect of reiterated speech acts.[14] Whether because Viola enters so thoroughly into her own masquerade of masculinity, or because that masquerade brings about its own transformation, many of the speech acts the printed text of 1.5 allots to Viola come more convincingly from Cesario. Which of them, for example, a woman, or a boy, more plausibly swears 'by the very fangs of malice' (178–9)? The oath is not particularly fearsome, but not particularly ladylike, either. Which is more likely to tease Maria as 'good swabber', calling her a 'giant' on the grounds of her diminutive stature (198–9)?

At the same time, Viola is never far away from the speech acts Cesario executes. Who, after all, has a compelling motive for seeing her rival's face? Who better than Viola knows the meaning of willow, emblem of unrequited passion, or has more reason to 'Write loyal cantons of contemned love,/ And sing them loud even in the dead of night' (264–5)? And who, for that very reason, has a motive for undermining with momentary irony her opening praise of Olivia's 'radiant, exquisite and unmatchable' beauty? The play thus complicates Judith Butler's analysis. If the speech acts in 1.5

are gendered, the gender in question fluctuates from moment to moment in a tantalizing display of discontinuity and deferral. This is not consistently either straight or a drag act.

Something of the riddle of Cesario's identity that fascinates Olivia is made perceptible – in slightly different terms – to the audience at the same time. Olivia does not know Cesario is *also* Viola; at any given moment the audience cannot be sure whether they are watching Cesario *or* Viola. Identifications are learnt, but from a variety of sources; the range of possible masquerades is wide. Joan Riviere's case history concerns a woman who moves back and forth between masculine authority and feminine submission. In *Twelfth Night* Viola/Cesario puts on display the paradox of gender as other than it is, at once defining and discontinuous.

No wonder Olivia is captivated. Desire is drawn to mystery, and its workings can be complex. Early modern drama shares with current psychoanalysis the view that our rigid dualities between male and female, gay and straight, or *bi*sexual, underestimate the complexity of attraction, too readily taking gender identifications at face value. What exactly is the nature of Antonio's devotion to Sebastian? The play does not specify, while indicating that it is powerful enough to make danger seem sport (2.1.46). Why precisely does Orsino attend so closely to a boy's narrative of his father's daughter, who never told her love (2.4.108–19)? Is it just because all lovers long to hear love stories, or on account of a deepening interest in the teller?

Twins

Orsino's question about the outcome of this tale of Patience on a monument is greeted with another riddle: 'I am all the daughters of my father's house,/ And all the brothers too' (121–2). Every Christmas, when I was a child, my father used to challenge us with a puzzle. Pointing to a photograph, a man says, 'Brothers and sisters have I none,/ But this man's father was my father's son.' Who is the figure in the photograph? Every Christmas we turned out to have forgotten the answer and had to work it out from first principles. The solution in this instance is perfectly logical, however, and there is, as far as I know, only one.

But is this true of Viola's riddle of identity? She is indeed the only sister and, as the sole apparent survivor of the shipwreck, 'all the brothers too'. The paradox names in the first instance the sad loss of her twin: she is all that's left. But perhaps, too, it indicates something about the construction of Cesario. As a boy modelled on her brother, who resembles him so closely, and who imitates him so perfectly, as to lead to a whole succession of mistaken identities, doesn't Cesario also partly incarnate Sebastian? The play suggests as much: 'I my brother know/ Yet living in my glass' (3.4.378–9). There are no identities, Jacques Derrida points out, only identifications;[15] we learn to be the cultural subjects we become by imitating others. To the degree that Cesario comes into being by incorporating a trace of Sebastian, he is both sister and brother, a paradoxical figure who embodies the difference within the interminable process of identification.

At the heart of the play a curious formulation draws attention to this difference, when Viola as Cesario says, 'I am not what I am' (3.1.142). She does not say, as we might expect, that she is not what she seems, thus reaffirming for the audience the simple and overriding truth of her female identity. On the contrary, she insists, much more paradoxically, that she is other than she is. Like Malvolio's initial account of Orsino's unusual messenger, this assertion depends above all on negatives. As Viola, she is not the Cesario that she also is; as Cesario, she is not the Viola she also is. There is and is not a distinction between the person and the masquerade; identity is both performative and not performative. Neither simply Viola, nor simply Cesario, this figure names for the audience the paradox at the heart of gender identification: the potential for masquerade depends not so much on a comprehensive androgyny as on a defining negative.

The little human animal, we might say now, is invested with a sexed body (even though this does not always conform in every physiological particular to one of the dualities of male and female). Sexual difference is given and is restrictive for both sexes: there is something each of us is not. When events require Cesario to get out his sword, Viola reminds the audience how much she lacks of a man (3.4.299–300). She cannot become one – or not without surgery. But the process of learning in culture to become a gendered adult opens up a range of possibilities way beyond the binary oppositions conventional in our own society. This process is effected at the price of a loss of continuity with the organic world the body continues, however uneasily, to inhabit, and it is never finished. We are none of us wholly or unequivocally what we are.

Riddles may have a single correct solution, but the right answer does not erase the trace of another meaning that made the question into a puzzle in the first place. The wrong side of meaning may be turned outwards to produce an unexpected answer, but the right side also survives to maintain its identity as a riddle. That it should be an onion that makes women cry is amusing – if it is – only because we remember our first answer was inclined to be a different one. Puns and paradoxes are witty to the degree that we acknowledge both meanings at once. Riddles that depend on puns and paradoxes are satisfying – when they are – to the degree that meaning is perceptibly turned inside out in the answer. Recognized as a woman, but still dressed as a boy when the play ends, Viola fascinates because she makes perpetual for the audience the trace of an alternative possibility, a gender not restricted by a binary opposition that isolates what we are from what we might be.

Class

The last of Olivia's questions about Cesario's identity in 1.5 concerns social class: 'What is your parentage?' (271). This enquiry follows her acknowledgement of Cesario's powers of romantic persuasion ('You might do much', 270), and is designed to discover whether he is of marriageable rank. Is he a possible husband for her? Class, the play makes clear, is not the impediment: 'Above my fortunes, yet my state is well:/ I am a gentleman' (272–3). Later, Orsino will confirm that Viola's twin brother is indeed of the appropriate rank: 'right noble is his blood' (5.1.260). The point is worth stressing because new historicism, taking romance for realism, has made it fashionable to believe that *Twelfth Night* is primarily about social climbing, as if Malvolio's aspirations to advance his status by marriage were the key to all the unions in the play. This confusion is no doubt encouraged by productions in Victorian dress, which turn Maria into a housekeeper, and divide Olivia's household between upstairs and downstairs.

Twelfth Night is not a documentary about social status. Indeed, the play is remarkably cavalier about the hierarchies it presents. At one point it seems as if Orsino outranks Olivia (1.3.106–7); at another Olivia indicates that her husband is by definition Orsino's equal (5.1.146–7). Contradiction is not the same as paradox. A play that cannot make up its mind whether Orsino is a duke or a count is not preoccupied with fine gradations of rank. Instead, just as there are in general two possible ages in Shakespeare, young and old, and it is not usually fruitful to calculate too minutely the stages in between, so in the idealized, chivalric world of most Shakespearean comedy, there are broadly two classes, those of gentle birth and those who are not. Gentlemen derive their income from the ownership of land and are entitled to bear arms; they are not expected to work with their hands. This meaning also holds for many in Shakespeare's culture, whatever the anxieties economic mobility was causing in social practice, so that in 1581 Richard Mulcaster, for example, was able to announce categorically: 'All the people which be in our country be either *gentlemen* or of the *commonalty*'. Among the commonalty he included merchants and labourers; 'gentlemen', on the other hand, included the gentry, the nobility and the prince, while the distinctions of rank between these three concerned no more than degrees of power: 'Their difference is in authority'.[16] Cesario is consistently identified as a gentleman; none of the characters seems to doubt this designation; it would not be appropriate for Sir Andrew to challenge him to a duel if he were not.

Class and wealth are understood as distinct. The shipwrecked Viola describes her social status as 'above my fortunes' (1.5.272); Antonio presses Sebastian to make use of his purse, since his current resources are not adequate 'for idle markets' (3.3.45–6). As in the case of Bassanio, whose estate is also impoverished (*The Merchant of Venice*, 1.1.123–5), Sebastian's marriage to an heiress resolves that problem, and Viola's to Orsino restores her fortunes, too, but these matches are not socially inappropriate. Outside the plays, the relationship between wealth and class might have been in question and in transition, but it is not always helpful to read off meanings from practice, or romantic comedy from social history.

In the aristocratic world of the fiction, 'service' is more likely to be understood in feudal than Victorian terms, as allegiance, attendance. Nobles enhanced their own prestige by supporting a retinue of high rank, like the young men who flock to join the exiled Duke in *As You Like It*, or the hundred knights and squires who originally form Lear's train. Courtly ladies, meanwhile, took as their companions ladies-in-waiting, such as those who attend Hermione in *The Winter's Tale*. Maria is a waiting gentlewoman (1.5.159–60) with access to Olivia's chamber, not a chambermaid in the Victorian sense of the term (1.3.50).

It is no doubt in a similar capacity that Viola initially wishes she might 'serve' Olivia (1.2.41). But since Olivia claims to admit no strangers, the only other household open to her is Orsino's. There she cannot respectably appear as a woman, because a bachelor has no place for ladies-in-waiting: Orsino's retinue, which includes Valentine and Curio, is all male. It is, however, as extensive as the size of the Shakespeare company will permit. Dispatching Cesario to woo Olivia, the Duke adds casually, 'Some four or five attend him;/ All, if you will' (1.4.36–7). The number included in this 'all' is not specified by the stage directions.

Nor are the ages of the people concerned. It is not always clear how many of the ubiquitous 'attendants' in Shakespeare are boys. Pages might or might not be of the same social rank as the master of the household in which they served. Aristocratic boys were sent as pages to other noble families, where they learnt obedience to authority, good manners, and the conventions of courtly exchange. The courtesy acquired in the process is part of the 'breeding' that Oliver withholds from Orlando (*As You Like It*, 1.1.1–24), or that the beef-witted Sir Andrew Aguecheek so notably lacks and so palpably envies: 'That youth's a rare courtier . . . ' (*Twelfth Night*, 3.1.87–92). Maria's letter cruelly misleads Malvolio on this issue: '*Be opposite with a kinsman, surly with servants*' (2.5.144–5); the '*singularity*' (146) of his yellow stockings instantly disqualifies him from the competition for Olivia's hand. By contrast, it is Cesario's eloquence, appearance, demeanour, and wit that confirm his social status for Olivia:

> 'What is your parentage?'
> 'Above my fortunes, yet my state is well;
> I am a gentleman.' I'll be sworn thou art:

> Thy tongue, thy face, thy limbs, actions, and spirit
> Do give thee five-fold blazon. (1.5.283–7)

Like the medieval quality of 'gentilesse', early modern 'gentleness' combines birth with the good manners and good taste that constitute its proper marks. It is almost as if the play, in reiterating and amplifying Cesario's own words here, wants to forestall the new historicist reading, instead registering with the audience the perfect social propriety of the marriages that will conclude it.

Plot as riddle

Desire's anarchic object choices, not class, defer the happy ending of *Twelfth Night*, and the text formulates the problem as a riddle, addressed to the audience. It is Viola who names the puzzle the plot is designed to solve:

> How will this fadge? My master loves her dearly,
> And I, poor monster, fond as much on him,
> And she, mistaken, seems to dote on me:
> What will become of this? As I am man,
> My state is desperate for my master's love:
> As I am woman (now alas the day!)
> What thriftless sighs shall poor Olivia breathe? (2.2.33–9)

'As I am man . . . As I am woman': how can the hybrid Cesario/Viola come out as a woman without abandoning Orsino's court? But how, as a man, can Viola hope to elicit Orsino's love? Or what, as a woman, can she offer Olivia? In other words, the play asks how the story can possibly end and, since the 'knot' is too hard for Viola to untie (41), the riddle constitutes a challenge for the audience, who are assumed to know enough about comedy to realize that it must end happily.

Early in Act 2, *Twelfth Night* makes explicit the degree to which the comedy enlists the audience in solving the riddle posed by the plot. But not before it has given, in the immediately preceding scene, a broad hint of the answer: Sebastian, whose twin sister (2.1.18) closely resembles him (24–5) is on his way to Orsino's court (40). The challenge to our intellectual powers is therefore to work out how *exactly* this will solve the problem. In the end, the answer turns out to be a paradox. As Sebastian explains it to Olivia,

> You would have been contracted to a maid;
> Nor are you therein, by my life, deceiv'd:
> You are betroth'd both to a maid and man. (5.1.257–9)

Just like the solution to the riddles that structure *The Old Wives Tale*, and conclude *Measure for Measure* and *All's Well*, this one depends on wordplay: Sebastian not only resembles his sister in every particular except the critical one; he is also still a virgin. Meanwhile, keeping Viola cross-dressed to the very end, the play emphasizes the visual pun that solves its structural and thematic riddle.

If puns make two meanings intelligible at once, and if Viola has been both maid and man, so too has Sebastian. His affirmation throws into relief the similarity, as well as the difference, between them. For sure, Sebastian knows what to do with a sword, while Viola does not. At the same time, however, he too is an object of desire for both a man and a woman. Wooed by Antonio and Olivia, Sebastian, like his sister, yields to marriage in the end, but without erasing the trace of another option, another possible identification.

The challenge for the play, meanwhile, is to delay the solution long enough to allow time to flatter our intelligence with a succession of dramatic ironies and a good deal of social satire. While Viola and Sebastian do not meet, the audience is in a position to know what the characters do not about Sir Andrew's defeat and Antonio's disappointment; while Olivia remains unmarried, there is comedy at the expense of her impossible suitors, Sir Andrew, who needs her money, and Malvolio, who wants her rank.

As every introduction diligently reiterates, John Manningham saw the play in February 1602, presumably some time after its first performance. He particularly liked the forged letter and its effects on Malvolio. But his first comment is on *Twelfth Night's* similarity to *The Comedy of Errors* and the *Menaechmi* of Plautus, though he goes on to say it is closer still to an Italian play. He would almost certainly be familiar with Roman comedy; he is less likely to have had first-hand experience of the Italian *Gl'Ingannati* (*The Deceived*). Nor is it clear that Shakespeare knew this bawdy citizen comedy directly: he probably came across his version of the story in Barnabe Riche's much more romantic tale of 'Apollonius and Silla'.

From Roman comedy Shakespeare inherited the five-act structure that shapes his comic plots, as well as the tradition of mistaken identity, disguise and misunderstanding on which many of the jokes depend. But the psychology of love that distinguishes Shakespeare's new genre of *romantic* comedy comes in the first instance from the native tradition of lyric poetry and the sonnets of Petrarch, as well as from Ovid, poet above all of unfulfilled desire. The Orsino of 1.1 displays the poetic paradoxes of Petrarchan passion, and invokes the suffering incurred by Ovid's Actaeon, by now an emblem of hopeless longing, since he was torn to pieces by his own hounds as a punishment for gazing at Diana naked (21–3).

Twelfth Night displays the character of the new form with particular clarity. Gone are the heavy fathers of the Roman tradition, and the clever servants who ingeniously find solutions where the young couple cannot. The lovers in *Twelfth Night* are self-determining adults with no living parents, and the obstacles to resolution are their own wayward desires. As the acknowledged sources make clear, a long tradition of romantic narrative also makes its way into the formation of the new genre, contributing stories of faithful lovers divided by consecutive adventures, until they are finally united in marriage. But criticism has paid less attention to the element that binds these disparate sources together in *Twelfth Night*. This is the popular tradition, with its delight in riddles as tests of ingenuity, wit, or virtue for the characters, and as puzzles for the audience.

Cruelty

Old wives' tales can be very unforgiving. Not everyone lives happily ever after, and the villains generally meet a cruel fate. The Red Ettin has all three heads cut off in the end. Tom Hickathrift, whose story goes back at least to the seventeenth century, heroically kills a marauding giant and cuts off his head. There is no discussion of compromise or reconciliation.[17] In its nineteenth-century version, 'Nix Nought Nothing' recounts how the giant's daughter caused a tidal wave out of her magic flask, and it grew and grew, until it reached her father's waist, 'and then his neck, and when it got to his head, he was drowned dead, and dead, and dead indeed'. Here the narrator adds laconically, 'So he goes out of the story'.[18] A Cornish giant made the mistake of falling in love with St Agnes. When he would not take no for an answer, she asked him to fill a hole with his blood as a proof of love. Sadly, the hole opened into the sea, and the giant bled to death in the process.[19]

Mr Fox, whose 'old tale' features in *Much Ado About Nothing* (1.1.200–1), is finally cut into a thousand pieces.[20] Mr Fox is a variant of Bluebeard who, in one of his German incarnations, is burnt to death in his own house,[21] while the witch in 'Hansel and Gretel' is roasted in her own oven, howling horribly.[22] The punishment often fits the crime. A wicked stepmother, who turned a princess into a fearsome dragon, was herself 'shrivelled up and shrivelled up, till she became a huge ugly toad'. Moreover, it is said that the loathsome creature haunts Bamborough Castle to this day.[23] No wonder, then, that Malvolio, blind to any interests but his own, should be confined in a dark house. The steward has not only taken a fustian riddle at face value but, worse, repudiated the spirit of fireside recreation appropriate to the climactic night of the Christmas festival that gives the play its title. In the end the benighted Malvolio, who wilfully entangled himself in Maria's word games, inevitably excludes himself from the general rejoicing: 'I'll be reveng'd on the whole pack of you' (5.1.370).

It is not only Malvolio's exit line, however, that calls into question the mood of the ending. The Clown's epilogue, whether an existing folk song, or Shakespeare's own in the mode of popular song, has the capacity to change our perspective on the preceding events. As Feste sings, the blazing chimneys of the last night of the Christmas holidays begin to give way to the wind and rain of a January morning. He invokes an altogether harsher 'folk' world, where 'wiving' is no more than a single episode in a bounded life. Thomas Campion's lyric about winter evenings acknowledges something similar: 'Though love and all his pleasures are but toys,/ They shorten tedious nights'. In their emphasis on transience, Feste's lyrics chime with a number of observations in the play itself, and in particular with his previous songs, most notably:

> What is love? 'Tis not hereafter,
> Present mirth hath present laughter:
>   What's to come is still unsure. (2.3.47–9)

The special place of the epilogue, at once inside and outside the action of the play, invests it with an undecidable status. Feste's final song does not change what has gone before, but it allows the happy ending to recede from the foreground, confirming that the most memorable romantic comedy is not all sugar. Four weddings may also encompass a funeral; *Shakespeare in Love* separates its lovers, even though it undertakes to provide a play in compensation.

Oddly enough, the last of these explicitly ends where *Twelfth Night* itself begins, on the edge of a new world and a new form. By bringing together popular recreations and the existing literary tradition, Shakespeare perfected in *Twelfth Night* a genre that would offer wish-fulfilment across the centuries. When the play draws attention to the momentary quality of present laughter, however, this new departure also offers to delight its audience precisely with the most transient of entertainments, making no promises fiction cannot keep to sustain its baseless fabric into the everyday world outside the theatre. The riddle this instance of the new genre poses concerning gender, meanwhile, is one our own culture has still not entirely solved.

8

Cultural Difference as Conundrum in *The Merchant of Venice*

Tradition

According to a folk tale that was still current in mid-twentieth-century Scandinavia, a merchant named a pound of flesh as security when he bought a bride in Turkey worth her weight in gold. After their marriage the husband came to believe his wife had betrayed him, and drove her into exile. But she disguised herself as a man and returned to Turkey to find the merchant in prison, while his creditor demanded the pound of flesh. Pretending to be a judge, the faithful wife had her husband released.[1]

No one has ever doubted the general resemblances between *The Merchant of Venice* and fireside stories. In a brilliant account of Shylock and his afterlife, John Gross attributes the international appeal of the play to the familiarity of the plot: 'Its folktale-like qualities enable it to cut across cultural boundaries, and it has proved a favourite with audiences in many different parts of the world.'[2] More than sixty years earlier, Harley Granville-Barker, actor, director, playwright and critic, had drawn a more specific parallel: '*The Merchant of Venice* is a fairy tale. There is no more reality in Shylock's bond and the Lord of Belmont's will than in Jack and the Beanstalk.'[3] Granville-Barker's analogy is not accidental: 'Jack and the Beanstalk' shows an unpromising antagonist confronting an ogre with a preference for human flesh. In so far as Shakespeare's play reproduces the structure of that tale, the role of the ogre is allotted to Shylock. The question for Granville-Barker, and a whole tradition of performance and interpretation since the Romantics first began to sympathize with Shylock, has been how far the play complicates the folk tale's straightforward moral opposition by humanizing its Jew.

For at least two centuries the great majority of actors and directors have chosen to exploit the paradox that is Shylock in individual ways. Although he appears in only five of the twenty scenes, in performance his role often overshadows all the others. Occasionally the ogre prevails: in Nazi Germany he vindicated anti-Semitism. But generally actors have preferred a more nuanced portrait. In the course of time Shylock has been variously located at most points along a continuum from scheming villain to persecuted victim, and from figure of fun to tragic hero. By the early nineteenth century, liberal critics were finding him grand, if damaged, while on stage in 1879 the formidable actor-manager Henry Irving stressed his pathos at every opportunity the script offered, as well as some it didn't.

Meanwhile, the part of the unlikely champion who puts an end to Shylock's bid for Antonio's flesh belongs in Shakespeare's version to a woman, as it does in the Scandinavian story. At the same time, Portia also has roots in other fireside narratives. She begins the play as a kind of Sleeping Beauty, immured in her palace in Belmont. And in the story of the three caskets, it is Bassanio who resembles Jack, the poor boy who wins the princess where others have failed.

The earliest printed text of the play, the quarto of 1600, indicates on the title page what the original publisher must have seen as its main selling points:

> The most excellent history of the *Merchant of Venice*. With the extreme cruelty of *Shylock* the Jew towards the said Merchant, in cutting a just pound of his flesh: and the obtaining of *Portia* by the choice of three chests.

There are two narrative strands here, one concerning the moneylender's bond, and the other about winning a bride. As far as the love story is concerned, this advertisement promises a happy ending. But already Shylock is listed first and, the title page slyly insinuates, the outcome looks ominous for the merchant of the title. Not surprisingly, it is Shylock's story that continues to preoccupy a Western world still struggling to come to terms with its own prejudice against anyone it perceives as an outsider.

The two tales come together in the court scene (4.1), and what links them is the fireside tradition of exchanging riddles. In their different ways, both Bassanio's test and Shylock's bond present the protagonists (and the audience) with this familiar form of conundrum. But there may be more at stake in each of these contests than we currently expect such verbal puzzles to entail.

A test

First, the caskets. Things in the popular narrative tradition commonly come in threes: three sons or daughters; three bears; three wishes; three heads in the well; third time lucky. *The Merchant of Venice* also opts for threes: Antonio borrows three thousand ducats for three months, the play insistently reiterates (1.3); he cheerfully agrees to Shylock's bond because he expects his ships to bring in 'thrice three times' its value (1.3.155). By the time we reach the moment of selection, Bassanio's success in choosing one of the three caskets seems a foregone conclusion. As the third of Portia's three suitors to risk the consequences, the poor man competes with princes; in accordance with the conventions of fairy tale, all he has to do is make the most unassuming choice.

Even so, the caskets represent a test of true love. Modern audiences, more familiar with the opposition between love and money as a staple of Victorian novels, are sometimes anxious about Bassanio's motives. In his initial account of Portia to Antonio, requesting a loan to enable him to appear in Belmont like a suitor, Bassanio stresses her wealth, attending only secondarily to her beauty and virtue. Does this make him a fortune-hunter, not to be trusted as a loving husband?

I think not. In medieval romance the ultimate object of desire of most good knights is a beautiful heiress. Similarly, when Jack marries the fairytale princess, he commonly goes on to inherit the kingdom. In the fireside tradition, love, wealth, and power are not in conflict with one another; on the contrary, they all play their part in the idea of what it means to live happily ever after. The wishes that fiction fulfils in a hierarchic culture include access to the pinnacle of the hierarchy itself. In *As You Like It* Orlando wins the Duke's daughter, and the implication is that he will in due course inherit his dukedom; from Florizel's point of view, the happy ending of *The Winter's Tale* includes the advantage that the woman he loves turns out to be the king's lost heir.

There was in this tradition no disgrace in wealth as such, which involved obligations towards others, including charity and hospitality. Misers were wicked not because they were rich, but because they hoarded their wealth, refusing to use it for good. (In a grotesque parallel, ogres were cruel because they betrayed the rules of hospitality, eating the guests they should offer to feed.)

At the same time, heiresses are an object of desire for fortune-hunters too. In fiction the difference, the guarantee of happiness, is virtuous love. Portia's father has devised the test of the caskets to distinguish among the many suitors sure to flock to Belmont. And as Nerissa explains to Portia, who knows it already, for the benefit of playgoers, in case they don't, the correct casket will 'never be chosen by any rightly, but one who you shall rightly love' (1.2.31–2). Her repetition of 'rightly' singles it out for attention. The casket will never be chosen 'correctly', as the correct answer, but also by the correct means (in accordance with the rules of the test), by anyone Portia will not love 'rightly', which is to say honourably, in the way of marriage. She will also love him truly, with the 'right' sort of love, and justifiably, as the right person to marry because he loves her. She is locked in one of the containers, Portia tells Bassanio, and, 'If you do love me, you will find me out' (3.2.41).

The marriage riddle

How can she be so sure? In accordance with the conventions of popular narrative, the test of the caskets takes the form of a riddle. The tradition of winning a bride by solving a riddle is well established by the Middle Ages and can be traced back to antiquity. Famous instances include the story of Oedipus, who solved the riddle of the Sphinx: 'what goes on four legs in the morning, two legs in the afternoon and three legs in the evening?' Suitors who failed to solve the riddle were devoured by the Sphinx. To the monster's dismay, Oedipus guessed correctly that the answer was 'a man', who crawls in babyhood, then stands upright, and finally walks with a stick in old age. Since his reward was to marry Jocasta, who turned out to be his mother, it could be argued that in this case the Sphinx had the last laugh. (Not for long, though. In most accounts, having lost the power conferred by her riddle, the creature killed herself in despair.) *Pericles* also begins with a marriage riddle, but here the incestuous King makes sure that he will not lose his daughter to any husband, by resolving to murder Pericles when he succeeds in solving it, at the same time making execution the official penalty for failure.

The riddle of the caskets seems to have been Shakespeare's own addition to *The Merchant*. There has been much discussion of a lost play called *The Jew*, but the main surviving source story seems to be *Il pecorone*. In this Italian narrative with clear folktale origins, the youngest and poorest of three sons seeks the hand of a rich lady. The condition of success is that he must make love to her overnight; if he fails, she takes possession of the ship laden with merchandise that his godfather has generously provided. But the lady drugs his drink so that he sleeps through the night and loses his goods. Nothing if not persistent, he returns with a new ship – and fails again. But the third time, when his godfather has had to borrow money to provide yet another ship, the lady's maid warns him not to drink. This time the night of love goes well, and the couple are married amid great joy and feasting.[4]

There is a test in the Italian story, but no riddle. As I indicated in Chapter 7, however, solving riddles was a popular winter pastime. Integrated into the fireside tales, meanwhile, riddles marked a well-trodden but risky path to successful marriage. The Brothers Grimm record the story of a princess who will marry the suitor who sets her a riddle she cannot answer. If he fails, his head will be cut off.[5] And 'The Innkeeper's Wise Daughter' tells of a young woman who marries a nobleman because she solves the riddles he sets her father. Dazzled by her wit, the nobleman eventually challenges her to reach his court neither dressed nor undressed, neither walking nor riding, neither hungry nor overfed, with a gift that is not a gift. She arrives in nothing but a net, leaning on a goat and hopping, with two almonds, to present her prospective husband with a pair of pigeons that she releases as she hands them over.[6]

Shakespeare's modification of his source to include the riddle of the caskets brings the play closer to this tradition. The father has set a riddle for his daughter's suitors, and their task is to solve it. As Nerissa puts it to Portia, 'who chooses his meaning chooses you' (1.2.30–1). But this is not just a test of wit. On the contrary, what is on trial is the proper motive for marriage. Wealth drives Morocco, it seems, and vanity Arragon; only Bassanio ventures his own happiness by investing it in another person.

If Portia's suitors fail, they are bound, predictably, by three commitments: never to reveal which casket they chose; never to marry; and to leave at once (2.9.9–16; 2.1.41). To succeed, they must choose from three metals and three inscriptions. Here again, Shakespeare drew on a widely familiar story, reiterated in a translation of the medieval *Gesta Romanorum* reprinted in 1595, a year or two before the play was probably first performed. In this instance, a princess confronts a choice among three caskets to prove her identity as the destined bride of the emperor's son. The metals are the same as they are in the play, but the third inscription reads, 'Whoso chooseth me, shall find that God hath disposed for him'. The princess demonstrates her virtue by opting for submission to God's will, and the couple live happily ever after.[7]

Bassanio chooses on different grounds. It seems that Shakespeare's audience is invited to try guessing the answer to the riddle of the caskets with him. At the beginning of this episode Morocco carefully reads out all three mottoes, naming the materials of the containers as he does so:

> This first of gold, who this inscription bears,
> *Who chooseth me, shall gain what many men desire.*
> The second silver, which this promise carries,
> *Who chooseth me, shall get as much as he deserves.*
> This third, dull lead, with warning all as blunt,
> *Who chooseth me, must give and hazard all he hath.* (2.7.4–9)

Then he reads them all out again in reverse order, pausing to reflect on their implications – and giving playgoers time to demonstrate their own wit by identifying the correct container.

In opting for the gold casket, Morocco chooses perfectly logically: what many men desire? 'Why that's the lady' (2.7.38); and the metal? 'never so rich a gem/ Was set in worse than gold' (54–5). But he fails to recognize the nature of the test. As Michael Wood points out in his excellent book on oracles, there is no chance of guessing the right answer without identifying the question as a riddle. 'A riddle often gives you help if you can crack it. But if you don't know it's a riddle, you can't even try to crack it – what would there be to crack?'[8]

This riddle gives some help, or perhaps a warning: many men desire Portia; they also desire gold. But without love, sought for itself, this cold metal remains ultimately barren, notwithstanding the usurer's capacity to make it 'breed' (1.3.94). In the end, gold serves only to decorate a funeral monument to the life wasted in its pursuit: '*Many a man his life hath sold/ But my outside to behold,—/ Gilded tombs do worms infold*' (2.7.67–9). The conundrum Morocco fails to crack relies on the capacity of the signifier to deceive. Both gold and inscription equivocate: gold is at once precious and deadly, deadly *because* precious; what many men desire may betray their best interests. When the Prince opens the gold casket, he finds an image of Death.

Riddles depend on equivocation. They invite us to think of the surface answer and then rule it out, in order to find one that depends on a quibble instead. 'What's brown and sticky?' 'A stick.' Knowing this to be a riddle, we are required to reject our first thought and produce an unlikely answer. Here is a cockney riddle: 'What's the difference between a buffalo and a bison?' It's no use bringing zoological information to bear on this one: 'you can't wash your hands in a buffalo.' The Prince of Morocco settles for the obvious meaning – and misses the point. He fails to crack the riddle because he ignores the duplicity of the signifier.

Portia's father's puzzle is as serious as the riddle of the Sphinx. The Old Testament included moral riddles; Samson set a famous one (Judges 14.14). Books of riddles mixing serious and trivial puzzles were popular in the sixteenth century. Only two leaves remain of John Rastell's *Book of a Hundred Riddles*, printed in 1530, but as early as 1511 Wynkyn de Worde had published *The Demaundes Joyous*, containing 54 questions. In practice, most of these are now little short of excruciating, perhaps because they are translated from the French. Since they exploit the duplicity of the signifier, riddles do not always work well in another language. As a sample, 'What thing is it that hath none end?' The answer is 'a bowl'. This would have worked marginally better then than it does now: to be without end was in the first instance to be everlasting, eternal. As usual, the form of the question is designed to send the addressee off in the wrong direction.

The Demaundes Joyous also includes the familiar conundrum about the chicken and the egg. Riddles are without origin; they are attributable to no single speaker. And in the contest they represent, the true antagonist we confront is language itself, which withholds the transparency of one fixed meaning for every signifier, whether this is a metal, a phrase, or a motto. It is always humiliating to fail to guess a riddle: signifying practice makes fools of those who believe it to be at their disposal. In the competition of the caskets the Prince of Arragon does no better than Morocco. In fact, he does worse. Treating the signifier as wholly transparent, he assumes he deserves Portia, but forgets that silver is the material of mirrors. This would have been more obvious to Shakespeare's original audience than it is now: medieval mirrors were made of solid silver and were correspondingly rare. It was only in the course of the sixteenth century that a thin coat of silver covered with glass gradually became more widespread in England. In his vanity the narcissistic Arragon, who rejects what other men desire, opens the silver casket to find his own resemblance in 'the portrait of a blinking idiot' (2.9.54).

Neither of the princes pays much attention to the humble lead casket or its reiterated warning motto: 'Who chooseth me, must give and hazard all he hath'. 'Must give, — for what? for lead, hazard for lead!', exclaims Morocco (2.7.17). 'You shall look fairer ere I give or hazard', Arragon insists (2.9.22). Only a lover would recognize that to enter into a lifelong commitment to another person is to risk everything. It is not clear that Bassanio solves the riddle. He knows there is more in the process than meets the eye, that things are not always what they seem (3.2.73–101); moreover, here he explicitly rejects mere wealth (101–4). But his own choice is intuitive, not logical: 'thou meagre lead/ Which rather threaten'st than dost promise aught,/ Thy paleness moves me more than eloquence' (104–6). Bassanio is not necessarily cleverer than the princes: instead, he is in love, and in consequence, he knows how easily unrequited desire endangers peace of mind. Love also equivocates in its own way; it too may constitute either a threat or a promise. Bassanio thus vindicates the nature of the test imposed by the former Lord of Belmont, which works to single out the suitor who knows the meaning of love.

Another test

In the court scene it is Shylock who is put to the test. Will the moneylender pursue his legal entitlement to the point of death, and cut out the heart of the merchant who is here brought to the point of giving literally all he has for Bassanio, or will Shylock finally relent and settle for the money? He is subject (inevitably) to three appeals: first the Duke urges compassion; then Bassanio offers double the original loan; and finally a young lawyer delivers a compelling plea for mercy. In each case, Shylock's answer is the same: the bond is absolute.

Many children would still recognize from 'Jack and the Beanstalk' the rhyme of the ogre who eats human flesh:

> Fee, fi, fo, fum,
> I smell the blood of an Englishman.
> Be he alive, or be he dead,
> I'll grind his bones to make my bread.

In the Britain depicted in *King Lear*, Poor Tom remembers it from the story of Child Rowland and the Elfin King (3.4.179–80). The fearsome Red Ettin, known in sixteenth-century Scotland, reiterates his own marginally more repulsive variant of the ogre's conventional utterance:

> Snouk but and snouk ben,
> I find the smell of an earthly man;
> Be he living, or be he dead,
> His heart this night shall kitchen my bread.[9]

Shylock has no desire to eat Antonio's heart. On the contrary, he explicitly distinguishes it from meat:

> A pound of man's flesh taken from a man,
> Is not so estimable, profitable neither
> As flesh of muttons, beefs, or goats. (1.3.164–6)

Human flesh is worthless precisely because it is not edible. At least, that is what Shylock apparently means. And yet, in a play full of linguistic duplicity, is there a sly equivocation here too? Is human flesh saleable as food after all, but less valuable because cheaper? Either way, in a kind of textual tease the imagery of the play repeatedly reverts to this prohibited possibility:

> SALERIO Why, I am sure if he forfeit, thou wilt not take his
> flesh,—what's that good for?
> SHYLOCK To bait fish withal,—if it will feed nothing else, it
> will feed my revenge. (3.1.47–50)

Invited to supper by the Venetians, Shylock grudgingly sets out:

> I am not bid for love, they flatter me,
> But yet I'll go in hate, to feed upon
> The prodigal Christian. (2.5.13–15)

Although analogue-hunters have unearthed a superstition that Jews ate Christian flesh,[10] Shylock's desire to devour his enemy is only metaphorical: to catch Antonio out will 'feed fat the ancient grudge I bear him' (1.3.45). And yet it is as if the trace of the fairytale ogre returns in the reiterated figurative cannibalism. The parallel gives a shocking twist to Shylock's casual observation to Antonio that they have been talking about him: 'Your worship was the last man in our mouths' (1.3.58).

Difference

How far does the play reproduce the fairytale motifs that constitute its structure? And how far does it diverge from the moral oppositions of the genre to enlist a sympathy that cuts across the conventional division between heroes and villains? What most evidently distinguishes the play from a folk tale is that Shylock's desire for Antonio's flesh is seen not as a natural disposition, but as driven by hatred and inflamed by oppression. Even before the loss of his daughter and his ducats, he has a grievance, with all that word implies of suffering and accusation combined.

Venetian law classifies Shylock as an outsider, an 'alien', not a citizen (4.1.347–9), and he himself begins by insisting that his own exclusion promotes hatred (1.3.46–50). The Venetians reproach him with usury, he complains; they spit on him, call him 'dog' (1.3.104–26). Antonio does not deny this (128–9), and the play confirms it. Solanio refers to him as 'the dog Jew' (2.8.14) and 'cur' (3.3.18); Gratiano reviles him as 'inexecrable dog!' (4.1.128). While in the early stages of the play most of the characters call him Shylock to his face, or 'sir' (1.3.2, 89), in the trial scene he is repeatedly addressed as 'Jew'. Mentioning him in the third person, the Venetians commonly call him 'the Jew'. Moreover, some of the original stage directions name him 'SHYLOCK the Jew' (2.5.0; 3.3.0), and a substantial number of the speech prefixes simply give 'Jew'. (It makes very little sense to blame the Venetians alone for a habit they evidently share with at least the printer of the quarto, as well as the editors of the First Folio, if not the author.) The effect is to draw repeated attention to Shylock's difference from the Venetians. When they set out to praise him, they call him 'gentle Jew', with a pun on 'gentile', as if querying the possibility of Jewish virtue (1.3.176; cf. 4.1.34).

What are we to make of 3.1, where Solanio and Salerio badger Shylock, apparently for the fun of it? Shylock is preoccupied by the loss of his daughter: 'My own flesh and blood to rebel!' (31). When Solanio ignores his distress to make a joke based on the double meaning of flesh (kin and penis), would the audience have found it comic? At this distance of time, it is hard to tell. As Portia demonstrates by her final comment on the Prince of Morocco (2.7.79), it is probably no use looking to the sixteenth century for political correctness. Venetian slavery is invoked, but not condemned (4.1.90–100).

How remarkable, then, that so soon after Solanio's taunt, the point of view swings round in the speech that above all constitutes the grounds of Shylock's continuing undecidability. For an instant, we see things entirely his way:

> he hath disgrac'd me, and hind'red me half a million, laugh'd at my losses, mock'd at my gains, scorned my nation, thwarted my bargains, cooled my friends, heated mine enemies, — and what's his reason? I am a Jew. (3.1.50–4)

Transparency

One striking element of this speech, in a play that depends so extensively on the instability of meaning and the duplicity of the signifier, is the impression of simple transparency the words create. In a work of fiction this perspicuity is a construct, of course, but an artful construct, the effect of everyday monosyllables and anti-thetical constructions ('laugh'd at my losses, mock'd at my gains'), as well as a list that piles up injustices, to juxtapose them with the single, stark, culminating explanation: 'I am a Jew'. The art is Shakespeare's, not Shylock's. By means of it, the play invests him at this moment with a tragic dignity that accounts for the sense the Romantics named, and many since have experienced, of Shylock's intense humanity. Shylock himself goes on to insist on the resemb-lances between all human beings that the Venetians are so ready to ignore:

> Hath not a Jew eyes? hath not a Jew hands, organs, dimensions, senses, affections, passions? fed with the same food, hurt with the same weapons, subject to the same diseases, healed by the same means, warmed and cooled by the same winter and summer as a Christian is? (54–9)

The continuing plain manner seems to render the issues with start-ling clarity, while the repeated patterns and oppositions duplicate the impression of mounting indignation. But what is new here is the emphasis on the common ground, a humanity shared between Jews and Christians, without repudiating the implied distinctions of culture and allegiance. Suddenly, we might after all be in the twenty-first century, acknowledging ethnic or cultural difference, while rejecting its association with inequality. No matter that the speech begins and ends with the threat of revenge. (If this is a shared impulse, it is not one to be proud of.) Regardless of any purely moral judgement we might be inclined to make, Shylock's appeal to our fellow feeling at this moment is hard to resist.

In *To Be or Not to Be* (Ernst Lubitsch, 1942) Greenberg, a minor Jewish actor belonging to the Theatre Polski, performs this speech apparently incidentally, as a display of his own acting skill. The film begins in Warsaw in 1939. At this point in the plot Greenberg is backstage, complaining that he only gets walk-on parts, when he would make a great Shylock. Later, after the German invasion of Poland, he invokes the speech again. This time the theatre has been closed, he is sweeping the streets, and he would give anything for the chance of a walk-on part. Our current awareness of the possible fate of a Polish Jew invests the first instance with a bleak irony and the second with intense pathos. The third time Greenberg rehearses the speech, however, he is acting for his life, in order to distract the German soldiers so that the entire company of the Theatre Polski can escape the Gestapo. Powerful when the movie was first made, these moments have a still deeper resonance in the light of what we know now.[11]

As the film demonstrates, meaning for any specific audience depends to a degree on an interplay between text and context. While the text of the speech remains unchanged, the implications of the performance alter each time Greenberg makes it. The actor selects the Shakespearean speech in the first instance for its tragic possibilities, but a history Shakespeare could not have foreseen confirms its continuing capacity to move emotion. The play's sudden shift of focus, the switch of point of view from Shylock as the butt of the Venetians' comedy to Shylock as victim of unjust oppression, must go some way to answer the question why Shakespeare continues to attract a special kind of attention.

It is not, in my view, that his play constitutes an unqualified plea for tolerance. On the contrary. Much as we might long to enlist Shakespeare's cultural standing on behalf of good causes, part of what gives his plays that standing in the first place is instead the differences within them. A prejudice conventional in its own period goes into the composition of *The Merchant of Venice*. At the same time, the play includes elements that radically unsettle the prejudice it reproduces. *It differs from itself.*

Trial by verbal combat

However we respond to Shylock's moment of tragic stature, when it comes to the trial scene, he has to be stopped. Execution is not a proper punishment for prejudice; we cannot, it seems to me, want Shylock to prevail at the expense of Antonio's life.

The play confirms its fairytale character in confronting Shylock with a most unlikely opponent. In the first place, Portia is not even the unpromising Jack, who sells his mother's cow for a handful of beans, but a cross-dressed woman only masquerading as a lawyer. And in the second place, she has done very little in the play so far but submit, with whatever wit and charm, to a dead father, however wise, and then to a husband, however loving, to whom she happily makes over her property, her power in her own household, and herself (3.2.149–74). Only Portia, however, who has reason to recognize one when she sees it, identifies the question at issue as a riddle. Her unexpected resourcefulness also confirms her popular ancestry. As the Scandinavian tale makes clear, folk heroines are by no means all helpless princesses. Molly Whuppie, for instance, ingeniously saves herself and her sisters from a murderous giant; the witty wife who marries Jack in 'Gobborn Seer' explains how to accomplish impossible tasks by turning them into riddles.[12]

Shylock's bond is absolute; the law cannot be broken without incurring anarchy; the moneylender must have justice; but justice also requires that Antonio should not die. In the view of Avraham Oz, the Israeli scholar and theatre director, the riddle posed by the trial scene is how Antonio's life can be spared without denying the legitimacy of Shylock's bond.[13] How, in other words, can the law be just to both Antonio and Shylock? And the answer, of course, is a quibble: flesh is not blood; a pound is not a jot more or less than a pound. Nowhere is the duplicity of the signifier thrown into clearer relief than in this exposure of the moneylender's worthless bond. Shylock's ultimate antagonist is the language in which his contract with Antonio is necessarily formulated – and he loses.

The difference within the signifier

In *Monolingualism of the Other*, Jacques Derrida describes his own childhood as a French-speaking Jew in Algeria. To an outsider, not Algerian, not in France itself and, during the Nazi occupation of France, not a citizen, the 'mother-tongue' was always located else-where. It was not that the young Derrida preferred or had access to any other language: on the contrary, his allegiance was to the very purest French. But his first language, the one he knew as his own, did not belong to him: 'I have only one language; it is not mine.'[14]

Derrida goes on to argue that in a sense this dispossession is exemplary: we none of us 'own' the language we speak, which was already there when we came into the world. The condition of our access to dialogue with others is that we learn to speak the existing language, make ourselves intelligible on the terms imposed by the language itself. It does not belong to us; indeed, it belongs to no one. In this sense, we are all aliens, all in exile from a state of perfect correspondence between what we want to say, or would want to say if we only knew what it was, and the signifying practices available to us. 'But it does not follow', Derrida continues, 'that all exiles are equivalent.'[15]

When language names the world, it also evaluates and legislates. In other words, the signifier defines what is good, true, right or lawful. Those at the heart of a culture struggle to impose on others the language they do not own themselves, in a bid to reaffirm its efficacy, while their victims, the more deeply alienated the further they are from power, seek to reappropriate in their own interests the language they have never owned, even though they own no other. Both parties are struggling to make language speak *on their terms*.

Although some modern productions give Shylock a foreign accent, Shakespeare's text does not allot him any alien speech habits, in contrast to the Welsh Fluellen, say, or the French Dr Caius in *The Merry Wives of Windsor*. Instead, Shylock speaks English with a peculiar purity, the simplicity that invests some of his speeches with so much dignity. His vocabulary is exact. And this exactness resists the word play, the waywardness, that allows for riddles. Shylock holds on to his own senses of the terms he uses:

SHYLOCK   My own flesh and blood to rebel!
SOLANIO   Out upon it old carrion! rebels it at these years?
SHYLOCK   I say my daughter is my flesh and blood. (3.1.31–4)

Shylock patiently explains his single meaning, as if to clear away the ambiguity that enables Solanio to mock him. In a similar way, he asserts control of 'good', confining the word to its singular, financial interpretation:

SHYLOCK   Antonio is a good man.
     BASS.   Have you heard any imputation to the contrary?
SHYLOCK   Ho no, no, no, no: my meaning in saying he is a
               good man, is to have you understand me that he
               is sufficient. (1.3.12–17)

In court he clings to the letter of the contract: 'Is it so nomin-
ated in the bond?' 'I cannot find it, 'tis not in the bond' (4.1.257,
260).

The letter, however, cannot be trusted to stay in place. Law is
inscribed in the signifier, but the signifier proves itself anarchic.
Derrida's point in *Monolingualism of the Other* is that his own practice
of deconstruction constitutes one possible response to the alterity
of language. Deconstruction invents a new idiom (the manner its
opponents ridicule as obscurantism), and exploits the undecidability of meaning in order to make language differ from itself, to
speak in another way, on other terms. By this expedient, perhaps it
can be brought to say 'what it does not know how to mean to say',
to name 'something else'.[16] Derrida's long-term hope has been a
language that does not yet exist, and that constitutes the inscription
of other values, hitherto unknown.

Portia's aims in the court scene, meanwhile, are more modest.
She wants to save Antonio's life, against the odds and in defiance of the written bond. But her effort to make the language
speak on her terms is closer to Derrida's than to Shylock's. She
exploits the difference within the signifier, makes it differ from
itself. Riddling, the 'tricksy word' that so frustrates Lorenzo when
he wants his dinner, will also be brought in to 'Defy the matter'
(3.5.67–8) of Shylock's deadly bond, and frustrate his knife before it
reaches Antonio's heart. The law is maintained on condition that it
equivocates.

Fantasy hate-figures

The play humanizes Shylock in the first instance by crediting him
with a context: a daughter, who deserts him; a dead wife, whom
he loved; a friend he confides in; a 'sacred nation' and a 'tribe'
(1.3.46, 49) he belongs to; and a society that despises him. The

same humanization is deepened by giving him a consistent manner and mode of address and, above all, an interiority, revealed in an eloquence that looks artless.

But it is worth remembering that Shylock is drawn mainly from fiction, not life. The play is not bound by the historical facts of what it was to be a Jew. At this time moneylenders were not necessarily Jews: usury was practised by Christians too. In Venice Jews were confined to the Ghetto after dark: Shylock could not have gone to supper with Bassanio, and Jessica could not have climbed out of the window into the arms of Lorenzo. Moreover, Shylock's folk-tale bond, so obviously against his business interests, would have had no contractual validity, and would have been laughed out of court if the case had ever been brought. The trial scene is pure fairy tale.

The play, in other words, is not offered as a documentary, and Shylock owes more to intertextuality than to observation. His attributes are assembled from a succession of textual types, including the ogre of popular imagination, but also the Herod of medieval drama, who massacred babies and ranted in the streets, and the Vice of the moral plays, who destroyed mortal beings out of pure malice. In addition, he owes something to the medieval miser, recreated in Ben Jonson's Volpone, and to the heavy father of Roman comedy, as well as to the austere stage Puritan, also incarnated in Malvolio. When he mentions 'the stock of Barrabas' (4.1.294), Shylock points to one major strand of his own textual genealogy: in 1596, shortly before *The Merchant of Venice* was probably written, *The Jew of Malta*, where the gloating atrocities of Barabas had so delighted Marlowe's audience, was revived for eight performances by Shakespeare's rival company, the Admiral's Men.

Societies, Slavoj Žižek argues, are impelled to create hate-figures. These cultural constructs, by definition products of fantasy, mask structural conflict. Always the location of power struggles of one kind or another, societies long, in Žižek's account, to imagine themselves as harmonious, unified wholes, where everyone who belongs there contributes to the well-being of the totality. To screen out the disunity that in practice composes them, societies produce a focus for resentment and imagine a single source of all the trouble, as if the exclusion of the hate-figure would restore a lost harmony. Historically, anti-Semitism has offered a recurring instance of the process:

> How then do we take account of the distance between this corporatist vision and the factual society split by antagonistic struggles? The answer is, of course, the Jew: an external element, a foreign body introducing corruption into the sound social fabric. In short 'Jew' is a fetish which simultaneously denies and embodies that structural impossibility of 'Society': it is as if in the figure of the Jew this impossibility had acquired a positive, palpable existence.[17]

Among other contemporary names for the object of social hatred, we might list traveller, immigrant, asylum-seeker, or terrorist. Some of these characters have a briefer history, and so have accumulated a less detailed mythology than the fantasy-Jew. The attributes that define them are not always so fully delineated, but they attract as much distrust, while effacing the real source of the problems their image is designed to obscure. Such hate-figures effectively mask a justified anxiety concerning actual social divisions.

Žižek's point is that the fantasy constitutes a symptom of social inequality and conflict, not the cause. The Venetians blame Shylock for disrupting the harmony of Venice as they imagine it, a leisurely world of feasting and good manners, as if his values are the real threat to the well-being of the city. But the play locates that threat elsewhere. In practice, Shylock's money plays an integral part in the romantic plot. Only in Belmont does wealth seem unlimited and without origin: in Venice, the play makes clear, money is won with considerable risk and (over)spent with remarkable ease (1.1). Shylock screens the precariousness of the Venetian way of life, with its uneasy combination of courtesy, generosity, carelessness, and danger.

It may be, as Lorenzo urges, that a divine harmony possesses immortal souls. In the world we know, however, such harmony remains inaudible, no more than a pious hope: 'whilst this muddy vesture of decay/ Doth grossly close it in, we cannot hear it' (5.1.64–5).

Prejudice

How surprising, then, that the play invests its fantasy-Jew with humanity. It is for this reason, however, that *The Merchant of Venice* does not just reaffirm prejudice, but draws attention to it.

We cannot reasonably, in my view, want Shylock to win: he lives the identification Venice has conferred on him: 'Thou call'dst me dog before thou hadst a cause,/ But since I am a dog, beware my fangs' (3.3.6–7). On the other hand, in so far as he also lays convincing claim to a human identity shared with the audience, we surely cannot want him further humiliated either. At end of the trial scene, two distinct imperatives come into collision. On the one hand, it is surely not enough to send Shylock home without his money: poetic justice seems to urge that his role as ogre deserves worse. On the other hand, in also stripping of his identification as a Jew a figure the play has invested with humanity, the Venetians effectively complete the process their persecution has inaugurated. Far from incorporating him into their own world, Shylock's enforced conversion finalizes his exclusion, isolating him from his community, the 'tribe' that has represented his only permitted social location.

As a result, he is silenced. Ironically, by their own lights perhaps the Venetians mean to be merciful in imposing on him Christian redemption. Why, then, do we find Shylock's final words so painful to hear? Identity, Derrida insists, is never attained, but only imagined. Without imagining it, however, how can we say *I*? How, in other words, can we *identify* ourselves in order to speak? There are in practice no identities, only identifications. These are produced in culture, as an effect of community, allegiances, beliefs. *I*, then, is always situated, even though that situation may be illusory.[18] A Christian Shylock has no place to speak from, real or imagined. What can he say of himself? 'I am . . . ?' In practice, he says, 'I am not well' (4.1.394). Not just in ill-health, Shylock is not at ease, not in good circumstances, not well *situated*. He has one language and it is no longer in any sense his. There is nothing of any importance he can say in it. A comedy, like a satisfying fairy tale, ends well. Shylock does not, and in addition he has lost his access to the eloquence that once enabled him to denounce the injustice of his treatment.

In a positive festival of riddles in Act 5 (how can a man give away his wedding ring to a woman without betraying his marriage? How can a wife sleep with a lawyer, without betraying her husband?), Portia reclaims a place of equality with Bassanio and affirms the supremacy of marriage over friendship. Shylock does not reappear. What could he contribute to the celebrations? The exclusion of Shylock enforces submission, but it does not create harmony. The social problem the Jew is invoked to screen has not been solved, merely shelved while the Venetians decamp to the fairytale Belmont. A similar problem remains to confront any society that would rather scapegoat a group than confront its own structural anxieties.

Some postwar productions of *The Merchant*, sympathetic to Shylock, have put all the blame on the feckless anti-Semitism of the Christians. This gratifying way out of the problem misses, it seems to me, the reason why Shakespeare's play continues to haunt the imagination of the West. The text does not settle for such simplistic moral judgements. Instead, it constructs, on the basis of two folktale motifs, a riddle that it does not answer: can a society preserve cultural difference and at the same time do away with social antagonism?

It is not entirely clear to me that we are in a strong position to answer it either. While enforced integration generates a justified resentment, our own well-meaning multiculturalism may inadvertently foster precisely the segregation, and thus the hostility, it was designed to prevent.

Postscript

Happy Ever After?

I should like to give this book a happy ending, in line with the fairy tales that have featured so prominently in its argument. I wish, in other words, I could produce a definitive answer to the question I set out to discuss, 'Why Shakespeare?' I have, after all, thought about very little else for the duration.

I do feel closer to a solution. Reinscribing familiar tales with a difference, the plays entice us into the worlds they depict, inviting us to feel as if we were already unaccountably at home there. In the process of reinscription, they pose serious problems – about race and gender, as well the character of fiction, not to mention language and what it can do – and they bring these issues to life with a wit and energy that remains unsurpassed.

Moreover, the plays do not close off the questions they raise. It is not the task of literature to solve problems or announce incontrovertible truths. Instead, faithful to the nature of the language that composes them, fictional texts at their most profound acknowledge a degree of undecidability, the incursion into the most firmly held point of view of an alternative way of seeing. The more determined the resolution to capture in language a nuance, a subtlety, a profound emotion, or a complex issue, the more irrevocably the chimera of a single, fixed, unalterable meaning retreats into inaccessibility, masked by the opacity of the signifiers themselves. Shakespeare's meanings disperse in direct proportion to the density of the language apparently designed to stabilize them. And this in turn generates new readings, productions, adaptations.

Their inconclusiveness does not imply, however, that any reading of the texts will do. On the contrary, in the light of close attention

Shakespeare's plays turn out to define the issues more sharply, not less. At the same time, they do not close off options and, most important, they do not preach: instead, they invite their audiences to think for themselves, to take a position, or to follow on with a contrary option.

They also, in my view, tell a good story, acknowledging the power of a well-told tale to capture and hold the attention of an audience. Such narratives offer the best of recreation; at the same time, they come to inhabit our consciousness. In Shakespeare's case, if I am right, to a degree they are there already, and in the end perhaps that, above all, is why.

Further Reading

Fireside recreation

Aesop's Fables, trans. Laura Gibbs (Oxford: Oxford University Press, 2002).

Katharine Briggs, *British Folk-Tales and Legends: A Sampler* (London: Routledge, 2002). More approachable than the same author's formidable *Dictionary of British Folk-Tales*.

Mark Bryant, *Dictionary of Riddles* (London: Routledge, 1990). Does what it says on the cover.

Angela Carter, *The Bloody Chamber and Other Stories* (London: Vintage, 1995). Traditional tales wittily updated.

Angela Carter ed., *The Virago Book of Fairy Tales* (London: Virago, 1990). Puts the heroines at the centre.

Jakob and Wilhelm Grimm, *The Complete Fairy Tales of the Brothers Grimm*, trans. Jack Zipes (Toronto: Bantam, 1987). This is probably the best edition, but it is out of print as I write.

Joseph Jacobs, *English Fairy Tales* and *More English Fairy Tales*, ed. Donald Haase (Santa Barbara, CA: ABC-CLIO, 2002). All the familiar stories, and some others, assembled in the 1890s.

Ovid, especially the *Metamorphoses*, is pervasive in Shakespeare. Editors, for the right reasons but with the wrong effects, usually print extracts from Arthur Golding's translation of 1567. Golding's translation makes Ovid virtually unreadable now, however. Shakespeare did consult Golding, but he could also read Ovid's Latin. A literal translation (with the Latin alongside) is available in the Loeb edition, trans Frank Justus Miller, revised by G. P. Goold (Cambridge, MA: Harvard University Press), vol. 1 (1977), vol. 2 (1984). For a more lyrical treatment, see the translation by Charles Martin (New York: W. W. Norton, 2004).

Maria M. Tatar ed., *The Classic Fairy Tales* (New York: W. W. Norton, 1999). Different versions of selected tales, with a selection of criticism.

Jack Zipes ed., *The Penguin Book of Western Fairy Tales* (London: Penguin, 1993). Includes literary renderings, as well as imitations and parodies.

Works on fairy tales

Graham Anderson, *Fairytale in the Ancient World* (London: Routledge, 2000). Traces some familiar stories to the classical period.

Bruno Bettelheim, *The Uses of Enchantment: The Meaning and Importance of Fairy Tales* (London: Thames & Hudson, 1976). A classic, and good on wish-fulfilment. I myself am less convinced by the detailed invocation of Freud to 'explain' fairy tales.

Angela Bourke, *The Burning of Bridget Cleary* (London: Pimlico, 1999). A true story, testifying to the survival of fairy lore in late nineteenth-century Ireland.

Marina Warner, *From the Beast to the Blonde: On Fairy Tales and Their Tellers* (London: Vintage, 1995). Wears its considerable learning lightly and stylishly.

Historical context

Peter Burke, *Popular Culture in Early Modern Europe* (Aldershot: Scolar, 1994). Offers a good corrective to the homogenization and idealization of 'the people'.

Adam Fox, *Oral and Literate Culture in England, 1500–1700* (Oxford: Clarendon Press, 2000). An illuminating account of what we know about the context in which the tales circulated, in print, as well as orally.

Stuart Gillespie and Neil Rhodes eds, *Shakespeare and Elizabethan Popular Culture* (London: Thomson, 2006). Includes informative essays on ghosts and ballads.

Margaret Spufford, *Small Books and Pleasant Histories: Popular Fiction and its Readership in Seventeenth-century England* (London: Methuen, 1981). A highly readable account of chapbooks such as *Tom Thumb*, cheap booklets sold to the poor by pedlars.

Shakespeare

From a huge range of possibilities, I have selected a handful of books that have made me personally see Shakespeare's plays in a new light:

Lukas Erne, *Shakespeare as Literary Dramatist* (Cambridge: Cambridge University Press, 2003). Not for the faint-hearted, but this book has made a significant difference to our understanding of the relation between theatre and print.

Marjorie Garber, *Shakespeare After All* (New York: Anchor, 2005). Sophistic-ated but accessible individual readings of all the plays.

Andrew Gurr, *The Shakespeare Company, 1594–1642* (Cambridge: Cambridge University Press, 2004). Backstage information, as far as we have it.

Frank Kermode, *Shakespeare's Language* (London: Penguin, 2001). Makes a persuasive case for a proto-modernist Shakespeare from 1600 on.

Stephen Orgel, *Imagining Shakespeare* (Basingstoke: Palgrave Macmillan, 2003). Elegant and beautifully illustrated.

Kiernan Ryan, *Shakespeare* (Basingstoke: Palgrave – now Palgrave Macmillan, 2002). This refreshingly independent take on Shakespeare also includes an extensive bibliography.

Tiffany Stern, *Making Shakespeare: From Stage to Page* (London: Routledge, 2004). Brilliantly assembles what we know of the way the texts made their way onto the stage and then into print.

Robert Weimann, *Author's Pen and Actor's Voice: Playing and Writing in Shakespeare's Theatre* (Cambridge: Cambridge University Press, 2000). A challenging account of the way increasing 'realism' curtailed the inde-pendent craft of the actor.

Abbreviations and References

AT	Antii Aarne, *The Types of the Folktale: A Classification and Bibliography*, trans. and enlarged by Stith Thompson (Helsinki: Suomalainen Tiedeakatemia, 1961).
Briggs, *Dictionary*	Katharine M. Briggs, *A Dictionary of British Folk-Tales in the English Language* (London: Routledge & Kegan Paul, 1970–1), 4 vols.
Bullough	Geoffrey Bullough ed., *Narrative and Dramatic Sources of Shakespeare* (London: Routledge & Kegan Paul, 1957–75), 8 vols.
Child	F. J. Child ed., *The English and Scottish Popular Ballads* (New York: Folklore Press, 1957), 5 vols.
EETS	Early English Text Society.
Ettin	'The Red Etin', Robert Chambers in *Popular Rhymes of Scotland* (London: W. and R. Chambers, 1870), pp. 89–94. (Reprinted in Briggs, *Dictionary*, Part A, vol. 1, pp. 463–70. Jacobs gives an adaptation, pp. 98–102.)
FQ	Edmund Spenser, *The Faerie Queene*, ed. A. C. Hamilton (London: Longman, 1977).
Grimm	The Brothers Grimm, *The Complete Fairy Tales* (Ware: Wordsworth Editions, 1997).
Jacobs	Joseph Jacobs, *English Fairy Tales* and *More English Fairy Tales*, ed. Donald Haase (Santa Barbara, CA: ABC-CLIO, 2002).
Marlowe, *Plays*	Christopher Marlowe, *The Complete Plays*, ed. Mark Thornton Burnett (London: Dent, 1999).
Marlowe, *Poems*	Christopher Marlowe, *The Complete Poems*, ed. Mark Thornton Burnett (London: Dent, 2000).
Motif	Stith Thompson, *Motif-index of Folk Literature* (Copenhagen: Rosenkilde and Bagger, 1955–8), 6 vols.
Ovid	*Metamorphoses*, trans. Frank Justus Miller, revised by G. P. Goold (Cambridge, MA: Harvard University Press), vol. 1 (1977), vol. 2 (1984).

Thompson   Stith Thompson, *The Folktale* (Berkeley: University of California Press, 1946).

All Shakespeare references are to the *Arden Shakespeare Complete Works*, eds Richard Proudfoot, Ann Thompson and David Scott Kastan (London: Thomson, 1998).

Notes

1 Shakespeare's Singularity

1. *Hamlet*, 4.7.42; *King Lear*, 4.6.106; *Macbeth*, 1.7.5; *Romeo and Juliet*, 2.6.35; *Hamlet*, 1.3.50; *Othello*, 3.3.168, *Hamlet*, 3.2.18, 1.2.231; *Macbeth*, 1.7.11; *The Tempest*, 1.2.401; *Hamlet*, 1.2.185; *King Richard III*, 5.3.12; *Macbeth*, 1.5.16, 4.1.117.
2. *Othello*, 3.3.357; *The Tempest*, 5.1.183; *Antony and Cleopatra*, 1.5.76; *Hamlet*, 3.1.65; *Macbeth*, 2.3.125; *Twelfth Night*, 2.3.114, 48, 2.4.52; *King Henry V*, 4.3.60; *King Richard II*, 2.1.45; *As You Like It*, 2.4.6; *Julius Caesar*, 3.1.273; *Hamlet*, 3.2.239.
3. Balz Engler, 'Shakespeare in the Trenches', *Shakespeare and Race*, eds Catherine M. S. Alexander and Stanley Wells (Cambridge: Cambridge University Press, 2000), 101–11, p. 107.
4. Yoko Takakuwa, '(En)Gendering Desire in Performance: *King Lear*, Akira Kurosawa's *Ran*, Tadashi Suzuki's *The Tale of Lear*', *Shakespeare and His Contemporaries in Performance*, ed. Edward J. Esche (Aldershot: Ashgate, 2000), 35–49.
5. See, for example, Henry Fielding, *Tom Jones*, Book 16, Chapter 5; Sir Walter Scott, *The Bride of Lammermoor*, especially Chapter 24; Jane Austen, *Mansfield Park*, Chapter 34; Charlotte Brontë, *Shirley*, vol. 1, Chapter 6; Charles Dickens, *Great Expectations*, vol. 2, Chapter 12; Mark Twain, *The Adventures of Huckleberry Finn*, Chapter 21. For a selection of the paintings, see Jane Martineau et al., *Shakespeare in Art* (London: Merrell, 2003).
6. Gary Taylor, *Reinventing Shakespeare: A Cultural History from the Restoration to the Present* (London: Hogarth Press, 1990 [1989]), 410–11.
7. Roland Barthes, *Mythologies*, trans. Annette Lavers (London: Vintage, 1993), pp. 140–1, 129 and passim.
8. Anne Olivier Bell, ed., *The Diary of Virginia Woolf*, vol. 3 (London: Hogarth Press, 1980), p. 301.
9. Marjorie Garber, *Shakespeare After All* (New York: Anchor, 2005), p. 3.
10. Folklorists preoccupied by taxonomy are more rigorous in their classifications, restricting fairy tales to stories that include magic. See, for

example, Steven Swann Jones, *The Fairy Tale: Magic Mirror of Imagination* (New York: Routledge, 2002), pp. 8–9.

11. *The Cobbler of Canterbury*, ed. H. Neville Davies (Cambridge: D. S. Brewer, 1976), p. 3.

12. *The History of Tom Thumb*, ed. Curt F. Bühler (Evanston, IL: North-western University Press, 1965), p. 2.

13. Quoted in Margaret Spufford, *Small Books and Pleasant Histories* (London: Methuen, 1981), p. 10.

14. Robert Burton, *The Anatomy of Melancholy*, eds Nicolas K. Kiessling, Thomas C. Faulkner and Rhonda L. Blair (Oxford: Clarendon Press, 1990), vol. 2, p. 79.

15. Bullough, vol. 1, p. 396.

16. *The Jew of Malta*, 2.1.24–6 (Marlowe, *Plays*).

17. Sir Philip Sidney, *An Apology for Poetry*, ed. Geoffrey Shepherd, revised R. W. Maslen (Manchester: Manchester University Press, 2002), pp. 95, 92.

18. *Tom Thumb*, p. 2.

19. John Aubrey, *Three Prose Works*, ed. John Buchanan-Brown (Fontwell: Centaur, 1972), p. 445.

20. *Cobbler of Canterbury*, p. 3. For a full account of this tradition see Marina Warner, *From the Beast to the Blonde: On Fairy Tales and Their Tellers* (London: Vintage, 1995), pp. 1–197.

21. Edmund Spenser, *Poetical Works*, eds J. C. Smith and E. de Selincourt (London: Oxford University Press, 1912), *Prosopopoia*, lines 33, 1388.

22. Lucius Apuleius, *The XI Books of the Golden Ass*, trans. William Adlington (London: 1582), fols 70r–103v.

23. AT 751. Briggs, *Dictionary*, Part A, vol. 1, p. 124.

24. Jacobs, p. 84.

25. *Tom Thumb*, p. 16.

26. The classic analysis is *Motif*.

27. Jacobs, pp. 89–94.

28. Jacobs, pp. 109–12.

29. Briggs, *Dictionary*, Part A, vol. 1, pp. 123–4.

30. See, for example, Joseph Ritson, *Fairy Tales* (London: Thomas Davison for Payne and Foss, 1831); J. O. Halliwell-Phillipps, *Illustrations of the Fairy Mythology of* A Midsummer Night's Dream (London: Frank and William Kerslake, 1875) (also reprints Ritson's essay); T. F. Thiselton-Dyer, *Folk Lore of Shakespeare* (London: Griffith and Farrar, 1883).

31. George Peele, *The Old Wives Tale*, ed. Patricia Binnie (Manchester: Manchester University Press, 1980), lines 68–92, 115.

32. 'The Entertainment at Elvetham', *Renaissance Drama: An Anthology of Plays and Entertainments*, ed. Arthur F. Kinney (Oxford: Blackwell, 1999), 139–54, lines 736–85.

33. J. W. Cunliffe, 'The Queenes Majesties Entertainment at Woodstocke', *PMLA*, 19 (1911), 92–141, pp. 98–9; John Nichols, *The Progresses and Public Processions of Queen Elizabeth* (London: 1823), 3 vols, vol. 2, pp. 211–13.

34. Ben Jonson, *The Entertainment at Althorp*, *Works*, vol. 7, eds C. H. Herford, Percy and Evelyn Simpson (Oxford: Clarendon Press, 1941), pp. 119–31.

2 *As You Like It* and 'The Golden Goose'

1. Grimm, no 64.

2. AT 556E, 577; *Motif*, Q2, L13, D822, H1242.

3. Briggs, *Dictionary*, Part A, vol. 1, pp. 507–9.

4. Jacobs, pp. 89–94.

5. Walter W. Skeat ed., *The Tale of Gamelyn* (Oxford: Clarendon Press, 1884), pp. viii–ix.

6. Jacobs, p. 278.

7. John Bowe, 'Orlando in *As You Like It*', *Players of Shakespeare*, ed. Philip Brockbank (Cambridge: Cambridge University Press, 1985), 67–76, p. 67.

8. Thomas Lodge, *Rosalind*, ed. Donald Beecher (Ottawa: Dovehouse Editions, 1997), pp. 116–17, 150–1.

9. J. K. Rowling, *Harry Potter and the Philosopher's Stone* (London: Bloomsbury, 1997).

10. Charles Dickens, *David Copperfield*, ed. Jeremy Tambling (London: Penguin, 1996), pp. 59–60.

11. Jacques Derrida, *Limited Inc* (Evanston, IL: Northwestern University Press, 1988), p. 40.

12. Jacobs, pp. 290–3.

13. Grimm, no. 89.

14. Jacobs, pp. 48–51, 314–18.

15. Richard Rastall estimates the likely age of male puberty as 17–18 in the late middle ages ('Female Roles in All-Male Casts', *Medieval Drama in English*, 7 (1985), pp. 25–50).

16. *Hero and Leander*, lines 672–3, 641, 147–8 (Marlowe, *Poems*).

17. Alan Sinfield, *The Wilde Century: Effeminacy, Oscar Wilde and the Queer Moment* (New York: Columbia University Press, 1994), pp. 26–33.

18. Lodge, *Rosalind*, pp. 134, 156.

19. Roland Barthes, 'The Death of the Author', *Image, Music, Text*, trans. Stephen Heath (London: Fontana, 1977), 142–8, p. 146.

20. For an authoritative overview of Robin Hood, see Stephen Knight, *Robin Hood: A Complete Study of the English Outlaw* (Oxford: Blackwell, 1994).

21. Ovid, 1.89–112, 15.96–103.

22. *The Jew of Malta*, 1.1.37 (Marlowe, *Plays*).

23. Ovid, 8.620–724.

3 *King Lear* and the Missing Salt

1. Jacobs, pp. 48–51.

2. AT 923. See Marian Roalfe Cox, *Cinderella: Three Hundred and Forty-five Variants* (London: David Nutt, 1893), nos. 208–26; Thompson, pp. 126–7.

3. Cox, *Cinderella*, nos 211, 222.

4. Geoffrey of Monmouth, *The History of the Kings of Britain*, trans. Lewis Thorpe (Harmondsworth: Penguin, 1966), p. 51.

5. Bullough, vol. 7, pp. 312–14.

6. William Shakespeare, *The History of King Lear*, ed. Stanley Wells (Oxford: Oxford University Press, 2000), pp. 11–12.

7. Jonathan Bate ed., *The Romantics on Shakespeare* (London: Penguin, 1992), p. 389.

8. *Motif*, L0-99.

9. Sigmund Freud, 'The Theme of the Three Caskets', *Art and Literature*, ed. Albert Dickson, The Penguin Freud Library (London: Penguin, 1985), 14, pp. 233–47.

10. Marina Warner, *From the Beast to the Blonde: On Fairy Tales and their Tellers* (London: Vintage, 1995), pp. 228, 202, 204.

11. Nahum Tate, *The History of King Lear*, ed. James Black, Regents Restoration Drama Series (London: Edward Arnold, 1976), pp. 1–2.

12. Tate, *King Lear*, p. 1.

13. *The Importance of Being Earnest*, 2.52–3, *Oscar Wilde*, The Importance of Being Earnest *and Other Plays*, ed. Peter Raby (Oxford: Oxford University Press, 1995).

14. W. K. Wimsatt ed., *Dr Johnson on Shakespeare* (Harmondsworth: Penguin, 1969), p. 126.

15. A. C. Bradley, *Shakespearean Tragedy* (London: Macmillan, 1957), pp. 205–6, 235, 204, 241, 253.

16. G. Wilson Knight, 'The *Lear* Universe', *The Wheel of Fire: Interpretations of Shakespearian Tragedy* (London: Methuen, 1949), pp. 177–206.

17. Sigmund Freud, *Beyond the Pleasure Principle*, *On Metapsychology*, ed. Angela Richards, Penguin Freud Library (Harmondsworth: Penguin, 1984), 11, 269–338, pp. 284–7.

18. I discuss some of the implications of this paradox in *Culture and the Real* (London: Routledge, 2005).

19. Jacques Lacan, *The Ethics of Psychoanalysis, 1959–60*, trans. Dennis Porter (London: Tavistock/Routledge, 1992), pp. 310, 305.

20. Jacobs, pp. 89–94.

21. Phyllis Gorfain, 'Contest, Riddle, and Prophecy: Reflexivity through Folklore in *King Lear*', *Southern Folklore Quarterly*, 40 (1977), 239–54, pp. 252–4.

22. Sigmund Freud, *The Interpretation of Dreams*, ed. Angela Richards (London: Penguin, 1976), pp 652–3.

23. Jacques Lacan, *The Four Fundamental Concepts of Psycho-analysis*, trans. Alan Sheridan (London: Penguin, 1994), p. 59.

4 The Exiled Princess in *The Winter's Tale*

1. H. H. Furness ed., *The Winter's Tale. A New Variorum Edition of Shakespeare*, vol. 11 (Philadelphia, PA: Lippincott, 1898), p. 373.

2. Robert Burton, *The Anatomy of Melancholy*, vol. 2, eds. Nicolas K. Kiessling, Thomas C. Faulkner and Rhonda L. Blair (Oxford: Clarendon Press, 1990), p. 79.

3. Thomas Campion, *Songs and Masques*, ed. A. H. Bullen (London: A. H. Bullen, 1903), p. 61.

4. George Peele, *The Old Wives Tale*, ed. Patricia Binnie (Manchester: Manchester University Press, 1980), lines 85–99.

5. John Lyly, *Campaspe*, ed. G. K. Hunter, and *Sappho and Phao*, ed. David Bevington (Manchester: Manchester University Press, 1991), 2.1.23–6.

6. *Motif*, J2070. Midas wished that all he touched would turn to gold. Unfortunately, his magic power turned out to transform his food and drink (Ovid, 11.100–45). For 'The Three Wishes', see Jacobs, pp. 258–9.

7. *The Jew of Malta*, 2.1.25–6 (Marlowe, *Plays*).

8. Ben Jonson, 'Induction' to *Bartholomew Fair*, ed. Suzanne Gossett (Manchester: Manchester University Press, 2000), lines 131–3.

9. *Pandosto* is reprinted in William Shakespeare, *The Winter's Tale*, ed. J. H. P. Pafford (London: Methuen, 1963), pp. 181–225, as well as in Stephen Orgel's edition of the play (Oxford: Clarendon Press, 1996), pp. 234–74.

10. AT 930, 931.

11. Longus, *Daphnis and Chloe*, trans. Ronald McCail (Oxford: Oxford University Press, 2002).

12. *FQ*, VI.ix–xii.
13. Ben Jonson, *The Entertainment at Althorp*, *Works*, vol. 7, eds. C. H. Herford, Percy and Evelyn Simpson (Oxford: Clarendon Press, 1941), pp. 119–31.
14. *The Mad Pranks and Merry Jests of Robin Goodfellow* [1628], ed. J. Payne Collier (London: Percy Society, 1841), pp. 5, 44.
15. *Folklore Record*, 4 (1881), pp. 176–7.
16. *The Winter's Tale*, ed. Pafford, 205.
17. Jacobs, pp. 234–8.
18. For the surviving evidence concerning Whitsun pastorals, see François Laroque, *Shakespeare's Festive World*, trans. Janet Lloyd (Cambridge: Cambridge University Press, 1991), pp. 136–9.
19. *The Lais of Marie de France*, trans. Glyn S. Burgess and Keith Busby (London: Penguin, 1986), pp. 61–7.
20. Ovid, 2.846–75.
21. Ovid, 5.391–408.
22. I discuss the sexuality of Perdita's flowers in *Shakespeare and the Loss of Eden* (Basingstoke: Macmillan, 1999), pp. 122–6.
23. Jacques Derrida, *Monolingualism of the Other; or, The Prosthesis of Origin* (Stanford, CA: Stanford University Press, 1998), pp. 28–9.
24. Thompson, pp. 165–70.
25. David Garrick, *Florizel and Perdita* (London: Tonson, 1758), p. 21.
26. Garrick, *Florizel and Perdita*, p. 63.
27. Jacobs, pp. 93–4.
28. Ettin. Lyndsay makes the claim in his 'Dreme', *Works*, Parts 1–5 (London, 1865–71), pp. 263–88, lines 44–6. The story is also listed among the tales told by shepherds in *The Complaynt of Scotland* (1549), ed. James A. H. Murray (London, 1872–3), p. 63.
29. Giovanni Francesco Straparola, *The Most Delectable Nights* (Paris: Charles Carrington, 1906), 2 vols, vol. 1, pp. 236–52.
30. Grimm, no.16; AT 612. See Thompson, *Folktale*, pp. 115–16, 255.
31. AT 311; Grimm, no. 46.
32. Emmanuel Cosquin, *Contes populaires de Lorraine* (Paris: Vieweg, 1887), 2 vols, vol. 2, pp. 1–7, 286; *Motif*, E55.
33. For examples see Joseph Quincy Adams, *Chief Pre-Shakespearean Dramas* (London: Harrap, 1924), pp. 353–64.

5   Fairy Tales for Grown-ups in *A Midsummer Night's Dream*

1. William Cornwallis, *Essayes*, ed. Don Cameron Allen (Baltimore, MD: Johns Hopkins Press, 1946), pp. 108, 109.

2. Child, no. 37. After his death Thomas evidently returned to fairyland. He reappears in the folk tale of 'The Tacksman's Ox' as an old man who advises the fairies on where they can best steal food from human beings (reprinted in K. M. Briggs, *The Anatomy of Puck* (London: Routledge & Kegan Paul, 1959), pp. 219–20). Tam Lin was rescued from the embraces of the fairy queen by Janet, the mortal mother of his child (Child, no. 39).

3. Cf. I Corinthians 2. 9.

4. *FQ*, I.ix.14.

5. *FQ*, p. 737.

6. Here I venture to disagree with Louis Montrose's influential new historicist essay, ' "Shaping Fantasies": Figurations of Gender and Power in Elizabethan Culture', *Representing the English Renaissance*, ed. Stephen Greenblatt (Berkeley: University of California Press, 1988), pp. 31–64.

7. Keith Thomas, *Religion and the Decline of Magic* (London: Penguin, 1973), pp 732–3. Such devices are parodied in Ben Jonson, *The Alchemist* (*c*.1610).

8. James A. H. Murray, Introduction, *The Romance and Prophecies of Thomas of Erceldoune* (London: EETS, OS 61, 1875), pp. xl–xli.

9. Ovid, 4.55–166.

10. Kevin Crossley-Holland ed., *Folk-Tales of the British Isles* (London: Folio Society, 1985), pp. 221–2.

11. Katharine Briggs, *British Folk-Tales and Legends: A Sampler* (London: Routledge & Kegan Paul, 2002), pp. 278–9.

12. *Aesop's Fables*, trans. Laura Gibbs (Oxford: Oxford University Press, 2002), no. 508.

13. *Caxton's Aesop*, ed. R. T. Lenaghan (Cambridge, MA: Harvard University Press, 1968), pp. 180–1. (Cf. *Aesop's Fables*, no 510.)

14. The authority here is Briggs, *The Anatomy of Puck*. See also Minor White Latham, *The Elizabethan Fairies* (New York: Columbia University Press, 1930).

15. Ovid, 7.198

16. Thomas Nashe, *The Terrors of the Night, The Unfortunate Traveller and Other Works*, ed. J. B. Steane (Harmondsworth: Penguin, 1972), 208–50, p. 210.

17. Bullough, vol. 1, p. 396.

18. *The History of Tom Thumb*, ed. Curt F. Bühler (Evanston, IL: Northwestern University Press, 1965), p. 5.

19. *FQ*, I Proem, 1.

20. Edmund Spenser, *Poetical Works*, eds J. C. Smith and E. de Selincourt (London: Oxford University Press, 1912), *Prosopopoia*, line 45.

21. *More Knaves Yet? The Knaves of Spades and Diamonds* (London: 1613), p. 114.
22. Geoffrey Chaucer, *Works*, ed. F. N. Robinson (London: Oxford University Press, 1974), *The Wife of Bath's Tale*, lines 861, 873–4.
23. John Aubrey, *Three Prose Works*, ed. John Buchanan-Brown (Fontwell: Centaur, 1972), p. 290.
24. Spenser, *Poetical Works*, *Epithalamion*, lines 315–52.
25. Angela Bourke, *The Burning of Bridget Cleary: A True Story* (London: Pimlico, 1999), p. 29.
26. Bullough, vol. 1, p. 396.
27. Cf. *Macbeth*, 5.5.24.

6   *Hamlet* and the Reluctant Hero

1. *Antony and Cleopatra*, 1.3.85, 4.3.21–2; *Love's Labour's Lost*, 5.2.583–8. See also Eugene M. Waith, *The Herculean Hero in Marlowe, Chapman, Shakespeare, and Dryden* (London: Chatto & Windus, 1962).
2. Jacobs, pp. 89–94, 131–5; Child, no. 34.
3. Stephen Greenblatt, *Will in the World: How Shakespeare Became Shakespeare* (London: Cape, 2004), p. 307.
4. *Johnson on Shakespeare*, ed. Arthur Sherbo, *The Works of Samuel Johnson*, vol. 8 (New Haven: Yale University press, 1968), p. 981.
5. Desiderius Erasmus, *The Praise of Folie*, trans. Sir Thomas Chaloner, ed. Clarence H. Miller, EETS (London: Oxford University Press, 1965), p. 41.
6. T. W. Baldwin, *William Shakespere's Small Latin and Lesse Greek* (Urbana: University of Illinois Press, 1944), 2 vols, vol. 1, p. 436.
7. Q1, 7.110, 115–36, 217–19, *William Shakespeare*, Hamlet: *The Texts of 1603 and 1623*, eds Ann Thompson and Neil Taylor (London: Thomson, 2006).
8. Kevin Crossley-Holland ed., *Folk-Tales of the British Isles* (London: Folio Society, 1985), p. 208.
9. Thomas Ady, *A Perfect Discovery of Witches* (London: 1661), p. 169.
10. Katharine Briggs, *British Folk-Tales and Legends: A Sampler* (London: Routledge, 2002), p. 197.
11. See, for example, Child nos. 47, 69, 78, 79.
12. Briggs, *British Folk-Tales*, pp 197–8; T. F. Thiselton Dyer, *The Ghost World* (London: Ward and Downey, 1893), pp. 64–84, 397.
13. *The Jew of Malta*, 2.1.26–7 (Marlowe, *Plays*).
14. Briggs, *British Folk-tales*, pp. 228–9.
15. Cf. Jacques Derrida, *Specters of Marx*, trans. Peggy Kamuf (New York: Routledge, 1994), p. 6.

16. Dyer, *The Ghost World*, pp. 81–4; Christina Hole, *Haunted England: A Survey of English Ghost-Lore* (Bath: Cedric Chivers, 1964), pp. 28–30.

17. Child, no. 78.

18. Briggs, *Dictionary*, Part B, vol. 1, pp. 416, 470–1, 480, 493–4, 497.

19. Briggs, *Dictionary*, Part B, vol. 1, pp. 508, 446–8.

20. Tiffany Stern, *Making Shakespeare: From Stage to Page* (London: Routledge, 2004), pp. 132–3.

21. William F. Hansen, *Saxo Grammaticus and the Life of Hamlet: A Translation, History and Commentary* (Lincoln: University of Nebraska Press, 1983), pp. 16–37.

22. Jacobs, p. 347.

23. See especially *FQ*, I.i.1.5, I.x.65–6, and p. 738.

24. AT 1642, 1643.

25. J. O. Halliwell-Phillipps ed., *The Merry Tales of the Wise Men of Gotham* (London: John Russell Smith, 1840), p. 4. See also W. A. Clouston, *The Book of Noodles: Stories of Simpletons; or, Fools and their Follies* (London: Elliot Stock, 1888), pp. 56–7.

26. Walter Raleigh, 'On the Life of Man', *Poems*, ed. Agnes M. C. Latham (London: Routledge & Kegan Paul, 1951), p. 52.

27. Jacques Derrida, 'Force of Law: The "Mystical Foundation of Authority"', *Deconstruction and the Possibility of Justice*, eds Drucilla Cornell, Michel Rosenfeld and David Gray Carlson (New York: Routledge, 1992), 3–67, pp. 5–6.

28. Dorothy Sayers, *Busman's Honeymoon* (London: Hodder & Stoughton, 2003), p. 449.

29. *Johnson on Shakespeare*, p. 990.

30. Derrida, 'Force of Law', pp. 26–8.

7   *Twelfth Night* and the Riddle of Gender

1. Thomas Campion, 'Now winter nights enlarge', *Songs and Masques*, ed. A. H. Bullen (London: A. H. Bullen, 1903), pp. 96–7.

2. Robert Burton, *The Anatomy of Melancholy*, vol. 2, eds Nicolas K. Kiessling, Thomas C. Faulkner and Rhonda L. Blair (Oxford: Clarendon Press, 1990), p. 79.

3. W. C. Hazlitt ed., *Inedited Tracts* (London: Roxburghe Society, 1868), pp. 56–7.

4. F. J. Furnivall ed., *Captain Cox, His Ballads and Books* (London: Taylor, 1871), p. 30.

5. George Puttenham, *The Arte of English Poesie*, eds G. D. Willcock and A. Walker (Cambridge: Cambridge University Press, 1936), p. 188.

6. Jacobs, pp. 19–24; Grimm, no. 55.
7. AT 927, 922. See Thompson, pp. 161–3.
8. George Peele, *The Old Wives' Tale*, ed. Patricia Binnie (Manchester: Manchester University Press, 1980).
9. Mark Bryant, *Dictionary of Riddles* (London: Routledge, 1990), nos. 987, 1397.
10. Bryant, *Dictionary of Riddles*, no. 339.
11. See M. Channing Linthicum, *Costume in the Drama of Shakespeare and his Contemporaries* (Oxford: Clarendon Press, 1936), pp. 106–9.
12. Bryant, *Dictionary of Riddles*, no. 541.
13. Puttenham, *Arte of English Poesie*, p. 188.
14. Joan Riviere, 'Womanliness as a Masquerade', *The Body*, ed. Tiffany Atkinson (Basingstoke: Palgrave Macmillan, 2005), 110–14, p. 113. Judith Butler, *Gender Trouble* (New York: Routledge, 1990, 1999).
15. Jacques Derrida, *Monolingualism of the Other; or, The Prosthesis of Origin*, trans. Patrick Mensah (Stanford, CA: Stanford University Press, 1998), p. 28.
16. Richard Mulcaster, *Positions Concerning the Training Up of Children*, ed. William Barker (Toronto: University of Toronto Press, 1994), p. 198.
17. Jacobs, pp. 223–8.
18. Jacobs, pp. 37–40, p. 39.
19. Katharine Briggs, *British Folk–Tales and Legends* (London: Routledge, 2002), p. 234.
20. Jacobs, pp. 109–11.
21. Grimm, no. 46.
22. Grimm, no. 15.
23. Jacobs, 131–5, p. 135.

8 Cultural Difference as Conundrum in *The Merchant of Venice*

1. AT 890. Thompson, p. 109–10.
2. John Gross, *Shylock: Four Hundred Years in the Life of a Legend* (London: Chatto & Windus, 1992), p. 227.
3. Harley Granville-Barker, *Prefaces to Shakespeare*, Second Series (London: Sidgwick and Jackson, 1930), p. 67.
4. The story is given in translation in William Shakespeare, *The Merchant of Venice*, ed. John Russell Brown (London: Methuen, 1959), pp. 140–53.
5. Grimm, no. 22.

6. Kathleen Ragan ed., *Fearless Girls, Wise Women, and Beloved Sisters: Heroines in Folktales from around the World* (New York: W. W. Norton, 1998), pp. 156–9.

7. *The Merchant of Venice*, ed. Brown, pp. 172–4.

8. Michael Wood, *The Road to Delphi: The Life and Afterlife of Oracles* (New York: Farrar, Straus and Giroux, 2003), p. 174.

9. Ettin, p. 92.

10. *The Merchant of Venice,* ed. Brown, 3.1.47n.

11. Cf Gross, *Shylock*, pp. 249–50.

12. Jacobs, pp. 94–7, 230–3. For other resourceful heroines, see Ragan, ed., *Fearless Girls*; and Angela Carter ed., *The Virago Book of Fairy Tales* (London: Virago, 1990).

13. Avraham Oz, *The Yoke of Love: Prophetic Riddles in* The Merchant of Venice (Newark, DE: University of Delaware Press, 1995), p. 161.

14. Jacques Derrida, *Monolingualism of the Other; or, The Prosthesis of Origin*, trans. Patrick Mensah (Stanford, CA: Stanford University Press), p. 1.

15. Derrida, *Monolingualism of the Other*, p. 58.

16. Derrida, *Monolingualism of the Other*, p. 67.

17. Slavoj Žižek, *The Sublime Object of Ideology* (London: Verso, 1989), p. 126.

18. Derrida, *Monolingualism of the Other*, pp. 28–9.

Index

Bold numbers indicate main discussion

Ady, Thomas, 115
Aesop, 13, 93
Allingham, Margery, 122
Apuleius, Lucius, 14–15
Aristotle, 51
Aubrey, John, 13, 96
Austin, Jane, and characters in, 11, 28, 46, 47, 73, 135

Barthes, Roland, 5, 36
'Beauty and the Beast', 15
Bluebeard, 16, 81, 83, 147
Bond, Edward, 51
Bourke, Angela, *see* Cleary, Bridget
Bradley, A. C., 17, 48, 60
Briggs, Katharine, 115, 116–17
Brontë, Charlotte, and characters in, 11, 28, 46, 47, 73
Brook, Peter, 51
Burton, Robert, 12–13, 14, 65–6, 129
Butler, Judith, 138–9

Campion, Thomas, 66, 129, 147
Cap o' Rushes, 29, 42, 71
Carter, Angela, 3
Chaucer, Geoffrey, 11, 22, 31–2, 40–1, 89, 91, 95, 96, 102
Christie, Agatha, 1, 122
Churchyard, Thomas, 19
'Cinderella', 11, 15, 22, 28, 29, 33, 43, 45–6, 48, 71, 72, 73, 77
Cleary, Bridget, 86, 99

Cobbler of Canterbury, The, 12, 14
Coleridge, Samuel Taylor, 17, 45, 91
Congreve, William, 135
Cornwallis, William, 85
Country Man's Comfort, The, 12
crime fiction, 121–4
cultural materialism, 4–6

Daphnis and Chloe, 70
Delacroix, Eugène, 110
Derrida, Jacques, 28, 75, 116, 122–3, 126–7, 140, 162–4, 167
'Dick Whittington', 11
Dickens, Charles, and characters in, 11, 26–7, 46, 116

'Entertainment at Elvetham, The', 18
Erasmus, Desiderius, 112–13, 120
Erne, Lukas, 7

Fielding, Henry, 11, 25–8
Four Weddings and a Funeral, 148
France, Marie de, 74
Freud, Sigmund, 45, 51–2, 59

Garber, Marjorie, 11
Garrick, David, 69, 78–9
Geoffrey of Monmouth, 43–4, 60
ghost stories, 114–18
'Golden Goose, The', 21–2, 23, 24, 25, 28, 120

Golding, Arthur, 95
'Goose Girl, The', 28, 29, 71
Granville-Barker, Harley, 149
Greenblatt, Stephen, 110
Greene, Robert, *see Pandosto*
Griffith, D. W., 2
Gross, John, 149

'Hansel and Gretel', 147
Hickathrift, Tom, 146

intertextuality, 36–41

'Jack and the Beanstalk', 149,
    157, 162
'Jack the Giant Killer', 11, 16
Johnson, Richard, 12, 13,
    16, 95
Johnson, Samuel, 48, 111,
    125–6
Jones, Bridget, 11, 28, 46
Jonson, Ben, 67, 80–1, 165
    Entertainment at Althorp, The,
    19, 70

Keats, John, 91
King Leir, 44
Kipling, Rudyard, 92–3
Knight, G. Wilson, 48–9
Kozintsev, Grigori, 1, 51
Kurosawa, Akiro, 2, 51
Kyd, Thomas, 112

Lacan, Jacques, 52–3, 59
'Laidly Worm, The', 109, 147
Lamb, Charles and Mary, 2
Lodge, Thomas, *see Rosalind*
'Love like Salt', 42–3, 44, 45, 46,
    48, 60
Luhrmann, Baz, 2
Lyly, John, 66, 95

Maclise, Daniel, 13, 14
Macnamara, Morgan, 69, 79
man in the moon, 16, 101

Manningham, John, 145
Marlowe, Christopher, 38–9
    Hero and Leander, 30, 33, 37
    Jew of Malta, The, 13, 14, 66, 115,
    165
Marston, John, 112
Mr Fox, 16, 147
*Merry Tales of the Mad Men of
    Gotham, The*, 120
modernism, 17, 67, 102
Munday, Anthony, 36, 37
My Fair Lady, 73

Nashe, Thomas, 95
new historicism, 5, 141–4
'Nix, Nought, Nothing', 146–7

Oedipus, 70, 73, 152–3
ogres, 16, 149–50, 157–8, 167
Old Wives Tale, The (George Peele)
    17–18, 66, 130, 145
Ovid, 36, 37–9, 74, 75, 89, 91–4,
    95, 96, 146

Pandosto (Robert Greene), 68,
    69–71, 72
pastoral genre, 37–40
Peele, George, see *Old Wives Tale,
    The*
performance criticism, 6–7
Petrarchan poetry, 37, 146
Porter, Cole, 2
Potter, Harry, 26, 28
Pretty Woman, 11, 46, 47, 73
Puttenham, George, 130,
    133

'Queenes Majesties Entertainment
    at Woodstocke, The', 19

realism, 17, 47–8, 67–8, 79–84,
    85–7, 101–2, 106–7, 141–2
'Red Ettin, The', 81, 83, 109, 130,
    146, 157
Revenger's Tragedy, The, 112

Riviere, Joan, 138, 139
riddles, 44, 60, 64, 71, **129–35**, 144–6, 148, **151–7, 162–4**, 168
Roman comedy, 11, 105, 145–6, 165
romantic comedy, 35, 37–41, 142, 146, 148
Rosalind (Thomas Lodge), 22, 23, 25, 30, 33, 40
Rowland, Child, 16, 22, 56, 81, 83, 109, 157

Saxo Grammaticus, 118–19
Sayers, Dorothy, 122, 123
Schlegel, A. W., 65, 67
Scot, Reginald, 13, 86, 95, 100
Shakespeare,
   language of, 8–11, 55–6, 62–4
   individual works,
      All's Well That Ends Well, 131, 145
      Antony and Cleopatra, 1, 9, 62, 108, 109
      As You Like It, 1, 10, 16, **21–41**, 102, 106, 129, 143, 151–2
      Comedy of Errors, The, 2, 145
      Coriolanus, 5
      Cymbeline, 28, 81
      Hamlet, 1, 2, 15, 100, **108–28**, 129
      Julius Caesar, 1, 5, 9, 116, 117
      King Henry V, 1, 119, 163
      King John, 2
      King Lear, 1, 16, 28, **42–64**, 81, 108, 109, 119, 121, 129, 143, 157
      King Richard II, 1, 66
      King Richard III, 1, 113–14
      Love's Labour's Lost, 73, 109
      Macbeth, 1, 3, 9–10, 17, 62, 66, 108, 115, 132
      Measure for Measure, 130–1, 145
      Merchant of Venice, The, 45, 131, 142, **149–68**

      Merry Wives of Windsor, The, 130, 135, 163
      Midsummer Night's Dream, A, 16, 17, 65, **85–107**
      Much Ado About Nothing, 3, 16, 135, 147
      Othello, 1, 3, 62, 68, 108
      Pericles, 28, 153
      Rape of Lucrece, The, 119
      Romeo and Juliet, 1, 2, 135
      Sir Thomas More, 8
      Taming of the Shrew, The, 2, 3
      Tempest, The, 1, 2, 5, 16, 98
      Titus Andronicus, 10, 112
      Twelfth Night, 1, 3, 28, 121, **129–48**
      Two Gentlemen of Verona, 106
      Venus and Adonis, 30
      Winter's Tale, The, 28, 47, **65–84**, 143, 152
Shakespeare in Love, 148
Sidney, Philip, 13
'Silly Jack and the Lord's Daughter', 22, 23, 24, 25, 27, 120
Sinfield, Alan, 31
'Sleeping Beauty, The', 71, 81, 150
Smiley, Jane, 3, 51
Sound of Music, The, 46
Spenser, Edmund, 37, 40, 95
   Epithalamion, 99
   Faerie Queene, The, 19, 44, 70, 87, 88–90, 96, 120
   Mother Hubberds Tale, 14, 96
'Snow White', 71, 73, 81
Stern, Tiffany, 118
Straparola, Giovanni Francesco, 15, 81

Tale of Gamelyn, The, 22–3
Tate, Nahum, 47–8
Tattercoats, 72–3, 77
Taylor, Gary, 4–6, 8
Thomas of Erceldoune, 87, 90–1
'Thomas the Rhymer', 87, 91
To Be or Not to Be, 160–61

Tom Thumb, 11–12, 13, 16   Warner, Marina, 46
Truman Show, The, 11   Wilde, Oscar, 48
                                  Woolf, Virginia, 9

Updike, John, 3   Žižek, Slavoj, 165–6